It Doesn't Have to be That Way

amy jo hawkins

Thank you so very much for your support and encouragement! You much my favorite uncle!!

amy jo hawkins

Remarkable Press
St. Charles, MO 63385

It Doesn't Have to be That Way / Amy Jo Hawkins. —1st ed.
ISBN 978-0-9862073-0-3
ISBN 0986207306

CONTENTS

Foreword ix

Macy xii

Luke xvi

"Boys of Summer" 1987 1

"Here and Now" 1990 21

"My, My, My" 1991 35

"This Woman's Work" 1992 47

"Love Is" 1993 69

"Loser" 1994 91

"Crazy" 1995 103

"You Oughta Know" 1996 127

   "Wonderwall" D I S S O L V E D 155

"The Freshman" 1997 161

"I'll Be" 1998 173

"I Will Remember You" 1999 183

"My Redeemer Lives" 1999 (cont'd) 197

"I Could Not Ask For More" 2000 213

   "I Still Believe" R E C O N N E C T E D 219

   "For The First Time" R E C O N C I L E D 241

   "Hallelujahs" R E M A R R I E D 255

For Taylor, Maranda and Ethan. Life is the most precious gift I have ever been privileged with and while my selfishness had taken that for granted during the early portions of your lives, I will strive the rest of my days to give you everything that your love and passion for life— your internal lights—has reflected onto and within me.
I love you with everything I am!

For Rick. With whom I've defied the odds...you're my best friend, my love, my king and I love you more today than I ever imagined possible. You have taught me to dream and for that I will always be your greatest fan!

"Love knows no limit to its endurance, no end to its trust. Love still stands when all else has fallen."

—1 Corinthians 13:7-8

Foreword

Flipping through the stations on his car radio couldn't keep the nagging impulses at a far enough distance. As if on autopilot, Luke took the right turn toward the casino instead of staying on the straightaway toward home. As he neared the entrance, he contemplated pulling out three hundred dollars. "But there's only three hundred twenty six dollars in the account," he said out loud shamefully to himself, an ill attempt for his conscience to talk him out of going. Rent was due the next day but that amount wouldn't cover it anyway. By the time he arrived, it didn't matter; the uncontrollable desire would seemingly take over the steering, the parking, the walking and the keying in of his PIN.

"When's Daddy getting home?" Avery asked her mommy while changing into her PJs.

"Pretty soon, sweetie. Daddy just finished work and is on his way home." Macy replied, trying to sound excited but the quiver in her voice betrayed the confidence she felt in that statement.

Luke made his way to the craps table while counting his twenties. *"Tonight I'm gonna win big. I can feel it. Just need to triple my money and we can catch up on rent, get the TV out of hock, and maybe pay back Al and Tucker. I got this."* He told himself the same familiar and justifying speech every time he set foot in the casino—regardless of the outcome—as if he were a quarterback pumping himself up before a big game.

Macy went through the motions—reading bedtime stories to the kids, cleaning up dishes, picking up wet towels left on the bathroom floor from bath time—all the while her nagging intuition twisting and pecking at her gut and heart. She sat down on the couch clutching one of Luke's shirts. She held it to her face inhaling his smell. The phone was staring back at her, *Where is he? Please God, don't let him be...* she trailed off as she picked up the phone.

He managed to keep the game going and keep his chips flowing at the craps table for a little over an hour. But it only took that one last roll for Luke to bet it all on the point of six; and lose. And then it only took a couple seconds to talk himself into winning his money back as he glanced down towards the poker tables, *Well that's crap. Damnit! I was up almost $500 too. Well, still got a little more than fifty in cash stuffed in my pocket. I'll make it all back playing some poker. I can't lose; I will not survive another loss.*

She called the bank and learned of his recent ATM withdrawal. As much as she wanted to throw the phone across the room, she fled in the direction of the kid's bedroom instead. She needed confirmation that their three babies were fast asleep...all the while her mind was screaming, *Go find him!* Macy slipped on her tennis shoes and quickly grabbed her purse, using her sickening rage as the fuel her body needed to get in the car and drive.

As he played hand after hand, Luke saw their number flash across the tiny gray screen of his pager. He heard the countless pages made over the casino intercom. Looking at his watch, he barely flinched when he noticed five hours had passed and he was down almost all of his money, all of THEIR money. He refused to acknowledge all of Macy's blatant in-your-face scoldings, but the only thing he could not ignore was the stabbing feeling in his heart.

It was the first time Macy showed up at the casino to face Luke. She found it hard to breathe with what felt like cement blocks sitting on her chest, hoping against hope that he had not been there for the past five hours. She walked with a purpose through the casino as if she knew exactly where she was going. Macy worried that everyone would read the rage and fury in her eyes, but not one person made eye contact with her as she stalked down the aisles. It felt like she was about to catch Luke with another woman, as if he'd been cheating on her, and she was not turning back now.

He was at the poker table in the middle of a losing hand when he looked up and saw Macy's eyes boring into him, a look of disgust on her face. She had been crying, her beautiful eyes big and blue now full of rage and sorrow. Luke, stunned, just looked back down at his cards and played with the two chips in his hand, flipping one over the other. He thought to himself, *Just look away, she's not really there.* He tried to maintain his poker face for the game's sake, but Macy read him better than anyone.

Macy's mind was racing, *Why do you not believe it? You knew he was here. This is no surprise whatsoever. But why?* She couldn't speak, although she wanted to shout at everyone in the place...most likely they were doing the same thing to their families. As she contemplated her next move, Macy's heart burst with pain—officially broken—bleeding out pure anger and rage. She ran down the smoke-filled aisles trying to escape, thinking, *I'll show him. If this is how he wants to live, then that's what he's gonna get.*

Why the hell did she come here? Luke thought to himself, even if he knew full well why she did. *I can't believe she left our kids all by themselves.* He maintained his defensive anger towards her as he threw back the last couple swallows of beer. He watched the dealer's hand push the pile of chips across the table and then looked at the two remaining in his hand—the last of their money. He stuffed them in his pocket—along with his guilt and shame—and got up from the table to catch up with Macy. But it was too late. She turned the corner and was gone....out of Luke's sight, for good.

Macy

Macy was the first-born daughter to the young Mr. and Mrs. Horn. With giant blue eyes and weighing in at just seven pounds, she was the perfect baby only waking to eat. Her mother often shared stories of how she would watch Macy as she was sleeping to make sure she was still breathing.

Peter and Leanne met in high school. Leanne fell in love with Peter's intense blue eyes and Peter was taken by Leanne's brighten-any-room smile. Both were from very large families—Peter had seven brothers and Leanne had four sisters and five brothers, with twins on each side; and, they both were the second oldest.

They were brought up with extremely conservative morals and a very strong work ethic—true baby boomers. At just twenty and twenty-one, the Horns were forced to grow up quickly. And, with a desire to provide more for their kids than their parents could for them, Leanne and Peter worked from this point forward. Peter worked full-time for a local car dealership, as well as having a second job on the weekends for as long as Macy could remember. He usually spent Saturdays doing construction, laying carpet or taking on all sorts of odd jobs. Leanne worked full-time as well, at the same dealership with Peter, forcing Macy to become accustom to daycares and babysitters at a very early age—all against her will.

Macy hated daycare—well, she hated her mom leaving her there. While the other daycare kids played, Macy was that sobbing toddler glued to the window hoping her mom would see her when she pulled away and maybe turn around to come back for her. Even worse, she often cried the entire time until Leanne arrived to pick her up.

Even though they would go from sitter to sitter, Macy and her sisters, Kyle and Miriam grew up in the same town their entire adolescent lives. Attending the same private elementary and high school, they had the same friends for the majority of their school years.

Although not many vacations were taken, the Horns had so many fond memories from traditional holidays to summers spent in the pool, playing softball and cruising on the river in their boat. Their house was fully decorated on every holiday. Macy's mom made their Halloween costumes and her dad built dollhouses. Christmas was always a plentiful event with gifts from the grandparents, aunts, uncles and cousins and, of course, Santa Claus. Birthdays were always celebrated with family, presents and cake. Macy and her sisters were provided every 'thing' they needed and then some.

Even though it was the 70s and Leanne worked full-time, that 'Leave It to Beaver' standard was still enforced in their house. Table set and dinner served by 5:30 every evening. House kept clean and kids reared. Macy, being the oldest, was cooking and caring for her younger sisters by the age of ten. Macy carried the adult role even further by buying and smoking cigarettes by the age of thirteen and taking swigs of alcohol on occasion. She was the adult, after all.

It was these memories that kept Macy sheltered. She feared attention but so longed for it at the very same time. She was extremely shy but sincerely witty, funny and exciting as she got to know others. While a young girl, Macy quit dance—something that she truly loved—shortly after joining the local dance company when she learned there would be a recital. She just couldn't get past the idea of being on stage but more so being 'looked at.' The decision to quit now gave others a new adjective to use for Macy, quitter.

As Macy grew into adolescence, instead of being proud or excited, she was embarrassed by the significant moments that came with this growth, such as getting her first bra. Instead of feeling private compassion it was a public announcement. Even though Macy had crushes on a couple of the boys she was in school with, she didn't like talking to them; she had this feeling of disgust toward them actually because she knew what they were interested in S-E-X. Besides she was pretty sure they had no interest in her and her frail, boyish figure. However, high school offered Macy much more attention the day she woke up in a woman's body and no longer resembled that of a twelve-year-old boy. And she liked it...No, she loved it, the attention that is. Trying out for the cheerleading squad was naturally the right thing to do. Leanne had been a cheerleader too.

Throughout her life, Macy often felt alone as if she wasn't important or understood or more so heard. These feelings were always reinforced when she'd remember the day that she stopped to take a second look at the anniversary plaque on her parent's entertainment center that she had seen day after day. The inscription read "Peter & Leanne 11-7-1970." Macy was born on April 6th 1971. *It's all my fault...they were pregnant before they got married,* she thought to herself. *If I hadn't been born maybe none of this would be happening. Maybe my parents wouldn't have married. Maybe they wouldn't be so unhappy.*

By Macy's junior year of high school, her parents divorced. She thought it would be a bit calmer than the previous years, but it was instead full of turbulence—arguing, disagreements, anger and confusion—and she wanted out from under all of it. It was this same time that Macy's life would be forever changed the night she met a stranger who would interrupt the family chaos and fill her space with overwhelming love and attraction. Nothing in the world mattered to her from this point forward. She was in love!

Luke

Luke was the first and only son born to Ron and Judy. With big brown eyes and lots of dark hair, he was instantly a charmer. Luke was a quick learner and always on the move. Even at just a few weeks old, he wiggled himself right off the changing table. From that point forward, Luke was a complete joy but truly a handful. He was so full of energy. By ten months old Luke wasn't walking… he was running.

Mr. and Mrs. Hawthorn met when Judy was only twelve. Ron loved her infectious laugh and Judy was completely smitten by Ron's sweet, quiet demeanor that came to life when he played his guitar. Both came from small families, Judy having a few siblings and Ron was an only child. Family was so very important to each of them.

Ron was a Vietnam veteran serving in the front lines witnessing more than Judy, Luke or anyone could ever fathom nor would ever hear about. Judy was in love and had a great talent for poetry. Both Ron and Judy were musically gifted. Ron played electric guitar in a band and Judy sang backup. Just as it is for most if not all musicians, his dream was to be a professional musician; but instead he would settle for selling cars. Not only did it pay the bills and help them build a new home in an up-and-coming subdivision, he was good at it. Ron was a true salesman with an entrepreneurial heart.

The Hawthorns had many great memories—from the basement parties where Ron's band would perform classic rock 'n roll hits—to swimming in their pool—to having nice cars. But it was only six short years later that those good memories came to a quick halt when Ron and Judy divorced. Luke was only five years old. An all-too-familiar experience for Ron, as his dad left home when he was a small boy too.

The one constant thing that remained in Luke's life from this point forward was moving: different homes in different states in different schools. Since they didn't have much, Luke and Judy were forced to move around a lot, living with family and friends. Judy did what she could to find work. Luke was talented in so many areas...his newest talent was to adapt, to become a chameleon.

Luke learned to make friends quickly but the relationships seemed as if they were over just as quickly as they were made. This included girlfriends. He loved girls and most always wanted to have a girlfriend and usually did. He gained experience with girls at a young age and enjoyed the feeling he got from kissing and feeling close to them. It somehow filled an emptiness that lingered within him. Or so he thought.

For many years, Luke and his mother went without. Living with family and in tiny apartments, they struggled financially. During the holidays, Luke watched his cousins open cool gifts like boom boxes and nice clothes, while he opened gifts that seemed less significant. He wanted to be grateful for getting anything at all, but it was really hard.

Judy's third marriage provided much-needed stability in Luke's life. He was 10. Growing up in the suburbs of Atlanta was a great time. The wonderful memories created there were filled with boat rides, waterskiing, football and being part of a champion little league baseball team. The energy never died within Luke. Stories were told by his family that Luke would just run in circles around the house. They'd yell to him as he made his way around to the back window again and again. This third marriage also gave Luke a younger brother and gave him more reason to be a great role model, even if there was a thirteen-year age difference.

Luke had also inherited his father's (and mother's) incredible talent for music. He had been playing drums since a very early age but it was around this time he found his voice. Finally being settled in the same high school, he would become a very talented musician and vocalist performing in musicals and district choir and drum line in the marching band. However, just like so many other things in Luke's life, his mother's third marriage came to an end and so did his hopes for having a future with music. The brokenness he was now drowning in caused him to run. It's at this time Luke moved to Illinois to attempt to build a relationship with his father. While feeling lost and unaccepted, Luke passed up many music scholarships to a number of universities and followed Ron's path by joining the US Marine Corps and the Drum & Bugle Corps.

Luke's heart was constantly broken and he had a difficult time determining what it was that he wanted to do. He knew in his heart what he wanted and what he needed to do but somehow he couldn't allow himself to make that happen.

Despite his incredible vocal gift and musical talents, Luke consistently felt inadequate and alone. He struggled with the belief that it was something he did to cause his father to leave. *Maybe if I try harder or get lots of awards or trophies, he'll see how good I am. I just need to be perfect, then he'll see me and be proud of me.* Luke thought to himself. He would often times wonder, *Why don't they care about ME or what I think?*

Despite the hurt and confusion that consumed Luke, there was only one thing that brought joy to his heart—simply thinking about the stranger he met simply by accident that warm summer night. He couldn't forget the feeling that he got when their hearts touched. It was a feeling he had never known. A feeling that would change his life. He was in love!

CHAPTER 1

"Boys of Summer"
1987

"No, I don't want to go cruising Regency movie theatre. I thought we were going to Mark's party," Macy said to her friends. Driving around in circles in the hopes of catching the eye of a good-looking guy just was not her idea of fun.

"Oh come on, Macy!" Misty pleaded. "Let's just go drive around for little while and then we can go to the party."

Kara, Misty and Macy all agreed it was a fair compromise. They continued to primp for the hot and humid July weather, making sure they had enough hairspray layered on so their mile-high hairstyles would last the entire evening.

It was a good 25-30 minute drive from their small-town homes to the movie theater. It didn't seem to take nearly as long as they laughed, told stories and danced and sang along with Salt 'n Peppa and Janet Jackson blaring on the radio in Macy's mom's Escort wagon.

Misty reminded Macy, "Don't forget to stop at the gas station. We're out of smokes and I want a soda." So they pulled into the Mobil right around the corner from the theater.

"I'll wait in the car. Get me a Pepsi," said Macy. Macy played with the radio skimming stations listening for a good song. Not two minutes had gone by before she felt someone staring at her. Macy looked up, turned to her left and saw a boy smiling at her from his car on the other side of the gas pump. He immediately started to wave at her. Macy did one of those, "Is he looking at me?" as she looked behind her. She tentatively waved back.

Misty and Kara made their way back to the car. It took only a few seconds for them to catch on to what was taking place. He had a friend getting back in his car too. He quickly pulled his car around to hers and not taking his eyes off Macy he asked, "Hey! What are you all doing tonight?" Macy replied, "Just driving around. Maybe going to a movie."

Now Macy wasn't one for meeting strange boys...she wanted to be at Mark's party. But her heart was doing the talking somehow. The boy excitedly responded, "Can we meet you there?" Macy loved questions that offered her the chance to be sarcastic, especially with boys who are forever labeled 'selfish heart-breakers.' "Well it is a public place, so you're free to go if you like." Macy replied with a coy smirk on her face.

Macy was feeling something she had never felt in those few moments and subconsciously feared being let down—she wasn't going to get her hopes up. The bright, brown-eyed boy replied, "Okay! I've got to drop off my friend and pick up another and then I'll be there. What movie you going to see?" For some reason, Macy believed him. She looked back at Misty and Kara to get their   approval (via a couple wide-eyed eyebrow raises and nods) and then looked back to reply, "Beverly Hills Cop II." He smiled, "See you in a little bit."

"Ooooh Macy, he's cute!" Misty and Kara teased her. "You think he'll show up?" Kara asked. "Who knows?" Macy replied while thinking to herself, *"but something tells me I hope so."*

"Dude, did you see her eyes?" Luke asked Joe. He was excited and thoughts were bouncing all over the place. "Oh my gosh. She's so hot. Do you think John will go back to the theater with me...did he have plans? I am so getting her number." Joe couldn't get a word in edgewise.

The girls bought their tickets and headed straight for the ladies room to check out their hair and makeup—a quick swipe of lip gloss and one last spritz of hairspray to seal the deal. The three found some open seats towards the back of the theatre. "Are they here yet? I don't see them. Macy wasn't getting her hopes up. But if I've just spent $5 on a ticket for nothing, I'm gonna be pissed." "Oh come on, they'll be here. We've got to make sure we sit where they can see us," Misty said. "Over there. There are six open seats," Kara   pointed.

It wasn't too far into the movie when Macy noticed the light from the hallway; someone was coming into the theatre.

"Is that them?" Sam asked.

"Oh yeah, there she is," Luke replied.

"Oh my gosh, you guys. They're here!" Macy whispered. She had turned around and caught Luke's glance. It was him and his friend, a different guy from before. Luke walked down the aisle to where the girls were sitting, stepped over all of them including Macy, saying "Hi there," giving her a sweet smile and sat on her left.

Only a few minutes had gone by before he and Macy started quietly   chatting.   "Where   are   you   from?"   Luke   asked. "Wentzville," Macy replied. "And you?" she asked. "Here. I mean St. Charles," said Luke.

Macy was never as comfortable with a boy as she was with him. She was drawn to his brown eyes and infectious smile. And likewise, Luke was just as drawn to Macy. Luke was enamored with Macy's big blue eyes and [big] blond hair. They studied each other in secret.

Luke was thinking, *Wow, this girl is gorgeous! Her eyes—I'm dreaming for sure.*

Macy noticed he had a keychain with the letter "L" engraved on it. She asked, "What's your name? Leroy?" He replied, "No. It's Luke." He grinned as he said, "My mom bought it for me." Luke and Macy were lost in thought, paying no attention to the movie even though they were gazing in that direction. Luke had his arms crossed but brushed his fingertips on the back of Macy's arm; Macy brushed back. She turned and grinned at him.

When the movie was over, the group of new friends all talked and laughed as they left the theatre. Luke walked with them to Macy's car. As Macy got in, Luke shut her door and she rolled down the window. Luke squatted down with his face at hers. "It was really nice meeting you, Luke," Macy said. "You too, Macy," said Luke. "Can I call you sometime?" he asked. Macy scrambled for a pen and wrote her number on his hand, and Luke wrote his on hers.

Macy started the car and pulled out of the parking spot. They waved and Luke was so excited he was bouncing around his car. It was as Macy drove away that she was contemplating something so not like her—her heart felt like it was going to explode. Kara and Misty were hounding her, "you want to kiss him, don't you?!" They repeated the dare over and over. With her heart racing and her mind scattered, Macy completely agreed.

She made a U-turn in the parking lot and yelled out the window in her best Rizzo (from Grease) voice, "Hey Luke, come here!" Luke looked over at her like "who me?" but ran over without hesitation. Macy leaned out the window and kissed Luke. Their hearts stopped as fireworks went off all around them. *WOW!* She thought to herself. *Holy crap!* Luke thought to himself. Both of them tried to act cool, ignoring the dazed feeling they couldn't escape. Luke was the first to talk, "I'll call you." Macy replied with a flirty smirk doing her best to hide the spell she was currently under, "You better."

The girls left. It was time to get to Mark's party. Another half hour in the car allowed for the three of them to discuss all the events of the evening so far. "Holy crap! How crazy was that? Pull into a gas station—not even for gas—and you meet a guy." Misty said excitedly. "And a pretty cute one too," Kara joined in. Misty just had to mention, "You know, Macy, if it wasn't for me you wouldn't have met Luke. You didn't even want to go cruising." Macy admitted it, Misty was right. Macy was in another world; her heart was beating fast and in shock from the jolt it just got. Her mind was swimming in his smile and eyes.

Luke too, was very taken by a new emotion that he was now feeling from this very beautiful stranger he had just met, exchanged numbers and kissed less than two hours ago.

The party was in full force by the time the girls arrived—a basement full of their high school friends playing pool, discussing very important topics like who's the better drummer, Tommy Lee or Alex Van Halen, challenging each other with the 'would you rather' game, and fighting over the radio.

Macy had an ulterior motive when initially suggesting they go to the party. She had a thing for Mark. Macy had hopes of spending time with him. Instead all she could do was study Luke's number on her hand, remembering their conversation in the movie theatre and studying his eyes and hands in her mind. That touch of his fingertips brushing the back of her arm would instantly send butterflies flying from every corner of her stomach.

Luke got home from dropping off Sam, showered and climbed into bed trying very hard to get to sleep so tomorrow would come. But thoughts of Macy and how his evening went from hanging with the guys to meeting a girl that had done something to him that he'd never known or felt, kept him wide awake.

Macy drove Kara and Misty home and made her way home and in to bed. She laid there wanting, trying to go to sleep in the hopes that Luke would be in her dreams, but the excitement of the night kept her wide awake and excited for what tomorrow would bring. *Will he really call? Will I even see him again?*

"Have I waited long enough? Is it too early to call? Crap, just pick up the phone and call her." Luke argued with himself.

It was around ten o'clock the next morning when Luke called. Macy was still lying in bed thinking of Luke when she heard the phone ring. She immediately turned to the table by her bed and watched the lights on her phone blink as it rang. She thought to herself, *what if that's Luke...Oh my gosh, I hope it is.* It was.

"Hi. Macy? It's Luke," he said. "How are you? I didn't wake you up did I?" Luke asked shyly.

"Oh no. I didn't sleep much anyway." They chatted a little bit more and then Luke asked, "Can I come see you?"

"Can you come see me? You can't drive all the way out here just to see me—"

"No really, I want to come see you." Luke interrupted.

"The guys I go to school with won't even come out here and they don't live forty-five minutes away like you do." Macy countered.

Luke insisted. Macy accepted and gave him the directions. Luke listened intently, memorizing every turn and street name; her words were like sweet music to him. "Are you writing this down?" Macy asked.

"What? No, no I got it, is that it?" Luke replied.

It was a dreary rainy day. As Macy hung up the phone it began it pour, strong thunderstorms took over the sky. Macy thought more and more to herself, *He's not going to come all the way out here. He'll find something better to do or get lost...especially in this downpour.*

Macy had all but talked herself out of Luke showing up when the doorbell rang. "Holy crap! It's him," Macy said jumping up off of the couch. She opened the door and there he was—that dark-headed, dark-eyed, bright-smiled, boy with the "L" on his keychain.

"Hi!"

"Hi! You made it. Even in the pouring rain. I can't believe it. Come on in." *Oh my gosh. I really can't believe it...he's really here.* Macy thought to herself as she closed the door.

Wow, what a big house, Luke thought to himself.

They hugged, well Luke squeezed. Both soaking in all their senses would allow. It was complete overload even in those few moments. Both Macy and Luke felt their bodies just fit like a missing puzzle piece. They stared in each other's eyes as they broke from their embrace somehow reading each other's thoughts, *you're thinking the same thing I am, aren't you?!*

"So, show me around, like, your room," Luke said smiling.

"Um, okay just for a minute." She hesitated but still walked him down the short hall to her room on the left.

Luke picked up some of the things on her dresser, played with the radio and then playfully grabbed Macy's hand pulling her on to the bed. They sat there for a minute giggling, flirting and then Macy stood up, grabbed Luke's hands and led him back into the living room and then to the kitchen holding hands along the way.

Luke was giddy—very much alive and couldn't sit still the entire time. "How long have you lived here?" Luke asked as he sat down at the kitchen table.

"Just a little while, almost two years." Macy was grabbing some drinks out of the refrigerator, more so hiding as she tried to understand the struggle she experienced with how much she was attracted to Luke. His smile, his eyes, his hands, the way he smelled, everything about him stimulated her senses and filled her heart in a way she had never felt before this very moment.

A feeling that she had known him forever but more so that he had always known her, almost overpowered her concern that they were in the house all alone, something Luke attempted to remind her a couple times during his visit. "So no one's home?" Luke would ask in that charming way, enticing and romantically, like "It's just us? Only you and me, right now?" Macy continuously heard her mother's voice repeating *'if he really loved you, he'd wait for you'* in her mind. But in her heart, she desperately wanted to test this promise; especially with the extreme attraction they both were feeling.

They sat down next to each other on the living room couch.

"Luke, you're not like the boys I know. There truly is something different about you. What is it?"

Luke, pulling his legs up onto the couch and turning to face her, just smiled, "I feel exactly the same way about you, Macy."

She did the same. Crossing their legs Indian style, their knees touching now staring face-to-face, "Like, where'd you come from?"

"All I know is that I want to know more of you." He said holding her hand. "When can I see you again?"

Macy smiled and felt her heart move to her throat.

It wasn't a long visit; it sure didn't seem that long. This would be the theme for the remainder of the summer, each time together flying by. Their time together was filled with so much but in such a small amount of time. Both were completely in awe of the emotions that were distracting them from the world around them. They were falling head over heels in love and their lives would never ever be the same.

Luke returned to Macy's a few days later with trunks and towel in tow. They planned an afternoon of swimming in the seven-acre lake behind Macy's house. Macy lived in a small, semi-private subdivision. Each home was on three or more acres creating privacy or seclusion or whatever you chose to call it but still close to town and neighbors available not too far off.

Macy's friends, Misty and Kara, were there too. The lake was so cool and refreshing that afternoon. Luke was the first to dive in and he swam a ways out, well farther out than Macy ever swam—which really wasn't that far. Luke yelled out, "Get in here, hottie!" and then he dove down to see how deep it was and if he could touch the bottom. He came back up with mud in his hands. All Macy could think was, *Damn! Impressive.*

Macy threw her raft out a ways and jumped in. She climbed on the raft and lying on her stomach swam out to meet Luke where he had been diving and wading. He quickly grabbed onto the raft and kissed Macy. His cool wet lips on hers. Undoubtedly the mushiest lips each had ever kissed. Luke went under the raft, blew bubbles and grabbed Macy's leg.

Moments of conversation would take place with Misty and Kara across the lake. But then quickly Luke and Macy would draw their attention back to each other. They were now on either side of the raft, holding hands and entangling their feet under the raft and water. The gazes seemed like forever but lasted only seconds. *Is it possible to know someone so well that you just met a few days ago?* They each found something new in the other every time they looked a certain way or said something. With every new discovery they loved even more than what they had already witnessed. They saw something in each other that no one had ever seen before—their absolute true hearts—and couldn't shake the 'fit,' that feeling of completeness that came with experiencing this unchartered exploration.

Macy studied Luke's hands and fingers, the flecks of green and gold in his brown eyes, the shapes his mouth made as he smiled. Luke studied the curve of her back and ankles and those amazing cheekbones that glowed especially when she smiled. He pulled her closer to him often and stole as many kisses as he could, sharing an occasional taste of his open mouth with hers.

"Hey, we want to get something to eat. We're starving." Kara and Misty yelled from across the lake.

"Yeah, I'm kind of hungry too. I have an idea. Do you have any pizza makings?" Luke asked.

"Uh yeah, I'm pretty sure we have a box of Chef Boyardee in the pantry."

"Okay, let's go back to the house and I'll make a pizza for us."

They all dried off and walked back to the house. Luke was working at Pizza Hut so his Chef Boyardee pizza was the best the girls had ever had. The friends all took pictures. Luke gave Macy his friendship necklace and his Pizza Hut nametag that read "Luker." "It's okay, I have two," he said. And there it was again, the overwhelming feeling of attraction and disbelief toward this boy.

Kara and Misty had left but Luke stayed. The hot sunny day turned into a cool starry night. Luke and Macy spent the evening laying on the chaise lounges on the deck talking and talking. At first a lot of light-hearted topics were covered.

"I'm in marching band on the drum line at school. I've been playing drums since I was like four," Luke said.

"Wow, you're a drummer?!" Macy replied with a coy smile as she checked off another positive quality in her mind...*Yes!* "I've always wanted to be a drummer—I love drummers," she replied.

"Yeah, right."

"I did."

Luke challenged Macy, "Then name five drummers."

"Phil Collins, Sheila E., Don Henley, Tommy Lee, Neil Peart." Macy met his challenge with ease and confidence.

"Wow! I'm totally impressed," Luke retreated as he checked off another positive quality in his mind... *Yes!*

The conversation grew more and more deep. Luke told Macy about his parents and their divorce when he was only five. He told her about his many moves and living in California and Georgia. "My mom remarried 5 years ago and I got a little brother out of it. Jason. He's four." He paused for a minute as he turned on his side and propped up his head, leaning on his elbow. "You know, even though I'm telling you all of this, I somehow feel like you already know it all. It's as if I've known you forever."

Macy smiled, "I feel the same way, Luke!" She turned to lay on her side as they held hands and just starred at each other.

Macy and Luke walked out to his car and sat in the front seat. It was still a little warm from the hot day. Luke took Macy's face in his hands and kissed her, so sweetly. A few more sweet pecks and it was time for Luke to go. "I love you, Macy." Luke said. Her eyes wide, she repeated the gesture. "I love you, Luke." Macy had never said this to anyone before, not even family. It was a term that she had only read on occasion in a birthday card.

Luke and Macy spoke on the phone numerous times a day.

"Hey there, beautiful."

"Hi Luke!"

"What are you doing?"

"Watching TV. What are you doing?"

"Getting ready to go to work."

"What are you wearing?" Luke would ask.

"Do you miss me? I dreamt about you last night. I could smell you on my t-shirt."

"What? You could? Really?"

"Hey, want to go to a church picnic this Sunday...with me?" Macy asked Luke. Luke of course accepted.

On the day of the picnic, he was there to pick her up as he always did. They went to the church picnic where Macy's grandparents were members and also where her father and uncles went to elementary school. Many of Macy's friends were already there. Macy gave Luke the tour walking by the kiddy rides, bingo games, grab bags, pull tabs and other gambling booths, the live band and most importantly the beer truck where they both ordered a bucket of draft Busch beer. Luke was the type that just could not hide his emotions. He was so excited that he was actually buying a bucket of beer and they were actually serving him and at a church picnic no less. This Catholic church picnic was unlike anything Luke had seen at his church functions.

Macy and Luke hung out with some friends for a little while, all laughing and having a great time. Macy's friends all loved Luke; he was accepted into their group immediately. They hadn't even finished all of their beer when the happy couple headed out to his neck of the woods. They rolled the windows down and sang along with radio...*oh, oh...livin' on a prayer.* Macy sat right next to Luke in the middle of his Ford Fairmont bench seat. Their laughter turned to quick silence and anxiousness when they saw the blue and red flashing lights in the rear view mirror. "Uh, I'm getting pulled over," Luke said.

Luke was still driving around with temporary license plates in his windows but the rear plate had fallen over making it not visible. The police officer let them go after getting many apologies from Luke and he hadn't even seen the bucket of beer sitting on the floor. Luke and Macy just laughed in nervousness as they pulled off.

Luke drove Macy through a subdivision and parked right past a corner street. He turned off the engine putting George Michael's "Faith" to a quick stop mid-song. Macy saw a big open field with this lone oak tree at the top of the hill. It grew darker as Luke walked around the other side of the car to let Macy out.

"Come on. And bring that beer."

"Where are we going? "

"Just follow me," Luke said.

He grabbed her hand and led her up to the top of the hill. Macy felt as if the stars were getting closer to them as they climbed. It wasn't steep, it was getting darker though, and if it weren't for the bright moon, they would have had a harder time maneuvering through the tall grass. They sat close sharing each other's warmth.

Luke and Macy spent the rest of their evening there in that cool grass wrapped up in each other's arms and legs. Luke was more 'experienced,' and he was only the third boy Macy had ever kissed. Macy felt so many new things when she was with Luke. His kisses gave her goose bumps and made her warm all over at the same time. Her heart would race and melt as he held her face in his hands or brushed the hair out of her face. Luke made Macy feel so comfortable. He kissed her mouth, her neck and then her hands. They both longed for the softness and warmth from each other's skin. But Macy would consistently end the arousal before it got them into trouble...even though she feared she might never see Luke again if she didn't allow herself to go all the way with him. That night ended with even deeper emotions and the love between them grew into indescribable proportions.

Macy laid in bed that evening unable to sleep thinking about whom she is and who Luke is and how could this be happening to her. She picked up a notebook and wrote a note to Luke expressing her feelings and how much she loved him.

Hi! Today is August 14 1987, and I've seen Luke three days in a row because he loves me and I love him. He is the greatest guy I have ever met. He's so sweet and not to mention gorgeous. He makes me feel so good I think I've finally found my true love. You know what? I forgot what I was going to say. You know why? Because he mesmerizes me - he puts me in a daze. In the last three days I have not been able to eat or sleep. Now that's got to say something right? Right! I love Luke!

Macy

They would spend the next day together; Luke had asked Macy out on an official date. Luke absolutely loved impressing Macy even if that was still partly due to the hormonal hunt he was on. And Macy loved the fact that he would come to her house to pick her up. While Macy was finishing getting ready, Luke found Macy's notebook and the note she wrote about him.

He picked up a pen and wrote her back:

Macy, Hi! How are you? I never really knew how much you loved me until last night August 13, 1987. I do really love you with all of my heart you are truly the best thing that has ever happened to me. I hope that our relationship lasts for....ever! You know Macy, last night was the best experience of my life. Truly! I know now that you truly love me (I don't know what my trip is with truly; but anyway). The reason I love you is not for S_ _. I love Macy for who she is and I mean that. I am totally sincere about this whole relationship. So you better count on being with me for a long time K? Well I guess I'd better sign off now. I love you, Macy.

Yours forever.

Luke and Macy forever and ever and ever.

The teenage romance blossomed as Luke and Macy did everything together. Their relationship grew intensely as the days went by. They were the center of each other's universe. Even though they had part-time jobs and hung out with other friends, Luke was all that truly existed in Macy's mind and Macy was all that really mattered to Luke. Even Macy's mother, Leanne, commented that it was as if "he has a spell over you."

One evening Luke and Macy drove out to Macy's friend's house for a party. Macy lived in the same town her entire life and grew up with the same kids all those years. Most of those kids were boys who liked to tease and taunt any outsiders, especially of the male gender. Macy believed they were just a little protective of her.

"Luke, this is Jay. Jay, this is my boyfriend Luke." Macy introduced the two.

"Do you drink Budweiser," Jay asked Luke.

"Knock it off, Jay? He's not applying to your club." Macy laughed.

Luke had no problems blending in with the group or making friends at all for that matter. Everyone loved him. They played games and blared the radio. "Here I Go Again" came on and Luke grabbed Macy, pulled her close and they started to dance, right there in Macy's friend's garage alongside the Camaro that he and his dad were rebuilding. Macy snickered thinking about the music video and said to herself; *it's actually pretty fitting*, when she looked around at the makeshift body shop. Most importantly, Macy loved that Luke didn't care what the others thought or wasn't embarrassed to dance with her.

"This is our song, Macy," Luke said. "I am so crazy about you."

"I'm crazy about you, too." Macy replied.

Nights like this continued to happen as often as possible. Macy and Luke enjoyed being with each other's friends. And, their friends liked them. They all had so much fun together.

As the summer was coming to an end, Luke asked Macy to go to Six Flags.

"Bring Kara and Misty too," Luke said.

They all met at Burger King and Luke drove the four to Six Flags. A common interest among the four was their love for music, dancing and singing. During this summer, Coca-Cola sponsored a dance theme at the park, the Coca Cabana.

The four rode rides, got soaked on Thunder River, ate food and danced as often as possible. On almost every corner, video vans would be playing music videos and Macy would join in with the circle of kids dancing to show off her moves. But, truly it was just a passion—one of the only things she felt she did really well—of hers that she really couldn't contain, especially when Janet Jackson's "Pleasure Principle" was on. Luke loved the energy that Macy put off when she danced. *She's so good and she looks so happy,* he thought.

He was distracted, however. "Oh there it is!" Luke said as he saw the dance club.

It was a huge outdoor pavilion converted into a huge dance club. Video screens were playing music videos in all the upper corners for dancers to dance along with. While the girls finished their snacks, the four all watched and checked out the crowd in the club.

"Oh my gosh. There's Tina," Luke said as he turned to Macy. "I heard she might be here today." Macy just watched him talk with this blank stare. "I'm going to go dance one song with her, okay?" he said to Macy. She just shrugged her shoulders, "Okay."

Macy's intuition instantly threw up a red flag with what was transpiring right before her eyes. *Is she the reason he invited us to Six Flags today? Is this what's been on his mind all day?*

Kara and Misty were like, "What's up with that? Who's Tina?"

"Tina is Luke's ex-girlfriend. They went out for a year or so before Luke and I met. But as far as what's up with him wanting to dance with her, I guess we'll find out," she replied.

"Ex-girlfriend? And, he's going to dance with her?" Misty and Kara were just as shocked.

When Luke returned to Macy and the girls, Macy pulled him aside, "Hey come over here and talk to me for a second."

"Oh okay, what's up? He was out of breath. Macy looked him in the eye and bluntly said, "Listen, if you still have feelings for Tina, you need to admit it right now." Macy had no desire to be second best or get in the middle of something else going on. More importantly, she didn't want her heart broken...she had completely fallen for him after all.

Luke quickly responded, "It's not like that, Macy, we're just good friends and have been for a long time now." Macy just looked to the ground, feeling worried. Luke picked her chin up and looked her in the eye and said, "Really, Macy. We're just friends, nothing more."

They stayed a little while longer at the park and then headed home. Luke dropped Misty and Kara off at their car and then took Macy back to his house. Luke went into his bedroom and yelled down the hallway, "Macy come here, I want to give you something."

"Sure you do," Macy said smiling as she walked to his room. When she got to his bedroom door, he was pulling his letter jacket out of the closet.

"With school starting in a couple days, I want you to wear this. Mainly so the other guys know you're taken but also so you don't forget about me."

Again, here is an act of kindness that no one has ever done for Macy. "Really?" she asked. "Of course, I'll wear it." They hugged and kissed.

A few days had passed and school had started. Luke had driven out to St. Dominic to see Macy one of those first days.

"Hey, baby."

"What are you doing here?' Macy asked with surprise as she kissed him.

"Coming to see you."

"I'm so glad!"

"Are we going to do something this weekend?" Luke asked.

"Of course."

It was her junior year and Macy had made the varsity cheerleading squad. SCW High, where Luke went to school, was hosting a clinic for all the local high school cheerleading squads that she and her teammates attended. Macy's squad sat right next to the SCW squad. While the clinic was going on, Macy leaned over to ask the girl sitting next to her, "Hey, do you know Luke Hawthorn?"

The girl to her left leaned over as she heard Macy ask the question, "Yeah, that's my boyfriend." It was Tina.

"Oh, I had just met him through a friend one night..." Macy said trying to cover up how she really knew him.

Macy was shocked and confused. *But he just gave me his letter jacket,* she thought to herself. Whatever was happening was creating a huge knot in her stomach.

The very next day was a Friday. Luke called Macy after school.

"Macy?"

"Hi, Luke."

"Macy, I need to ask you a favor." *Oh geez, I can't do this. How am I going to tell her?* Luke struggled silently.

"What is it, Luke?"

"I need my letter jacket back."

"What? What for?"

Luke, searching for an excuse... "Well, it can get pretty cold down on the field."

"Really? Like you're going to wear your letter jacket while you're marching?" Macy asked with sarcasm. Luke was silent, knowing she was right, but he couldn't tell her the truth about Tina. "Fine, Luke. I'll bring it to you tonight." She hung up the phone and cried.

"Mom, Dad, I'm going to Kara's for a little bit. I'll be back later on." Macy yelled down the hall as she grabbed her keys.

Macy's anger somehow gave her the courage to make the forty-minute drive SCW. She knew this was about Tina and wondered just how much Luke didn't tell her. Macy pulled into the crowded parking lot.

One of the first people she saw was Luke's friend Sam. Sam saw Macy and walked over to her. "Hey Macy, what's up? What are you doing all the way out here?" he asked.

"Oh hey, Sam," Macy replied. She got out of the car and then opened the back door to reach in to get Luke's jacket. "I came out here to well—well, would you just give this to Luke," handing over Luke's letter jacket. She paused for a second as she went to get back in the car, "And, Sam, one more thing...tell him to stick it where the sun don't shine."

"Uh, sure. Okay." Sam replied with confusion.

Macy got back in her car and headed back home. That was it. Macy and Luke had broken up. Macy was so hurt, almost every song on the radio would remind her of him. Her emotions would go from hurt and sadness to anger and confusion. The long drive home initiated a few sleepless nights. The nights she couldn't sleep, she'd smell the t-shirt she put on and wore home from one of their dates, she read the notes they left to one another and eventually she packed away his necklace, name tag and the movie stub from the night they met.

How did this happen? I can't believe I did this to her. How am I ever going to get her back? Luke was very confused and distraught with how he had hurt Macy.

It was a couple months later when Luke walked in the front door of his friend Joe's house that he saw Macy sitting there on the couch with Joe's brother Sam. Sam and Luke were in the same class and all three of them were on the wrestling team together, so they hung out pretty often. But now, to Luke's surprise, Macy and Sam were dating. It hurt Macy's heart to see Luke again. She missed him but she was also still very angry at how things had ended. But, she also couldn't help feeling a little guilty seeing the disbelief and hurt on Luke's face. Luke was feeling a double dose of betrayal thanks to his friend Sam dating his ex-girlfriend.

Macy and Sam continued to date off and on for almost two years. She liked Sam but he would never compare to Luke. And probably subconsciously she felt close to Luke through dating Sam. Selfishly, dating Sam meant that Macy wouldn't have to completely let go of Luke. She could see his face and he could maybe feel a little of the pain he put her through; especially since he was still dating Tina.

CHAPTER 2

"Here and Now"
1990

It had been almost exactly three years since Macy and Luke had met the day he decided to call her. Even though the structure and discipline was exactly what Luke had been longing for, Camp Lejeune and the Marine Corps was now a thing of the past as was his girlfriend since he left North Carolina to move back home.

Macy and Sam's relationship was no more. One evening she and Sam were together, Macy 'changed her mind' and that was the last time she saw him. She was now doing her best to focus on work and saving her money to someday have a new Mustang and a place of her own.

Luke heard that Macy's parents had divorced and looked up Macy's mom in the phone book. Macy was living with her father in his apartment while her younger sisters lived with her mom. One afternoon Macy was hanging with her sisters at her mom's house when the phone rang. Macy's sister, Kyle, jumped off of the couch leaving their Uno game and ran to the phone. Macy arranged her cards and out of the blue her intuition revealed a feeling that she couldn't believe, however was completely confident that it was Luke on the other end of the line. She said out loud to herself, "Oh my gosh, that's Luke Hawthorn."

"Hello," said Kyle.

"Is Macy there?" the caller asked.

"Who's calling please?" she asked.

Kyle put her hand over the phone, "Macy, it's him, you were right." She heard Macy say that it was Luke. "How did you know it was Luke Hawthorn?!"

21

"I really don't know. I just did!" Macy confused at how she knew that but excited, jumped up from the couch and picked up the phone. "Hello? Well, Luke Hawthorn, how are you?" Not once did it even cross her mind why the heck he was calling her, or how she knew it was him after all this time.

"I'm good, Macy!"

"Awesome. Happy Birthday by the way," Macy said.

"Holy crap. You remembered. It's really good to hear your voice. How are you?

"Of course, I remembered! I'm doing pretty good. How'd you know to call me here?"

"I had heard that your parents separated, so I figured I'd look up your mom in the phone book."

"Wow, that's crazy. You lucked out because I live with my dad now. I just happened to be here this afternoon hanging with my sisters."

"No way! So, Macy, I'm wondering...would it be okay if I came to see you?"

"Sure, it'd be nice to see you too."

Within an hour, Luke pulled up out front to Macy's mom's house in his RX7. He had a new haircut under that white ball cap (no more business in the front and party in the back), a great tan and was looking extra fit. He was always thin but the Marines had given him much more definition. Thankfully the two things that remained the same were those brown eyes and his infectious smile.

It was love at first site all over again. Luke admired Macy's long and thick and curly blond hair, giant blue eyes and that incredible smile of hers. *Oh, how I've missed her* he thought to himself. They talked and hugged and laughed as if not one day had passed.

"God, you look amazing, Macy! Better than I remember!"

"You look good too, Luke. Obviously the Marines have been good to you."

"Are you doing anything tonight? Can I take you out?" he asked.

"Um, no I'm not doing anything and, yes, I'd love that," Macy replied. "I'm heading back to my dad's in a little bit so can you pick me up there?"

"How's 7 o'clock?"

"Perfect. I'll see you then."

"Wow, Macy. He's cuter than I remember," her mom said as she came back in the house.

"I would have to agree with you, Mom. I guess I better get going so I can get ready."

"Alright. Have fun!" Leanne said.

Macy was just about finished getting ready when she glanced out the second story window and saw Luke getting out of his car. "Crap! He's here and he's all dressed up." She quickly ran to the closet but stopped to take one more look, "Damn, he looks so good!" *I can't wear shorts and a top when he looks like that,* she thought to herself and changed as fast as she could.

Luke came to the door. Macy gave him a welcome hug. He smelled so good and looked even better. "You look awesome," Luke told Macy. Luke's teenage hormones were on fire at the sight of Macy. *Damn, she is so hot and my God, she smells amazing,* he thought to himself.

"Thank you, Luke."

"Hi Mr. Horn." Luke reached out for Macy's dad's hand.

"Hello, Luke." Peter replied.

"It's good to see you again."

"And, you too. All good with your mom?"

"Yes, sir. She's doing great." He tried to make eye contact with Peter, but found it hard to take his eyes off of Macy.

"You ready to get going? I made reservations."

"Oh okay. Yes, I'm all set," Macy replied surprised and excited by his chivalry.

They walked down the staircase to the parking lot hand in hand. Luke led her to his car and opened the door for Macy and shut it behind her.

"Nice car, Luke. What happened to the Fairmont?" Macy asked with a chuckle.

"Thanks. I like it. It's a lot of fun but needs some work."

"So where are you taking me?"

"Somewhere nice. I'm sure you'll love it as much as I do."

He drove her to a nice restaurant on the riverfront for dinner. Luke got out first to walk around and open the door for Macy— taking her hand, not letting go until they made it to the door of the restaurant. They had a table waiting for them on the sun porch of a very popular restaurant. It was a beautiful early summer evening. Not too hot and not too cold. Macy and Luke picked up where they left off three years ago.

"So tell me what you've been up to, Luke."

"Well, a lot has happened, too much to share tonight. But the most obvious and most recent would be being discharged from the Marines. I enlisted right after graduation, specifically to join the Drum & Bugle Corps. Had boot camp in San Diego and then transferred to Camp Lejeune in North Carolina. But was honorably discharged earlier this month for medical reasons and decided to move back home. So here I am. What about you?"

"So, here you are." Macy smiled. "Well, Mom and Dad divorced, which you obviously figured out by now. That was a pretty terrible time. It happened right before graduation. I moved into my friend's basement for a little while. My sisters were staying with other family. We had to sell our house. Mom and us girls lived in a very tiny apartment for a while until she found the duplex she's in now. But when Dad was selling the house, he showed me the apartment complex he was going to move into and at the request of my mother, I decided to move in with him. She thought it would be a good idea for me to 'get to know' Dad. Even though my relationship with Mom hasn't been the same ever since moving in with Dad, he and Mom have been working on reconciling, so we'll see."

"So now that you're out of the Marines, what are you doing?" Macy asked, changing the subject.

"After getting discharged, I moved to Atlanta for a little while. While I was there, I worked at Ronnie's Sports. So when I came home, I was able to get a Manager-in-Training position at Champs at Northwest Plaza. I'm staying with my mom in St. Peters for now. Are you working?"

"Of course. I've been working at DoubleTree hotel ever since graduation. Misty and Tess, remember you met her at the church picnic, work there too."

"Oh my gosh! How are they?"

"They're great. Crazy as ever."

Luke and Macy spent the rest of the evening walking along the riverfront, holding hands, kissing and catching up. Luke drove Macy back to the apartment complex where they continued their conversations and rekindling the very same sparks that generated so much connection between them before. They listened to music and Luke sang to Macy.

"I don't want this night to end," Macy confessed to Luke.

"Me neither," Luke replied.

"Come on," Macy grabbed Luke's hand.

"Where are we going?"

"Just for a little walk."

Macy led Luke to the lighted tennis courts. They were the only two awake in the complex, so they believed. The two sat on the warm court and made out.

And so it was; Macy and Luke were back together as if they had never parted.

They spent the next couple of months reconnecting. Macy visited Luke at his store when she was off work. Luke would visit Macy at the hotel. They'd stay up all night long talking and end up sleeping over at each other's homes. They went to the movies, they ate out—Macy had never stepped foot into a Subway or Taco Bell until Luke took her there. They met new friends. They found new hangouts. They shared their hopes and dreams and fears with each other.

"So what happened with your mom and step-dad? Why'd they divorce?" Macy asked. They were lying on the living room floor of Judy's condo, Macy's head resting in Luke's arm.

"Um, well, it's a pretty messed up story."

Luke rolled over to face Macy, "Shortly after the time you and I broke up, my dad came back in the picture. He and my mom met up a couple of times."

"Wow! Really?" Macy asked.

"Knowing this caused me to smart off to Timothy. You know that 'you're not my dad' stuff. A part of me was happy that my mom and dad were talking again. I guess there was a little bit of excitement thinking they could get back together. But when Timothy heard of my mom and dad meeting up, he ended the marriage immediately."

"Holy crap. That really sucks. Well, what's the deal then with your real dad?" Macy asked.

"Oh, he's in Alton. Nothing ever came of it between them. So on top of all that, my mom being heart-broken all over again and losing her husband, Tina and I broke up. I moved out to Alton with my dad and two half-brothers. Even spent my last semester of school struggling with, well everything—I almost didn't graduate. I hated school and skipped a bunch and my dad did nothing. He'd be like, 'Luke it's time for school,' and I'd just say,

'I'm not going,' and he'd do nothing, absolutely nothing. That's when I decided to go into the Marines, like he did."

"I'm so sorry that happened to you and your mom and geez, little Jason. How old are your two half-brothers?"

"Justin's 10 and Ryan's 8."

"And they live with your dad?"

"Yeah, Patricia, his ex-wife...their mom, decided to move to Mexico and left the boys with my dad."

"Oh my gosh, Luke. Things have just been pretty inconsistent for you for a long time, huh?"

"Yeah, I guess you could say that."

"I want to take care of you, Luke." Macy ran her fingers through Luke's hair and along his face. She kissed him on the mouth. Luke kissed back.

"I want you to too, Macy."

The work that Macy's parents had done to resolve their marriage over the past couple of months was now becoming reality. They found a home in St. Peters and got remarried in the courthouse. Peter and Leanne were a very good-looking couple, however, their new wedding photo gave off a perception of nervousness and exhaustion. Leanne in her off-white suit was very thin from the ulcers she suffered during their divorce. Peter was a new man, in his navy sport coat and tie, now that he left his anger and cigarettes where they belonged, in the trash out on the curb.

With Peter and Leanne remarried, Macy had the option of moving in with them or getting a place of her own. It was a couple days before Peter and Leanne's move when Luke came over to help Macy pack up her things. "I made you something," Luke said as he came in the door.

He headed straight for the stereo and popped in a cassette tape—a compilation of all of their songs. He pushed the play button. Luther Vandross' "Here and Now" began to play. Luke reached out his hand to Macy, "Dance with me?" She took his hand and he pulled her close and they danced. She always loved the way he smelled and how warm he felt.

Luke sang a couple verses to Macy but then stopped. He starred at her for a brief moment.

"Macy, will you marry me? I want you to be my wife."

Macy pulled back to look at Luke's face. He had a tear in his eye.

"What? Really, are you serious?!"

"I don't have a ring or anything." He paused. "I love you more than you know," Luke told her.

"Yes! Absolutely. Yes, I will marry you. I love you so much," Macy replied. "And, I want nothing more than to be your wife."

"Let's move in together," Luke suggested.

It had only been two months since Luke and Macy were dating again and they were progressing with their future at lightning speed.

They found an apartment right across the street from the very spot they met three years prior. They both signed the lease and it was theirs. They would move in in a couple weeks.

"Come on, let's go to the mall. We're gonna need some stuff for our new place," Luke said.

Luke and Macy went to the mall and both of them opened some department store credit cards. They bought towels, a phone, dishes and some CDs and, of course, Macy picked out some engagement rings at the jewelry store.

They stopped by Macy's parent's new house to share the news of their engagement and decision to move in together. Peter and Leanne were totally put off about them living together—which is putting it lightly. In fact, Peter even had reservations about the engagement. Leanne, although very reserved, was sweet and hugged both Macy and Luke in congratulations.

Luke and Macy headed back to Macy's apartment to do more packing. Luke called his mom to tell her the news. She too was excited about the engagement but not pleased whatsoever with the moving in together part.

"You really think living in sin is the right thing to do?" Judy asked.

"Ma, I love her and we're going to get married. Nobody else has ever made me feel like this. She is all I ever want to be with." he replied.

They ordered a pizza and watched the movie they had picked up from Blockbuster when they finished packing; sharing in occasional hopes and wishes for the future.

"I can't wait to call you Mrs. Luke Hawthorn," Luke said as he came from the kitchen with plates and drinks.

"I can't wait for you to see me in my dress as I walk down the aisle," Macy replied. "You're going to lose it," she said smiling.

"You're absolutely right. I'll be crying like a baby, too."

Macy and Luke headed to their new place the next day with their boxes and new purchases to spend their first night together in their apartment. They were both so excited to have a place of their own. They unpacked and made decisions on where everything would go...which didn't take too long since they didn't have much.

While eating pasta by candlelight and listening to CDs on the boom box, they tried to soak in just where they were in that very moment and both felt a great sense of excitement for where they were heading. They didn't have a bed yet, so they crashed in each other's arms on the living room floor listening to their Johnny Gill, Black Crows, Seal, Slaughter and Whitesnake CDs, as the 6-CD changer played over and over.

Tomorrow came and more furniture was delivered thanks to Peter and Leanne, including Macy's old bedroom set. They spent the next few days living together as a couple—going to their jobs, washing each other's laundry, making each other dinner, taking out the trash, buying groceries, etc. They took care of each other.

"You okay, Macy?"

"No, I'm miserable. I can't breathe. I've got the chills and can't sleep."

"Want me to get you something? I can get you some medicine?" Luke offered.

"No, Luke. That's okay."

Luke got out of bed, put some clothes on, and headed to the local Walgreens to pick up some meds for his ill Macy. He got home and gave her a dose.

"I'm sorry I woke you up, Luke."

"It's okay, Macy. Get some sleep now," as he kissed her on her forehead.

"Thank you, baby."

Macy woke up to the phone ringing the next morning. It was her boss.

"Macy, you coming into work today?" he asked.

"Oh my gosh. What time is it?" she replied. "I'll be there as soon as I can."

It was almost 11:00am and she was supposed to be at work at 7:00am. Luke had already left for work. Still feeling ill, she showered and got ready for work. She stood there thinking about what Luke had done for her the night before. It was his little acts of kindness that touched her the most—the cassette tape, his notes, an occasional flower and now this.

Several months passed by as the weather grew colder. Luke was offered an Assistant Store Manager position at a new Champs store that was opening in a town not far from Chicago. It was a better paying position and a move up, but it was in another state.

"Really, Chicago?" Macy asked, knowing this was a possibility.

"I know, Macy. You can come and see me when you're not working. It'll be okay, I promise."

"Where will you stay?" Macy asked.

"I'll probably get an apartment with the other guys that are going to be in training with me. I'm not sure, though."

"Well, I don't think I can afford this place all on my own. I guess I'll ask if I can move back in with Mom and Dad until we see how things go. We can save up some money for the wedding and a new place."

"I love you, Macy, and I do want to take care of you," Luke assured her.

The night before Luke headed out for Chicago, he and Macy had dinner at Leanne and Peter's. Luke and Peter had gone into town to run an errand and returned as the girls were setting the table. The family made casual conversation over Leanne's wonderful spaghetti.

"So where are you going to be living in Chicago, Luke?" Peter asked.

"I'm going to share an apartment in Shaumburg with the two other guys I'll be working with." Luke replied. "It's a two bedroom so I'll have to share a room. But that will help keep rent low."

"And, have you guys discussed any wedding plans yet?" Leanne asked.

"We want to get married in the fall so we're thinking next October. Pretty sure it's hard to find a hall any sooner than a year, and with Luke's job transition that should be a good time." Macy shared.

"Well, just let us know how we can help with the plans," Leanne said.

The four finished dinner. As they got up to put their dishes in the sink, Luke began saying his good-byes.

"Peter, thank you so much for everything," Luke said shaking Peter's hand. "Leanne, thank you for dinner and all you do for us. I'll be talking to you all soon."

Macy and Luke walked out to his car.

"Macy, I really don't want to leave you. I wish you could just come with me. I truly hate this. You're going to come visit me, right?" he asked sarcastically.

Macy had her head in Luke's chest. "Of course, as soon as I can." She looked up to his eyes, "How am I going to sleep without you next to me?"

Luke grabbed her hand and put an engagement ring on her finger, "I'm going to marry you, Macy. I can't wait to call you my wife!"

It was the pear shaped solitaire Macy had picked out. They hugged and cried with one another.

"I love you, Luke Hawthorn. I will always love you. Come home to me soon," she said.

"Oh, Macy. I will. I promise you! I love you with everything I am."

Macy drove to Chicago to visit Luke as soon as she had a couple of days off. It was a long, quiet drive. It had snowed in Chicago. Macy finally found his building despite the wet packed snow that hadn't been cleared yet. She climbed the couple flights of stairs to Luke's apartment. It was full of new smells and sounds that would become a permanent fixture in her memory. She was so excited to see Luke again—to touch his face, to smell his neck and kiss those mushy lips of his. She knocked on the door and there he was.

Luke gave her the tightest hug yet. "Get in here," he said to her. "God, you look awesome!"

"So do you," she said. "I've missed you so much."

"Oh my God, I've missed you!"

Luke introduced Macy to his roommates and showed her around the apartment. His room was the back bedroom, which he shared. It was a typical bachelor pad complete with hand-me-down furniture, a nasty bathroom, no food in the pantry or fridge, pizza boxes piled up on the trash can, empty beer cans everywhere and dirty dishes in the sink.

Luke and Macy hung out in his bedroom for a while for some long-overdue time to reconnect. Luke had brought the boom box and CDs with him so he put in Johnny Gill. They spent the next couple hours lying with each other.

"Oh, baby, it's so hard to fall asleep without you here. I miss your smell and feeling you next to me," Luke told Macy.

"Same for me, Luke. I just feel like a part of me is missing when you're not near me."

When Luke's roommate got home, they decided to go out for a while. Luke took Macy to see his store at the mall right before it closed. Then they stopped for a late dinner at Steak 'n Shake.

"I put a deposit down on a dress." Macy told Luke.

"Oh my gosh, really?" Luke said with much excitement. "You are going to be my bride," Luke said sweetly. "What does it look like?"

"I can't tell you, but you are going to love it."

"That's awesome. You are going to be the most beautiful bride. Macy, you are the most beautiful woman I know."

Luke reached out across the table for Macy's hand so he could kiss her ring. There were other people in the restaurant, but as far as Luke and Macy were concerned, not even a waiter or cook could've been there.

"Can you believe it, Luke? Before we know it, we are going to be Mr. and Mrs. Hawthorn. What are you going to do when you're a husband?"

"Take care of you. Make babies with you."

"Make babies, huh?" Macy replied with a coy grin.

"Yes. Three babies." They both smiled and held hands and then at the same time said, "Three—a boy, a girl, and another boy."

"How perfect would that be?" Macy replied amazed that they said the exact same thing.

"Add a couple of dogs and a cat and we're a family!"

"I just can't wait to marry you! To be your bride."

They spent the rest of the weekend going out dancing, laughing and holding each other. Macy got back in her car to head home—home with her mom and dad, who were becoming ever more impatient with Macy as she wanted to live her life by her rules and not theirs despite living under their roof.

It was a huge struggle to be away from Luke and getting grief from Peter and Leanne all of the time didn't help. The late nights talking on the phone only lasted so long since Macy's parents weren't having the excessive long-distance charges on their phone bill. The house rules and the distance made Macy want to be near Luke even more. So, Macy used her dad's credit card to fly back and forth to Midway a couple of times. It was the credit card he let her use during a visit to (then) Southwest Missouri State to see some of her friends from high school who were attending there. "Here, take this and use it only in case of an emergency," Peter had said.

It was hard for Luke to be away from Macy. And being so young, temptation was everywhere. Luke and Macy were engaged but living five plus hours apart. Going out to the clubs made it hard to maintain commitment, *besides flirting and dancing with other girls isn't so bad and doesn't really cross any lines, right?* Luke would ask himself at times.

Macy too found herself flirting with temptation at times. Partying and going out with friends and meeting new people kept Luke even further from her thoughts. Even though Luke made it home for the holidays, there was a growing absence between she and Luke both.

CHAPTER 3

"My, My, My"
1991

By February, Luke moved back home with his mom and started working at a local Champs store. This was mostly an attempt to keep the waters calm while Macy and Luke were still engaged, and besides, Macy was living with her parents too.

One night while sleeping over at Luke's, Macy was awakened by Luke standing in front of the basement support pole shaking his head and pointing in various directions. She sat up, rubbing her eyes, "Luke?" She got out of bed to get a closer look at what he was doing. He was talking to the pole. "We're having a buy one get one free sale on all of the team sweatshirts and, oh, all of our accessories are two for $15 or three for $20."

Oh my goodness, he's sleepwalking. Don't wake him up, Macy told herself. She remembered seeing a documentary on how you should just calmly get them back to bed. "Baby, come back to bed with me," she whispered, while gently putting her hand on Luke's back to direct him to the bed. He climbed back in bed and never remembered selling to the pole when Macy asked him about it the next day.

This was another example of Luke's restlessness and continuous excitability. He rarely ever sat still.

That April, Macy turned 20 and the following month Luke turned 21. They celebrated Luke's 21st birthday over dinner at Racquets Club, a casual restaurant at the hotel where Macy worked. They each had a giant cheeseburger, Macy had a Pepsi and Luke had a beer.

"You okay?" Macy asked Luke. "You seem quiet."

"What? Huh? Oh no, I'm fine." Luke came out of his daze to respond but then looked back at his watch.

"Okay." Macy said not believing him.

"You ready to get out of here?" Luke asked.

"Sure."

As they pulled out of the parking lot, Luke made the right turn on to the highway toward home.

"Why are you going this way? I thought you wanted to go do something? Did you want to go to a movie? Or rent one and go back to your place?" Macy asked as she looked in the visor mirror reapplying her lip-gloss.

"Macy, I'm taking you home." He said matter-of-factly.

"What? Why?" Macy looked at him concerned fearing the impending abandonment.

"It's my twenty-first birthday. I'm going out with the guys. I get free drinks."

"Seriously, Luke? Wow!" Macy's disappointment and hurt came out as sarcasm. "Why the hell didn't you tell me that's what you wanted to do instead of dropping a bomb on me like this?"

"I shouldn't have to tell you." Luke said sheepishly.

"You're right, I should know that free shots are more important to you than I am. I get it."

"Give me a break, Macy."

Luke pulled up to Macy's house. She got out of the car without looking at Luke and said, "Have a great birthday."

Luke said nothing as he drove off.

Macy went straight to her room—passing her mom, dad and sisters in the kitchen.

June came and with it came a new job for Luke at Merry Go Round clothing store. Macy hated it. They sold guys and girls clothes, which were not her taste; and worst of all, the dressing rooms had no mirrors and a curtain for a door. There was, in Macy's opinion, a 'loose' sort of vibe in the store.

What worked in Luke's favor, however, was the commission that came with running the store. He was an excellent salesman and motivator. The employees—and the customers—loved him. Luke always knew how to say exactly what they wanted to hear. He was confident and outgoing and that charm of his won each and every one of them over—one more thing that set off Macy's insecurity.

That same month, Macy was a bridesmaid in one of her best friend's wedding. She had known Tess since high school. Luke had met Tess back when he and Macy first met. Unfortunately, Luke had to work that day and wasn't able to attend the festivities.

"I wish you could go to the wedding with me," Macy confessed.

"Yeah, sorry. You get that I can't ask off since I just started working here, right?"

"I know." Macy paused. "But I could pick you up after work and then you could go to the reception with me."

"Um, yeah. I could probably do that." Luke hesitated.

The day of the wedding, Macy and eleven other bridesmaids took part in the wedding ceremony and then went to a nearby park for pictures.

Meanwhile, Luke got a phone call from his manager to chat about the day's sales. "Luke, you should go to Roger's tonight. We're all going after work for drinks."

"Oh yeah? What's Roger's?" Luke asked confused.

"It's a dance club downtown. Donnie, Sarah, Aaron and all the other store managers will be there too. You should go."

"Yeah, that sounds awesome! I'll see you all down there." Luke hung up the phone and finished his close-up tasks. On the way to the club, Luke remembered that Macy was going to pick him up after work to go to Tess' reception. *Crap! Macy's going to hate me,* he thought as played with the radio. *I didn't really want to go to the reception anyway. It's probably better this way. She'd just be upset that she couldn't go with me to the club. It'll be all right.*

Macy went to pick up Luke after wedding pictures. "What the hell? Where is he?" Macy exclaimed as she pulled into the mall parking lot. His car was nowhere to be found. She drove to his mom's house thinking maybe he was going home first. But he wasn't there either. Macy was left behind without any explanation. She didn't really know what to do but eventually headed back to the reception alone and upset.

Turning twenty-one had created a new and exciting time for Luke filled with a new, outgoing group of friends who could all legally drink together. He was constantly torn but usually chose to hit the clubs to do shots rather than spend time with Macy. He'd party and dance and drink at the clubs while she'd have to stay back.

There were a few times that Macy would get in to the clubs by using someone else's ID, but sometimes that didn't work. One night she went to meet Luke at a club, and the bouncer ripped up her (fake) ID—sending her home in tears. She had no way of letting Luke know that she was stranded in the lobby; she wanted nothing more than for Luke to feel badly and take her home and be with her. But that didn't happen.

Now another type of wedge was growing between the couple all thanks to their age difference. While they still did things together, the unspoken and unresolved concerns kept Luke and Macy emotionally separate. Macy didn't like how Luke would invite her to work parties out of what felt like was obligation. Luke didn't like how he was made to feel badly that he wanted to go have fun. This was not the sort of engagement Macy had ever envisioned.

With this new type of distance between them, Macy became more and more uneasy and frustrated. She wanted out of her parent's house and back into her own place so badly. She wanted her independence and privacy, no curfews and freedom to talk on the phone or listen to her music (as loudly or softly as she wanted) when she wanted to. She realized picking up a second job would allow just that.

One sunny summer afternoon, Luke called Macy at the hotel before her shift was over. "Hey, Macy! How's your day going?"

"Hi Luke. Not bad. What's goin' on?"

"You have plans tonight?"

"I'm not sure yet, why?" Macy actually was planning on going to talk to the manager at Glamour Shots to apply for the open position they had, but she didn't want to tell Luke.

"Well, my mom's in Iowa visiting with Jason, so I invited some friends over."

"You're having a party at your mom's house?" Macy asked in disbelief, knowing Judy would have a conniption if she knew.

"Yeah, it'll be fun. Come over, okay?"

"Um, okay. Sure, I'll try."

After applying for the open position, the manager hired her on the spot. She spent the next couple of hours getting to know all the procedures involved in setting up appointments, sittings, etc. She really enjoyed talking with CJ, one of the stylists who immediately took her under her wing.

"Girl, you are awesome. I just know we're going to have a blast working together," she told Macy on her way out. I'll see you in a couple days.

Macy made the drive from the mall to Luke's mom's house tentatively; worried Judy would come home at any moment. The party was in full swing when she arrived. She had been thinking on the way there about how Luke invited her to the party as if she was just another guest. *Did he forget that he asked me to marry him? That I said yes? He's really pissing me off lately. It just feels like he's just kicked me and my under-age status to the curb.*

She walked in the front door and into the kitchen, walking by a bunch of people that she didn't know playing drinking games. Then she walked through to the TV room where she saw Luke. He was at the radio putting in a new CD before returning to the girl sitting on the couch. There was no question in Macy's mind that they were a little too chummy. She made the step down into the sunken room and plastered a smile on her face.

"Well, hello there!" she said catching Luke off guard.

"Hey, what's up, Macy?" Luke stammered with regret in his eyes. "Do you, uh, know Jamie?"

"Oh, hi, Jamie. You work at Contempo now, right?" Macy realized that most of the people she didn't know were from other stores in the mall.

"Hi Macy," Jamie replied and looked away.

"Luke, I'm not feeling it. Think I'm gonna head out."

"Yeah? Well, all right. I'll talk to you tomorrow."

"Sure."

Macy stopped at the front window to take one last look at Luke before she left. She felt like a stranger to him. It was as if they were broken up but neither one of them officially called it off. Adding insult to injury, *oh my God, NO!* She saw Luke kiss Jamie. "NO!" she cried. "He's *my* fiancé!" She didn't know who to be angrier with.

Macy went home; but instead of crying, she wanted revenge. She dug through her nightstand until she found Sam's phone number.

"Hi, is Sam there?"

"No, I'm sorry he's doesn't live here anymore. Can I ask who's calling?"

"Hi, Mrs. Trisson. It's Macy Horn."

"Oh, hi Macy. It's good to hear from you. Sam and Joe have their own apartment now. Here, let me give you the number."

"Thank you and sorry to call so late." Macy wrote Sam's new number in her book.

"You're welcome, Macy. Take care."

Macy fell asleep while contemplating whether to call Sam or not.

The next evening, Luke showed up at Macy's house with a rose.

"Macy, can I talk to you?"

"Are you kidding me? Right now?" She walked out onto the porch closing the front door behind her. "I saw you kiss her, Luke!"

"You did? Oh, Macy. I'm not going to lie. I did, and I feel awful for it. I don't know what the hell I was thinking. But it was a huge mistake!"

"Luke, how would you feel if you saw me kissing someone else?"

"I'd be really, really pissed off and probably wouldn't be speaking to you like you are with me right now."

"I just absolutely can't believe you would do that to me."

"I really am sorry, Macy."

"Well, awesome. I'm glad. Your sorry doesn't change how angry and hurt I am right now."

Luke kissed Macy on the cheek, setting the rose on her lap. "I am sorry. I'll talk to you tomorrow?"

"Sure. Whatever."

Seeing Luke made Macy angry all over again. She had that picture of him kissing another girl burned into her memory, and seeing his face instantly replayed the moment in her head over and over again—causing her stomach to turn and twist in a knot. She went to her room to make a phone call.

"Sam? Hey it's Macy."

"Macy Horn. What the hell are you doin'?"

"Nothin' much. What about you?"

"Just watching movies with my brother and some of his friends. Why are you calling me? Where's Luke?"

"Oh, Luke? I don't really know where Luke is. But, I was just thinking about you and thought I'd give you a call. Your mom gave me your new number."

"Sweet. Well come on over if you want."

"Yeah? Sure, okay. Sounds great."

Macy got directions and headed over to Sam's. She was hoping Sam would make a move on her and she'd let him...the same way Luke did with Jamie. But Sam never made a move—although his brother Joe did. Macy reciprocated, only it didn't make her feel one bit better; but instead full of shame and regret.

After that night, Macy and Luke continued to drift apart—wanting to believe that the other was somehow responsible for the distance and loneliness that continued to grow between them.

Work certainly kept Macy busy in the meantime. The holiday season was quickly approaching, so it was the perfect time for her to earn some extra money with her full-time and part-time jobs. It didn't take long for her to save up enough to put a deposit down on a loft apartment in St. Charles. It came furnished, so Macy just had to pack up her TV, clothes and dishes and she was back on her own—just the way *she* loved it. Macy's mom even bought her a vacuum cleaner...Macy believed it was more a 'thank you for moving out' gift more than it was an apartment-warming gift. With her new job and new apartment, Macy finally had the independence she longed for...but something was missing. Luke was missing.

"Macy, can we talk?"

"About what?"

"What are we doing?"

"Nothing."

"Yeah, well, I don't want us to be like this anymore. I love you, Macy."

"No you don't. You'd rather be with your girlfriends from the store."

"Macy, that's not true. I don't know what my deal is, but no one will ever do to me what you do. I'm sorry I've been a dick. I want to come see you."

Macy conceded. When Luke arrived, Macy let him in and barely made eye contact. Not only was she feeling extremely guilty, she was also feeling really sick.

"This loft is pretty cool. I'm sure you love having your own place, huh?" Luke asked as he sat down on the couch.

"Yeah, it's nothing special, but it's mine! I love knowing that I pay the bills and I have the key."

"Luke, what *is* going on with us? I am so confused. Is all that happened this past summer and fall your idea of being engaged?"

"Absolutely not. Macy, I really feel awful for how I've been treating you. I've taken every advantage available being twenty-one now and tried to ignore how that must make you feel."

"Luke, you were with Jamie and that has nothing to do with our age difference."

"Macy, I crossed a line in a bad way. But I owned up to it and apologized. How much more are you going to rub my nose in it?"

"It hurt so badly, Luke. To see you put your mouth on someone else's. I felt kicked and stepped on. You made me—"

He cut her off. "Macy, what can I do?" Luke pleaded.

"Do you know why Sam and I broke up?"

"Sam? What's he got to do with anything?"

"He walked out on me, Luke. He left me in his bedroom while his parents were downstairs. I led him to believe I'd sleep with him and then I didn't. So he got up and walked out, and that was the last time I saw him."

"He what? Are you freaking kidding me, Macy—?"

Macy wasn't finished and cut him off, "—until the other night."

"I'm not following...what did you say?!"

"I went to see him. When I saw you kiss Jamie, I lost it and wanted to hurt you back."

"Macy what the hell are you talking about?"

"But nothing happened...with Sam. I...I was with Joe." Macy broke down and cried. She was so ashamed.

"Oh my God. You're kidding me, right? I cannot believe you're telling me this right now. I apologized, Macy!"

"Yeah, but I didn't believe you, Luke. I knew you and Jamie did more than kiss."

"Macy, I told you—"

"Luke, I'm sorry!" Macy was sobbing, kneeling on the floor and holding her face in her hands. "I'm so sorry. I don't want us to do this. I don't want to hurt you. I love you so much and YOU are the only one I want to be with. YOU, Luke. No one else." Macy was screaming now. "Do you hear me, Luke? You, I only want YOU."

Luke kneeled down beside Macy and pulled her close. "Macy, I'm so sorry. I did this to you. I pushed you away. I love you so much and don't want to hurt you. I want to marry you. I don't want anyone else, either. I only want YOU, Macy." Luke was crying too.

Macy's rigid body became relaxed as she heard Luke say that he still loved her and wanted to marry her. "Luke, I'm so sorry. I'm embarrassed and ashamed with what I've done."

"I know, Macy. Me too." He kissed her forehead and wiped her tears.

The holidays quickly came, as well as the colder winter weather. Luke and Macy exchanged many gifts over the Christmas holiday and had Christmas with each other's families, which they always had so much fun doing. Being part of name exchanges and dinners gave them much excitement for what their future would hold.

They had also agreed on a banquet hall for their reception, a DJ and a church: they were going to get married at St. Patrick's where Macy grew up attending. Leanne put a deposit down on the banquet hall for them and the contracts were signed. A fall wedding was in the works!

Luke and Macy made big plans for a New Year's Eve outing with a couple of Luke's friends. They both got dressed up—Macy in her little black dress and black blazer and Luke in his black suit. They made several stops at parties and clubs. What fun it was to make appearances and be crazy and dance all night. While in a crowded downtown loft apartment, just like something straight out of the movie *Less Than Zero*, with drinks in hand and their arms around each other, they counted down till midnight. Luke and Macy kissed as the clock struck midnight.

"I love you so much," Luke told Macy. "I truly cannot wait to spend the rest of my life with you."

"I love you, Luke, more than you'll ever know."

"Happy New Year, baby."

"Happy New Year."

The two couples returned to Luke and Macy's friend's house. They said their goodbyes and Luke and Macy headed back to their apartment. While Luke drove, Macy kissed his ear and his neck; the excitement between them both had been growing all night and they just couldn't wait to get back to the apartment. It was an evening full of passion. The connection that they had together, physically and emotionally was intense; the lovemaking was overwhelming. Luke and Macy began their new year in each other's arms.

CHAPTER 4

"This Woman's Work"
1992

The year was 1992, and Luke and Macy would be getting married in just ten short months. Luke was doing well managing his Merry Go Round store while Macy was taking on more in her front office position at the hotel. After a day of working the front desk and doing a little training in the sales office, Macy went straight for the couch as soon as she got home. *What time is it?* Macy asked herself as she sat up on the couch, rubbing her eyes. "Oh my gosh...it's like eleven o'clock. I've been sleeping for almost seven hours!" She stretched as she made her way to the kitchen, trying to shake off the exhaustion she felt. Macy made herself a bite to eat but could barely stay awake. She finished her sandwich and returned to bed shortly after.

Luke was working until close at the store and ended up going out with the guys. He got home early in the morning and then crashed on the couch in hopes of not waking Macy or, worse, pissing her off. She would have read him the riot act for his cigarette smoke-covered clothing and beer breath.

Macy woke up later that morning, and as she put on her robe and went to the kitchen for some juice, she shook her head at Luke sleeping on the couch. She could smell the stench of alcohol and clothes saturated in cigarette smoke as she walked down the stairs. "God! Nothing like a liquored up fiancé passed out on the couch—love it." Macy muttered under her breath.

Luke woke up as Macy's toast popped up.

"Hey."

"Hey. Late night?" Macy replied with sarcasm, not looking up from smearing jelly on her toast.

47

"Yeah, guess so." Luke crinkled up his eyebrows to the rhetorical question but also to shield his eyes from the sunlight peering in from the curtains. His head was pounding.

"Really can't stand that crap," Macy sneered under her breath. "I'm taking a shower." *Getting in the hot shower should help me get out of this funk*, Macy thought as she closed the bathroom door behind her.

She stepped in the shower and put her face in the shower stream. "Ouch! Holy crap that hurts!" The water seemed to pound on Macy's chest, and it felt like sharp needles piercing her breasts—something she had never felt before and painful enough to bring tears to her eyes. She quickly turned her back to the water. "What the hell?" She asked and she stood there, arms crossed over her breasts, analyzing the thoughts racing through her mind. That's when the thought hit her like a ton of bricks...*could I be pregnant?*

Her mind immediately went to the pregnancy test she had bought a while back for a previous scare. She turned off the water, stepped out of the shower and immediately found the one remaining in the box. Macy peed on the test strip, and then with her head in her hands, she sat there on the edge of the tub for those fifteen excruciating minutes.

Already certain of the results, Macy thought to herself. *What am I going to do if I am pregnant? What about the wedding? What will my parents think? What will Luke think? How could this be happening to me?* The scared thoughts flooded Macy's head and heart.

"Macy? Are you okay in there?" Luke asked, knocking on the door.

With hesitation Macy responded, "Uh yeah, I'm fine."

"You've been in there a really long time. Can I come in?"

Fifteen minutes was up.

Macy opened the door. Luke smiled at Macy, "You okay, honey?" he asked.

Macy directed his eyes to the test that sat on the sink and thought, *I'm pregnant. Of course, the test was positive...I have every classic symptom in the book.* So fearful of Luke's response, Macy just sat there.

"What? You're pregnant?!" Luke asked with reserved excitement picking up the test stick and looking back at Macy.

"I'm afraid so," Macy said, nodding her head as she stared into his eyes.

Luke looked into her eyes, staring off a bit but seeing the fear in Macy's eyes. With that giant grin of his, Luke rejoiced, "Oh my gosh...we're going to have a baby!" He picked Macy up and squeezed her.

"Hey! Ouch! Don't squeeze so hard." Macy yelped as she half-smiled. *How can he be so excited?* Macy wondered. *Doesn't he realize what this does to everything...all of our plans, the wedding, jobs, etc.*

"Oh my God. There is just no way I'm walking down the aisle a pregnant bride. Shoot, the priest won't even marry us now. Holy crap, we can't get married in the church! What are we going to do??" Macy cried to Luke as they walked out of the Birthright center. "I mean when I woke up from the couch the other night after sleeping for seven hours, I knew something was up. But now that we know for sure, what are we going to do?? How are we going to have a wedding now? I'm going to have to return my dress. My parents are going to be so disappointed. It wasn't supposed to happen to this way."

Confused and scared himself, Luke searched for the words Macy needed to hear. He shut the car door behind her and walked around to the driver's side while thinking to himself, *what are we going to do? I don't know how to be a dad; I don't even know how to be a husband.* "Baby we'll make it work! We could get married at my mom's church," Luke said, trying to console Macy (and himself).

"No, no one from my family would come. I just don't get how this happened? I've been on birth control for a while now. What went wrong?"

"What about that medicine you were on from your hospital stay? Did they tell you any side effects?"

Macy had fallen ill with a pretty bad infection and spent the night in the hospital after running high temperatures for a couple of days. They wanted to keep her for observation and treated her with fluids and antibiotics.

"That was just a strong form of antibiotics, that's what they told me any way. You know, I do remember them asking if I was sexually active. They're a Catholic hospital and do not believe in or support birth control. Could antibiotics really screw with birth control and would they really keep that from me?"

"Whatever happened, the fact is we're having a baby. We're having a baby, Macy! Aren't you excited?"

"Yeah, I guess so. But, I'm just so scared!"

"Maybe he or she will have your blue eyes and my brown hair. You know we're going to have a beautiful baby! Not to mention just how beautiful you are—you're glowing, Honey!"

"Wow!" Macy smiled. "You always know just what to say, don't you?" She didn't feel very beautiful. More like a giant disappointment.

Luke, Macy, Peter and Leanne all sat around the kitchen table after finishing a meal together. "Mom and Dad, Luke and I need to talk to about you something," Macy said.

"Oh okay. What's going on?" Leanne raised her eyebrows.

Luke anxiously started the conversation off. "Well, we're going to have a change of plans somewhat."

Peter pulled his shoulders back and sat stiffly in his chair. Leanne took a deep breath.

"We're pregnant," Macy blurted out.

"You're kidding me," Leanne snarled sarcastically.

"No, I'm afraid we're totally serious." Macy confirmed looking up from her plate.

Peter sunk in his seat and looked at Leanne, "There go our deposits."

The ride back to the apartment was a quiet one. Macy and Luke feeling like complete disappointments kept the conversation at a standstill.

When they told Judy, she was compassionate but worried. "Oh you guys. It's going to be so very hard. I'll help however I can." She said with great concern.

Along with the news of becoming parents, the next couple of months brought Macy and Luke other changes as well. Macy started a new position in the sales office at the hotel. She was very excited for the opportunity, as it was a step up from her front office responsibilities that she had been working for three years now. She couldn't wait to trade in eight hours of standing and for a desk and comfy rolling chair. Luke's team continued to grow at the store as did his responsibilities. He was making a great name for himself thanks to some great sales volume.

They both looked forward to those first couple of visits to the OB. Macy hated the weigh-ins but always loved seeing the sign hanging in the office that read, "There could never be enough Dr. Ederings." Below that line listed Dr. Greg (Dad), Dr. Greg Jr. (Son), Dr. Charlie (Son) and Dr. Patrick (Son). Seeing this somehow made her nervousness subside and gain some hope that her baby's life was in good hands.

"You are progressing very nicely, everything's going as it should, Miss Macy. In a couple weeks, we'll be able to hear the baby's heartbeat." Dr. Charlie said putting his hand in Macy's as he helped her to sit up. "Do you have any questions for me?" he added.

"How far away do you live?" Luke blurted out with complete seriousness.

Dr. Charlie and Macy looked at each other. Macy just shrugged her shoulders.

Dr. Charlie looked back to Luke and said, "Just about ten minutes away."

He barely finished his sentence when Luke said, "It's just when we go into labor, I want to know that you're not far away."

Macy said, "I'm sure he's done this a few times before, Luke."

"Understood. It's a good question, Luke. Anything else?"

"Nah, I'm good." Luke confirmed.

Dr. Charlie always had something for Luke and Macy to take home with them such as pamphlets and videos. He also had them sign up for a Lamaze class and an epidural overview session. "Oh, I won't need that." Macy told Dr. Charlie. "I am not getting an epidural."

Dr. Charlie responded with, "It's a mandatory thing, Macy. We need you to go so no getting out of this one. Besides, it's extremely informative."

It was almost March now. Just a couple months had passed since the news of her baby. Macy was accepting the fact that she was going to be a mommy. *But what about our wedding plans? When and how are we going to be married?* Macy would wonder. One night she and Luke went out to dinner to discuss their plans.

"I've cancelled the hall and DJ. And, I've returned my dress," Macy shared with Luke "We're out the deposits, unfortunately, so those amounts will most definitely be added to the list of IOUs my father keeps for me."

"Honey, what about this…How about you and I elope? Let's just get married. We can do it just you and I at the courthouse. I know it's not the big wedding you had dreamt of but I also know how important it is to you and me for us to be married—especially before the baby is born."

Macy put her fork down and took a drink of her tea.

"What do you think? Say something."

Macy thought about how much she loved Luke. It made her sad to know that their plans had completely blown up in her face, but the worst part was she felt like a disappointment to so many—including herself. None of this changed the fact that she dearly loved the young man sitting across the table from her. She loved his brown eyes and that they could see so deeply into her. She loved his hands and his mouth, his smile, his voice, his excitement and spontaneity. She wanted so badly to be married to him—she had dreamt about it for years. And, he loved her, desperately loved her.

"I think it's a wonderful idea, honey! I really do. Let's do it."

Wedding Day. (If you can call it that.)

"Luke, get up. You need to get ready." Macy was out of the shower and had just finished blow-drying her hair. She had even eaten a nice breakfast, but Luke was still passed out from his bachelor party the night before. Luke's friends (the ones Macy didn't care for) kept him out very late and got him very drunk—no doubt they hit the strip clubs too. "So flipping disgusting," she muttered. "Luke, GET UP!" Macy yelled again as she kicked the bed. "Yeah, this is exactly how I had always envisioned the morning of my wedding," she mumbled as she finished getting dressed.

After a shower and a couple aspirin, Luke and Macy headed to the courthouse with their marriage license in hand and, of course, baby too. They waited out front in a waiting area along with numerous other couples waiting to tie-the-knot. It was the farthest thing from romantic. It was more like the DMV. Take a number and wait until it flashes up on the screen for your turn to say, "I do."

Their name was called and they entered what might as well have been the cafeteria of the local legion hall. Smelled like one too, dank and old. "Did you bring witnesses or will you be using court appointed witnesses?" the judge asked. "We'll use court appointed witnesses," Luke replied. The judge read from a sheet of paper and Luke and Macy repeated after him. Ten minutes later they were married. No long, mushy, romantic kiss; no pronouncing husband and wife or introducing Mr. and Mrs. Luke Hawthorn; no family or friends to throw bird seed or blow bubbles for them—they hadn't told a soul.

"How 'bout we have our own little reception?" Luke asked Macy.

"Okay. What did you have in mind?"

Luke drove them to Pizza Hut. He parked the car and Macy just laughed. "I'm hungry for pizza. That's what I would've preferred at our reception anyways," Luke joked with Macy.

They shared a pepperoni and jalapeno pizza. Luke picked up his glass, "I'd like to propose a toast." Macy picked up her glass. "To my bride, Mrs. Hawthorn, may I be the best husband to you forever and ever. I love you so much!" They clinked glasses and snickered at the clack sound, as best as two plastic glasses could.

"I love you so very much," Macy replied as she leaned across the table to give Luke a kiss.

"By the way, I'm keeping this," Macy said to Luke, putting her glass in her purse. "It will be our wedding gift."

Luke headed home but then put on his blinker. "I think we should pay my mom a visit to share the news with her. She'll feel so much better knowing we're officially married."

"What? You did what?!" she asked in that 'are you out of your mind' tone.

"Ma, we eloped. There was just no way we were going to make a big wedding happen."

"And, I am not going to be a pregnant bride." Macy chimed in.

"Besides, we want to be married before the baby comes."

"Well, I get it. I just wish I could've been there."

"I know, Ma. But we wanted it to be a surprise. If we told one person, we'd have to tell everyone else too."

The next day Luke and Macy shared the official news with Macy's parents. While at Peter and Leanne's for dinner, Macy asked her mom, "Do I have something on my cheek?" as she scratched her cheek using her ring finger—flashing the new wedding band next to her pear shaped solitaire.

"Um, what is this?" Leanne asked as she took Macy's hand and pulled it in Peter's direction.

"Well, we made it official yesterday morning—we're married." Macy replied smiling at Luke.

"Really?" Leanne's voice squeaked. "Oh my goodness. Well, congratulations you two!" Macy's mom hugged her and then hugged Luke. "Take care of my baby, Luke...and that grandbaby of ours."

"I will, I promise."

That following Tuesday, Leanne called Macy. "Dad and I want to have a reception for you. We can have it here at the house. I already talked to Judy about it, and she's going to help. We need to do it next month before dad and I go on vacation. We'll invite family and friends."

"Wow! Okay! Thanks, Mom! That would be great." Within just a couple of days, the invites were mailed out to all of their immediate family and friends.

Peter and Leanne's house was full of relatives and friends, young and old alike. "I don't know some of these people, do you?" Macy asked Luke.

"Um, not really," Luke concurred.

All of Macy's immediate family was there for the reception along with many of her aunts, uncles and cousins. Many of Luke's cousins had made it in from out of town including his dad, Ron. Ron's mother and step-dad, both made it to the party as well. Luke was always so excited to have his dad around. It was just one of those special wishes that rarely came true for Luke.

The buffet was set up with so much food. Having come from such large families, the food line ran like a well-oiled machine. The garage was set up with long tables and decorations. It was April and despite the chill in the air, Peter grilled and all the bodies crammed in the garage kept the temperature comfortable.

Peter was at the stove putting hot dogs and hamburgers into an aluminum pan when Judy joined him. "What a nice party, Peter," Judy said as she gave him a side-hug. "Thanks so much for opening your house to do this for the kids."

"Ah, thanks. It was the least we could do. Kids are having fun, don't ya think?" Peter replied.

"Yes, I think they are very happy!" Judy answered.

"I give 'em six months," Peter snickered.

"Now Peter, let's hope not." Judy laughed, not really knowing how to respond.

Inside the house, Macy and Luke were getting ready to cut the cake. They positioned themselves between the table and the china cabinet while some of the immediate family watched on. It was a white sheet cake that read, "Congratulations Luke & Macy," along with a couple red roses and green stems and sugar wedding bells. They both took a small piece and fed the other politely. No cake smashed in each other's faces, not today.

"Congratulations, Luke and Macy! We wish you all the very best and may God bless your marriage and new family." Judy said lifting her glass to toast the newlyweds. Luke kissed Macy on the cheek and a few moments later, Judy came around and kissed each of them on the tops of their heads. "Love you both," she whispered to them.

After extending many thank yous and hugs, Luke and Macy's day came to an end. When all of their guests had left, Peter, Leanne and Judy all stayed to help Luke and Macy open their gifts. Macy and Luke opened appliances, gift certificates, picture frames, cash, towels and some baby items. "This is all so wonderful," Macy said.

"Yes, thank you so very much for doing this for us today," Luke said as he and Macy both made their way off of the couch and across the room to hug their parents.

With all of the festivities over, it was time to find the new family a place to live. The studio loft apartment was just not going to accommodate their new family. "You ready to find ourselves and the baby an apartment?" Luke asked Macy.

"With our lease being up this month, I guess the timing is good, right?" Macy asked, seeking Luke's approval.

"Yes! It is time for our own place. Let's get dressed and go do some looking. With the cash we've got from our wedding gifts, we can afford to put down a deposit too."

They found a nice two-bedroom, two-bath apartment on the ground level really close to both of their jobs and, most importantly, their families. Luke and Macy signed the lease and fronted the six hundred dollar deposit that included one and a half month's rent.

They'd get to move in the following month.

During the end of her fourth month of pregnancy, Macy got a call from her favorite Aunt.

"Macy? It's Aunt Joan."

"Hi, Aunt Joan! What's up?"

"I have some really bad news. It's about Grandpa."

"Okay," Macy responded tentatively.

"Grandpa's passed away. We're trying to get a hold of your mom and dad now."

"Oh no, Aunt Joan. They're on the cruise ship!"

"Don't worry about that. Macy, get your sisters and go to your mom and dad's house. Your mom will want you all there when they get home."

When Leanne got the call on the cruise ship, she was devastated. She was on a boat so far away and felt helpless. Somehow she blamed herself for his death even though it was years of smoking and heart disease that had taken this sweet man's life at such an early age. "I know CPR. If I would have just been there, maybe I could have saved him," Leanne cried.

That night after the funeral, Macy got ready for bed and slid under the covers next to Luke. She was exhausted. She lay there thinking what a very sad day it had been; seeing all of her aunts and uncles, all the flowers and so many unknown faces whose lives had been touched by her grandpa. He was loved by so many. But the image that was ingrained in Macy's mind was that of her grandmother. She didn't cry the entire day—she was a rock. This woman had birthed ten babies with this man and stood by the side of his casket the entire day. She ended her time at the funeral by leaning down over the casket to give a sweet and gentle kiss to her deceased husband's forehead. She stood up, closed her eyes, and walked away. That was it.

As Macy finished pondering that moment, a sensation went through her womb. It was like nothing she had felt before. She wasn't hungry, she wasn't sick. *Oh my gosh, it's the baby. The baby just moved!* Macy realized. She held her belly in her hands and quietly woke Luke. "Luke, it's the baby. I felt the baby move!" She grabbed his hands and with hers they held her belly and felt the flutter of tiny feet or hands. And at that very moment, tears filled Macy's eyes as she thought to herself, *life goes on.* She couldn't help but smile knowing that her baby is healthy and somehow her grandfather was there with her too; perhaps to let her know that he was okay now. Luke kissed Macy's belly and they slept through the night wrapped around one another.

A couple of days later, Macy and Luke would be back at Dr. Charlie's office and cried as they heard their baby's heartbeat—the sound of what was like being underwater and hearing a helicopter overhead. It was another reminder of the recent loss of Macy's grandpa and the miracle that was growing inside of her. She had life within her—something no one could ever explain or prepare someone for. It's an emotion that comes with a unique definition that confirms you are officially a mother now that all of the senses have been acknowledged. That's exactly what Macy felt.

May had come and Luke and Macy were now settled in their new apartment. They bought a big couch and a couple tables and chairs from various garage sales. All that was left was the baby's room. Macy's parents pulled her old baby crib out of storage, the same crib she and her sisters had slept in. They also gave Macy the old rocker she loved so much. Both pieces were good as new after a fresh coat of white paint thanks to Peter. Leanne made all the bedding and curtains.

Macy and Luke (more so Macy) were not interested in finding out the sex of the baby, so Macy decided on yellow, blue, pink and green for the nursery décor. Dreaming about the sex of the baby and what he or she would look like and picking out boy and girl names was what would make those nine months of waiting, much more exciting. Finding out would be the finale to the long awaited ending for them both.

About this time, Luke and Macy started Lamaze classes. "This is so weird and uncomfortable. I don't like this. I don't want to sit with my legs spread in front of all these other couples," Macy whispered to Luke.

"Oh Macy, I'm sure they probably feel the same way." Luke reassured her. They practiced breathing techniques together while Luke got tips on how to comfort Macy during labor. It was during this time they learned about epidurals too. "I am not getting a needle stuck in my back," Macy insisted. "I hate needles, let alone one going in my spinal cord. I am going natural—especially if *that's* how I have to get pain meds." Macy also planned on using cloth diapers and breastfeeding. She wanted to give natures best to her baby.

Despite having the life that they created growing in Macy's womb, they both tried to live life as normal as possible. Macy was doing well with her recent promotion in the hotel sales office where she answered phones, assisted with scheduling customer visits, typed correspondence and other admin tasks. She enjoyed it and worked hard, as she saw it as an opportunity for growth. But, she could never shake the feeling that the Sales Manager had something against her or just plain didn't like her. It was always unsettling the way she'd talk to Macy as if she was doing something wrong.

Being pregnant didn't impact Luke and Macy's social life too much, either. They continued hitting their favorite dance clubs. This was Macy's favorite thing to do—just let loose and dance the stress away, and they both were so good at it. Music was a major part of their lives. Luke would sing and plays drums and he often sang to Macy. Luke was the musician and Macy was the dancer. Their growing baby would have to put up with loud, bass-pumping house music from the alternative grunge era, as well as R&B and Hip Hop. Songs like "Smells like Teen Spirit," "Head Like a Hole," and "Rhythm is a Dancer" were songs that were sure to keep Luke and Macy on the dance floor. It wasn't until that seventh month that dancing became more uncomfortable than fun for Macy. "Yeah, I think I'm done dancing," Macy told Luke as she let go of his hand and left the dance floor one night. Macy never really started 'showing' until that month.

Other than all that dancing, Macy's baby grew just as all the textbooks said he or she would. She craved meat and potatoes, and ice cream was the only thing that would cure her unbearable heartburn. "Luke, please go get me some ice cream. This heartburn is killing me!" became an all-too-familiar request from Macy—sometimes at three in the morning. Macy woke up one morning and realized that she couldn't see her feet. The baby was growing and so was her belly!

In September, only one month to go, Macy started her workday in a somewhat awkward manner—something seemed 'heavy' in the office. The week prior, all the employees threw Macy a baby shower in the office, cake and all. It was a sweet surprise and she felt appreciated. But that feeling was obviously gone today. As all the sales reps filed out of the boss' office, not a word was said and some would just look at Macy with this odd look. Soon afterward, Macy got a call from Tracy, her boss. "Macy, can you come to my office, please?" Macy's heart was in her throat. *Something's not right*, she thought to herself. She grabbed her notebook and pen and took a seat in Tracy's office.

"Macy, I'm not happy with the way this is working out. You're not doing your job." Tracy addressed Macy rather abruptly as she got up to shut the door. She didn't even tell her to have a seat or say hello. Just, "Macy, I don't like you." That's all Macy heard anyway.

"Excuse me? I'm not sure I understand what you mean." Macy replied.

"Well, I am not getting my messages," she said with heavy sarcasm. "Customers tell me that they call, leave a message, but I never get it from you. You were also seen with the MOD (Manager On Duty) keys to get soda out of the conference area closet. And, we just can't keep you here when these types of things are taking place."

"What? I only had the MOD keys because Barb said it was okay. I had asked her for caffeine free Pepsi out of the closet and she said no problem. In regards to your missing messages, I write down every call that comes in for you. I don't really understand why this is happening or why you're saying these things!"

Tracy finished the meeting with, "Macy you'll need to get your things and head down to the HR office. I've said what I need to say."

Macy did all she could to pick up her purse and keys without throwing the giant 10-line phone across the office. "BITCH!"

I cannot believe this is happening. What are we going to do now? Macy thought to herself as she went downstairs to the HR office, hands shaking and heart pounding. She did all she could do to hold back the tears—the anger stirring in her gut definitely helped.

When she got to the HR office, of course they were waiting for her and had all the necessary paperwork setting there ready to finalize Macy's termination. They asked Macy if she had any feedback. Macy shared the same replies with the HR manager that she had with Tracy, in addition to adding, "Tracy just doesn't like me and is looking for any reason she can find to kick me out. Could you not just move me back to the Front Office? Why do you have to terminate me?" Macy began to cry. The HR person just stared at her giving no response. "Oh, what difference does it make how I feel or what my feedback is. It obviously isn't going to change anything." Macy blurted out.

Of course, Luke had taken Macy to work that day so she had to call Luke and ask him to come pick her up. She waited in the front lobby for him—humiliated, disgusted and fearing the future. *How could they do this to me? Especially right before our baby is born.*

Luke took Macy home. "What happened, Macy?" Luke asked.

Macy was so angry. "That bitch hates me, she always has and she completely made up lies to get me fired. She has no heart whatsoever. I'm giving birth next month and she had no problem adding this stress in my life. What are we going to do now, Luke? What are we going to do about insurance?"

"We'll figure it out, honey. You'll find another job."

Not having a job gave Macy time to focus on the baby. She finished getting the nursery decorated; got all of the tiny clothes and diapers washed, folded and put in their assigned drawers; sterilized the bottles; and finished up her reading. Macy's family threw a surprise shower for her too. They had her come to what she thought was a bridal shower for her cousin. *What is Kimberly's car doing here if it's her bridal shower?* Macy wondered as she got out of her car. But when she walked in, everyone yelled surprise and she realized this was all for her. She opened so many wonderful gifts. A new Pack n Play, high chair, clothes, clothes, and more clothes, diapers, bibs, and so much more. They played games and enjoyed lots of good food.

Luke showed up at the end to help get all the gifts home. As Macy and Luke finally sat down from putting everything away that night, Macy laid her head on Luke's shoulder, "This was an awesome day. I'm so grateful for all we have—especially our family." She was still scared to death. They both were.

October arrived, and little baby Hawthorn was due on the 5th. The doctor visits continued to go well and the baby was right on schedule. Macy was getting bigger and growing more impatient. "I just want this kid out of me already," she'd say to Luke.

"I know, sweetie. I can't wait to meet her or him either!" Luke would respond.

The morning of the 7th, Luke and Macy decided to go walking around the parking lot of their apartment complex in hopes to kick start contractions. Nothing was happening, so Macy sent Luke to work. "Just go ahead, honey. I'll call you if anything changes."

Not an hour after Luke headed to work, Macy felt her first set of contractions. She drank some water and sat with her notebook and watch as she timed the next one and the next one after that. *Could this be it? Could I really be going into labor?* Macy wondered.

A few hours later, Macy decided it was time to call. "Luke?"

"Hey, baby. You okay?"

"Uh yeah, I think so. You'll never guess what?"

"What? Is it time?!"

"I think it is." Macy replied, excitedly *and* apprehensively.

"I'm coming home!"

Macy was ready to leave as soon as Luke arrived.

"Here we go, honey. We're gonna have a baby." Luke said as he fastened his seat belt and pulled out of the lot.

Like some finely-tuned production line, the labor and delivery unit got Macy a room, a gown to put on, strapped on monitors, took vitals and began instructing them both on what was to come. "This could take a couple hours or many hours, so get comfortable," the nurses said.

After hours of painful contractions and slow progression, the nurses sent Luke and Macy out to walk the halls in the hopes of speeding things up a bit. They returned to the room an hour later and Macy fell back into the bed. Some progression had been made, but still lots more to go.

The hours went by and family members were beginning to arrive—anxiously awaiting the new arrival. Macy's contractions got harder and stronger and she struggled with managing the pain. The nurses were constantly telling her to slow down her breathing and control it more, "like they taught you in Lamaze," they'd say.

Macy's doctor finally arrived; well actually it was her doctor's older brother, Dr. Greg Jr. as he was on call that evening. At this point, modest Macy was on show for no less than four nurses, six interns, and a couple doctors; it was like one, big happy party— just not to Macy. As the contractions got stronger, Macy's breathing got worse. The nurses finally got fed up and told Macy she needed the epidural. "If you don't slow down your breathing, you are going to hyperventilate, Macy. And, if you pass out, then you'll be in surgery and I know you don't want that. Macy, the epidural will help you relax."

"Okay, fine. Give me the freaking epidural," Macy cried as she gripped her pillow trying not to hold her breath.

While sitting on the edge of the bed, the anesthesiologist was cleaning off Macy's back in minutes. "Okay, now just bend over and sit as still as possible." Macy leaned against Luke with much fear. "How am I supposed to sit still while I'm having a contraction?"

Luke watched intently as the guy did his magic. "That is so freaking cool. You should see this, Macy," he said.

Macy now had thin tubes taped up her back, coming out her uterus, taped around her arms. In minutes, the epidural kicked in and Macy was able to relax and joke around a little. "I feel like a giant marionette," she chuckled, making Luke and the nurses laugh. "I just want to take a nap for a little bit," she told Luke.

"Okay, go ahead get some sleep."

Thirty minutes later, Macy awoke to a sudden urge that instinctively told her, "I need to push." Again, like some amazing magic act, doctors appeared, the bed was torn apart, and bright lights now blinded Macy while putting out some serious heat too.

In just a couple pushes, their baby was born; Luke and Macy's new son. Luke ran out the waiting room, "It's a boy!" he shared with everyone as tears ran down his face. He smiled, "He's a seven pound three ounce healthy little boy!"

Luke quickly came back to the room and continued taking pictures as the nurses were cleaning him all up. To hear his little cry made Macy cry. She knew this sound meant he was okay. Once he and Macy were all cleaned up, the nurse handed him to her. At first, Macy held him in her hands away from her as she studied his little face. *Oh my God! We made this little person—we made this perfect little person. What am I supposed to do now? How am I supposed to take care of this little life when I can barely take care of myself?* Macy was scared to death. She pulled him up under her chin on her chest and smelled him. She kissed his forehead, and as he wrapped his little fingers around hers, she looked up at Luke, "We're a family now." Luke kissed Macy on top of her head and whispered, "Yes, we are. I'm so proud of you lil' mama." It would be his new nickname for her.

Those first few days at home were very trying to say the least. As with any first-time parents, there was a big difference between what the books and videos said to expect and what was reality. They just didn't answer all those immediate questions.

Oh my gosh! It's taking too long to get these frigging pins in here. How did I do this when my sister was little? Now I have my own baby and I can't remember nor can I do it fast enough, Macy fussed to herself as she changed Travis. Macy was struggling with breastfeeding too. "I just don't think he's latching on and my chest is killing me." Macy cried to Luke. "I'm a complete failure. I can't even feed my own baby."

Luke tried to console her, "You're not a failure, and I hate not knowing how to help."

With her hormones out of whack and all of the struggles that come with being a new mom, stress began weighing down on Macy. She was scared and depressed more now than ever. Luke was too.

Thank God Travis was such a good baby. Macy would often sit in front of his crib watching for his back to rise and fall because he never cried and only woke to eat or have his diaper changed. She would also just stare at this tiny human being lying there so pure and innocent; taking in this miracle of life that lay before her. His only means of survival was she and Luke. He needed them. A tear rolled down her cheek.

It wasn't too long before Macy was able to get Travis on some routines. Everybody loved little Travis with his big blues eyes and sweet, calm disposition; what wasn't to love? But, Macy was extremely protective of him. She rarely allowed anyone to hold him especially the in-laws. When they would ask to feed him, Macy would reply, "No that's okay, I got it." With the holidays coming up, it was even worse. Everyone got maybe five to ten minutes of time to hold him. "I just don't want anyone breathing on him," Macy explained to Luke.

With the New Year upon them, Macy landed a job as an Administrative Assistant with a small financial company not far from the hotel. She was working for a man who was an ergonomics consultant. He'd instruct people on poor posture while sitting at their desks and how they would eventually develop carpel tunnel syndrome if they didn't use his wrist pad for their keyboard. Although they needed the extra income, Macy didn't want to have to deal with finding a sitter for her sweet baby Travis. She hated letting anyone hold him, let alone someone else having him all day long.

Judy offered to watch him, and Macy reluctantly agreed to just a couple days a week. While dropping off their rent payment, Macy saw an ad for a babysitter on the community bulletin board in the leasing office. A lady in the complex was offering her babysitting services. Macy immediately called. Her name was Jean, and she lived right across the street from them. "You're more than welcome to come over and chat. And I'd love to meet your little one," Jean said sweetly on the phone.

Luke, Macy and Travis took the short walk to Jean's apartment. Jean opened the door before Luke could even knock. "Oh there you are, please come in." Jean mushed over Travis. She was an older lady with such a sweet personality. Travis immediately took to her and Luke and Macy both loved her caring warmth. It was a perfect match. Macy asked that she take care of Travis the other three days a week.

By December, Macy started her new job and Travis started his time with Grandma Judy and Jean. Macy had a very difficult time leaving him, especially with Judy.

"Hi Grandma," Macy said as she walked in the house.

"Oh where's my perfect little grandson," Judy oozed as she reached out for Travis.

"Here he is." Macy would say as she unloaded him and all of his supplies. Travis smiled as he went to his grandma.

"Okay, I made this list for you of feeding times and how much formula to make and when and what time he needs to lay down for naps and so on. Here is my number at work, so please call me with any questions."

"Of course I will, honey. We'll be fine and have lots of fun." Judy assured Macy.

Things seemed to go pretty well for the most part, especially with Jean. Travis loved her. The only thing that bothered Macy was how Jean would hold onto Travis when she came to pick him up, saying, "No, he's *my* baby, he's *my* baby."

It was cute the first couple of times but after a while, it drove Macy nuts. *No, he's MY baby,* Macy told herself walking out of Jean's apartment.

Grandma Judy on the other hand created some frustration for Macy. She seemed to care for Travis in her own way instead of following Macy's instructions. It became more and more difficult for Macy, and Jean began watching him full-time.

CHAPTER 5

"Love Is"
1993

Things between Luke and Macy were going okay considering all they had on their shoulders. They were still crazy in love with each other, an attraction that never quit. But, neither did the arguments. Although their struggles usually revolved around finances and lack there of; a bigger issue became Luke's consistent late nights out with friends.

"Luke please, please don't leave," Macy cried holding on to him.

"I want to go out, Macy. If I want to go out, I should be able to just go."

"But, Luke, we have a baby to take care of now. How is it fair that you leave us to go party, and I'm stuck here all the time?" Macy begged.

Luke turned away and headed out the door.

Macy ran to the front window, crying, "Please don't leave me, Luke!" "Please, Please!"

Luke pulled away. Macy would sit on their bed and cry herself to sleep; the next day would be full of anger and silence between them both.

They eventually sought counseling, as the fighting seemed endless. Luke and Macy had a couple sessions with the young female counselor; but the afternoon she said, "Luke is only 22. He should be going out and enjoying this time." Macy took one look at her and thought, *Are you insane, lady? What about me? I didn't create this child all by myself!*

Meanwhile, Luke sat back in his chair crossing his arms, self-satisfaction written all over his face.

Macy walked out.

Luke followed soon after.

Macy stomped the whole way to the car wanting to beat the shit out of anything. "We are never going back to this place again!"

"Of course we're not," Luke said. "You didn't get your way."

Macy called him an asshole under her breath, and nothing was said between them for the next two days.

The constant arguments were always followed up with making up. But there still were the nights they enjoyed going out together and just being with each other. Their first anniversary would be one of these nights. Peter and Leanne kept Travis overnight so Luke and Macy could spend the evening eating a nice dinner and then dancing at their favorite club. They even bought a bottle of wine to bring back home with them. The evening went on into the early hours with drinking, dancing and, of course, love making. There was no doubt in either Luke or Macy's minds that this was the one person they were meant to be with.

"I'm so in love with you, Macy! There is no one more beautiful than you nor could anyone ever make me feel the way you do."

"I feel the very same way, Luke! I love you so much."

A couple weeks later, Macy realized she was late. It had been five months since Travis was born and Macy had been on three different types of birth control pills, none of which seemed to regulate her properly. The thought of getting pregnant again never even crossed their minds, but there it was again: double lines. The pregnancy test was positive. *Oh dear God, how? Why? I can't do this again—not this soon!* Macy sat on the toilet sobbing with her face in her hands. *This cannot be happening!* She cried as she finished getting ready and headed off to work.

It wasn't too long after they learned they were pregnant (again) that Macy got a call at work from Luke.

"Macy?"

"Yeah, Hi Luke. How are you?"

"Not so good. I have some bad news."

"Oh no, what is it?"

"I just got fired."

"What, why? What happened?"

Luke just cried.

The store's register was short too many times with no explanation and that was enough grounds for Luke's termination.

"Honey, we'll figure something out. I'll see you in a little bit," she said as they hung up the phone.

Macy cried the whole way home. *What next? What are we going to do? We're already behind on bills from when I was out of work. How will we ever catch up now? Why is this happening to us? Why?* She slammed her fists on the steering wheel, "Dammit!"

Luke was home when Macy got there. Macy hugged Luke, "Oh, honey, I'm so sorry."

Luke sobbed, "I'm so sorry too. I don't know what to do. How are we going to take care of us?"

"I know. I just don't understand why this is happening to us."

Luke and Macy had to move out of the apartment. Their bills were just too much and their income way too little. Luke went to his mom to ask for a place to stay.

"Ma, with me losing my job, we can't afford our apartment anymore. We could really use a place to stay."

"Oh Luke, I'd love to have you but you know I don't have much room."

"I know, Ma. Maybe Macy, Travis and I can all sleep in the front room and we won't bring any of our stuff. We can put it in storage."

"It's fine with me, honey. But I'm going to need your help with bills and chores."

"Of course, Ma!"

Luke looked for work while Macy forced herself to the office every day. Luke would find himself learning the art of car sales at a local Nissan dealership. Although having to wear ties every day wasn't really his thing, Luke was always energized by the challenge of learning something new. Plus his dad was a car salesman; that offered a bit of internal motivation.

For Macy, it was becoming more and more difficult to work for Chuck. She noticed him staring at her sometimes when he'd be walking into his office. It just didn't feel right. Macy spent more time working with the other ladies in the back office with whatever she could help with to avoid her creepy boss. One of the ladies took Macy under her wing and gave her lessons on processing orders and making accounting entries.

One afternoon, all of the girls were working on a company-wide mailing—sticking labels, stuffing envelopes and such. Cheryl asked Macy, "You know what you would be so good at, Macy?"

"I don't know. What?" Macy played along, thinking she was going to make a joke about licking envelopes or where glue comes from.

"I go to Vegas a lot and I think you would be an awesome black jack dealer. You just have a great personality for something like that." Cheryl agreed that Macy's boss was a big freak and wanted to help her come up with some other job alternatives.

"What? A black jack dealer? I've never even been to a casino."

"Well you should take Luke to go check out the Alton Belle some time. You'd have fun, and while you're there, watch the dealers. You'll see what I mean."

Macy had just finished giving Travis a bath and was getting him ready for bed while Luke was picking out a story to read to him.

"So, Luke, listen to this. All the girls in the office were working on a mass-mailing today, and Cheryl suggested you and I go to the Alton Belle to watch the black jack dealers. She seems to think I'd be a good dealer for whatever reason?'

"Really? A black jack dealer? But you never even play cards...much less hang out at a casino."

"I know. That's what I said. Want to check it out anyways?"

"Sure. Sounds fun."

That Friday night, Luke and Macy took the forty-five minute drive to the Alton Belle. It was a Riverboat casino. For gambling to be legal in Illinois, the casino had to dwell on a body of water. Luke parked the car and they walked through the gravel parking lot to wait in line on the ramp. They each bought a ticket and followed the seasoned gamblers aboard the riverboat.

They made their way through the lobby and up the stairs to where the games were. The cigarette smoke got heavier as they reached the top of the stairs. "Those damn smoke eaters aren't working. I can barely breathe," Macy said, holding her nose while thinking how bad this was for the baby.

The carpet was deep red with gold diamond designs. The floor had wall-to-wall games—slot machines with seizure inducing flashing lights and deafening ching-ching-ching noises; black jack tables; craps tables; roulette tables and people everywhere. The place was packed with hopeful gamblers. Some had necklaces made out of their passes...they had been there for hours. It was sensory overload for Macy; but for Luke it was a dream world—a place where his dreams of big money could all come true.

Macy stopped a young lady with a nametag on. "Excuse me, would you have a minute to help me? It's our first time on the boat, in a casino actually, and I was just curious if you could tell us a little bit about getting a job here and maybe becoming a dealer?"

"Well, I'm a concierge. I assist our VIP players with whatever they need—meals, drinks, hotel accommodations, etc. But I'm not sure what you have to do to be a dealer. I guess you'd have to check with the HR department."

Luke wasn't paying too much attention to Macy and the Concierge's conversation; he was enthralled with watching all the games taking place around them. Luke elbowed Macy, "Do you see all the chips that guy has? He has a couple thousand dollars sitting there. Oh my gosh. This is just crazy."

"Come on, let's look around some more," Macy said.

They went up the flight of stairs to the lookout deck. "Now this is what I'm talking about. Fresh air and peace and quiet." Macy said, as she found a good spot to watch the water. The full moon was reflecting on the river.

"What a beautiful night," Macy said to Luke.

"What? Oh yeah, it sure is. Let's go back downstairs. I want to see how that guy with all the chips is doing." Luke said as he took her hand and led back inside.

Luke studied the game and the player's moves while Macy people watched and found herself feeling sorry for just about every person there.

The boat was finally making its way back to dock when Macy said, "We better get heading home, honey, we've got a long drive," and reached for Luke's hand.

"Yeah, I guess so. Let's check out the Casino Queen next time, okay?!" He stared off while the wheels were turning in his head. "Honey, I could so do that." Luke was captivated with excitement and grinning from ear to ear. "I mean I would be great at dealing black jack."

"I agree, baby. You definitely have the outgoing personality for it," Macy smiled.

While Macy slid off to sleep soon after getting in to bed, it took Luke a while longer to come down from the excitement and stimulation.

The following weekend, Macy and Luke took fifty dollars each to the Casino Queen to test their strategies with gambling. *(Oh come on...they were desperately hoping for a big win.)* This casino was even larger than the Alton Belle, which meant even more sensory overload for Macy and seemingly more opportunity for Luke to make a killing.

"I'm stopping here," Macy told Luke. "I'm going to watch this roulette game for a while."

"I'm gonna find a black jack table." Luke kissed Macy as he walked off.

Macy watched the people around the table drop their chips on random numbers on the board. Then her eyes were drawn to the dealer, as he got ready to spin the little white ball. They all watched it, eyes and head following the ball, until it finally dropped into one of the slots. The numbers would light up on the electronic display screen behind the dealer. Macy studied the numbers trying to find some pattern to help her with her strategy. All the while, the same thing kept bothering Macy: she didn't want anyone taking her money. If she lost, that was it. *The dealer will sweep my money right off the table and I'll never get it back*, she thought to herself.

Nevertheless, Macy changed out a twenty-dollar bill for four five-dollar chips. Instead of randomly picking a number, Macy put two chips down on black. She felt her chances were better sticking to a color versus all those different numbers. *It would be almost a 50/50 chance, right?* Macy figured. The dealer spun the ball on to the wheel. It went around and around and Macy's heart raced and moved farther and farther into her throat. "Red nineteen," the dealer called and then swept up all the losing chips, including Macy's. Macy just stood and watched; feeling like a part of her body had just been ripped from her.

"Macy, give me $40," Luke came running up behind Macy.

"Where's your money?" Macy asked anxiously.

"I lost it...but I'm going to win it back. Just give me your money so I can go back to the table."

Macy was already feeling anxious from losing some of her money and growing more and more fearful of the demanding, desperate tone in Luke's voice.

"No, I'm not giving you my money. I've already lost ten dollars and I don't want to lose the rest of it."

"I'm not going to lose it, though. I'll win back what I already lost." Luke was doing all he could to insist that he was capable of winning their money back. But it wasn't working.

"No, Luke."

"Just give me the money, Macy."

"I said, No."

Macy ran out to the car and locked herself in it. *What is happening to him? That's not Luke!* Macy cried to herself. She didn't recognize this man and she was really scared of what she just saw in him.

Eventually Luke calmed down and the two drove home in silence.

The next couple of days, Luke called around and researched what he needed to do to become a dealer—his determination at times was truly impressive. He found a training facility for a new casino that was going in closer to their house. They offered a six-week training program that taught dealers-in-training how to deal black jack, craps and roulette. He signed up for the next available class. It was to begin in just a couple of weeks.

When Macy found an administrative assistant position at a marketing fulfillment company, she left her job working for Chuck. She couldn't stand his constant and inappropriate peering anymore. It just wasn't worth it. By the time she paid the sitter and gas, there was nothing left of her paycheck anyway. This new job was a little closer to home.

While Macy trained at her new job, she grew excited for Luke's new career path and the chance of Luke having an income again. She daydreamed of having their own place where they all could enjoy some freedom. She couldn't wait to buy their own food and have means to pay their own bills again. But the day he wasn't there to pick her up after work created an uneasiness that she would—from that point forward—be unable to shake.

"Kyle, are you doing anything at the moment?" Macy called her sister.

"Just hanging with David. Why? What's up?"

"Luke dropped me off at work today, and he's not here yet. I've paged him like ten times but he's not responding. Can you come pick me up from work? I've been waiting almost forty-five minutes now, and I have to pick up Travis by six o'clock."

"Hold on a sec, Macy."

Macy heard Kyle whisper to David, "It's Macy, Luke hasn't shown up to pick her up from work and she has to get Travis."

"Macy, we'll be there in ten minutes."

"Thanks so much, Kyle. I'll be waiting out front!"

Kyle and David picked up Macy and then went to pick up Travis from the babysitters before taking them home.

Luke got home shortly after.

"Hey, baby!" Luke said rushing up behind Macy, wrapping his arms around her waist and kissing her neck.

Macy shrugged him off. "What the hell have you been doing, Luke? Why didn't you respond to any of my pages?"

"Oh my gosh, Macy, I'm sorry. I went to the boat. I was up a hundred bucks but then made a big bet and lost that hand. So, I picked up my chips and left. I didn't lose anything. But holy crap,

I couldn't believe how awesome I was doing. I'm sorry I couldn't leave the table to call you back."

"Really, Luke? You couldn't leave your precious game to call your wife back?! You can't just leave us hanging like that! If Kyle wouldn't have been available, what would I have done?"

"Baby, seriously. It wasn't my intention to leave you hanging like that. I really am sorry!" Luke turned her around from cleaning off the counter to get her to look at him. "Do you believe me? I just want to help us out. I want our own place again." He kissed her on the cheek and then the other cheek and then on her lips. Then he squatted down to kiss Macy's belly. "How's my little baby doin' in there? I love you and can't wait to see you!"

Macy's frustration was again remedied by his warm mouth and tenderness. Luke wanted Macy's support and encouragement and felt that her reciprocating his advances was just that.

"Macy, I have to quit working at the dealership."

"What are you talking about, Luke."

"Honey, I can't very well do both. I want to focus on training as much as possible. Plus they're not going to let me have enough flexibility during dealer school."

"So you quit?"

"Yes. But, honey I just know that I am going to get through dealer training sooner than six weeks and I'll be bringing in a good income. I've already been talking to some people at Alton Belle about getting a job there. So, please trust me. I'm going to take care of you and our babies. I promise, lil' mama."

Like everything else in his life, Luke picked up dealing quickly. He was always the sort of kid who could watch someone do something and then just do it. Golf, baseball, wrestling, anything. One summer, Macy and Luke went boating with a friend and Glen had gotten out on his wake board and did all sorts of tricks. "Hey man, I want to try that," Luke said. So he put on a life jacket, jumped in the water, grabbed hold of the rope and popped right up as soon as Glen took off. There were no two or three tries; Luke watched him do it and then he turned around and did it. It drove Macy nuts, since she was the type who had to try everything ten times and practice and work at it to be able to do just about anything, especially sports related.

With everything else going on in their lives, Macy and Luke couldn't believe it was already time to celebrate Travis' first birthday. They scrounged up all they could to buy some decorations and a gift for their little boy. They had a cowboy-themed party at Judy's with Luke's side of the family. Kim took pictures of little Travis in his cake-covered jeans and plaid shirt. The family enjoyed showering him with clothes and toys. Watching him work at opening his gifts would be a feat for the non-patient aunts and uncles, "Rip it open, Travis!" Aunt Rose would shout.

Then they did it all over again with Macy's side of the family. Travis did better ripping open his gift this time around and a little stuffed Barney doll would be a favorite. Plunging into that yummy cake wasn't as much of a challenge this time around either. That night, Travis went to sleep (after crashing from his sugar-high) in a new car bed from Peter and Leanne. He was a big boy now. *Where did the past year go?* Macy thought to herself as she laid him down for the night.

Back at dealer training, Luke would go to class and then practice with Macy and Jason at home all the time. Within two weeks, Luke passed his dealer tests—four weeks ahead of schedule. The instructors told some of the trainees about a new boat that was opening in Savannah, Georgia, that needed dealers. Luke had fond memories of Georgia since he had lived there for a while when he was a kid. "Georgia, no way! I want to go," Luke blurted.

"Macy, I'm going to get us to Georgia," Luke couldn't wait to share the news with her. He had rushed home and ran down the steps calling for Macy. She was on the floor changing Travis' diaper.

"What? Georgia? What you mean?" Macy was excited but confused.

"I passed my dealer tests today and our instructor told us about a boat opening in Savannah that needs dealers. So, I am getting a position on the boat there. Honey, isn't it awesome? You're going to absolutely love Georgia. I can hear you picking up the accent already." Luke was bouncing off the walls, he was so excited.

"Oh my gosh, Luke that's so awesome. You've seriously already passed your tests? What about the baby? Where would we live?"

"We could just rent an apartment. There are some other guys going too." Luke paused a moment. "Well, maybe it would be best if I share a place with them and then look for a place for us. I could send you money to put away so when I found a place, we would have it."

"But, I don't want to be away from you, Luke...not again. And especially not while I'm pregnant."

"I don't want to be away from you either, Macy. But this could be a great opportunity for us. Georgia is so incredible."

"Well, I guess I need to ask Mom and Dad if we can move in with them." Macy mumbled dejectedly.

With their tails between their legs, they went to Peter and Leanne once again, "We're in need of some help." Leanne just looked at Peter with that look of 'uh oh, here we go' as if they saw it coming or knew about it already.

"With what?" Peter asked with his short, stern voice. Peter and Leanne were still struggling with the fact that they were pregnant again. "Obviously, they weren't planning on doing what was necessary to not get pregnant again either," Peter shared previously with Leanne.

"Well, Luke completed his training—four weeks ahead of schedule—and has an opportunity to work on a new boat in Georgia." Macy started.

"Okay?" Peter said, looking in Luke's direction.

"I won't start on the boat for another month, and unfortunately, we don't have the means to move us all down to Georgia right now. So, we'd like to ask if we can move in with you until I can build up some savings and find a place for us to live." Luke asked shamefully. Macy, too, felt more shame in her heart than she ever remembered having before. Luke was scared to death that Macy's dad was going to strangle him right then and there.

"I've picked up some work at the MP station—"

Peter interrupted the painful conversation, "fine, you can move in downstairs but you will be paying rent, phone, etc."

Luke answered, "Of course, we wouldn't expect it any other way. It's just until we can get back on our feet. We don't want to add any more stress."

Leanne just stared at nothing and said nothing.

As promised, they closed off a room in the unfinished basement for Luke and Macy. The large room now became their bedroom, baby's room and living room.

The first night in their new basement dwelling as Luke stripped off his smoke-drenched uniform and slipped into bed, Macy lay there wanting to speak, but the worry and guilt kept her silent. A few minutes later she rolled over to Luke's direction.

"Luke?"

"Yeah?"

"I'm sorry."

"Sorry for what, honey?" She wanted to apologize for her parent's attitude towards them. The shame and guilt she and

Luke were carrying was enough without their noses being constantly rubbed in it.

"All of this. I can't believe we are living in my parent's basement. I hate it. This constant walking on pins and needles is just ridiculous. One day here and Dad's already yelling at Travis. I can't stand it. This is his house so he feels like he can be the disciplinarian of my child." She paused a moment, "I guess it's his way of taking his anger out on me, but little Travis doesn't deserve it. And, he and mom are always bickering. I don't want us to be here."

"I know Macy. I hate it too. I feel like your parents *really* don't like me now. Just no pleasing anyone it seems. We're just going to have to suck it up and follow their wishes." He stared at the ceiling in the dark and told himself he was inadequate. He was deeply ashamed and depressed, but made the conscious decision to push it down and keep it hidden from Macy and everyone else. Worse...he hid it from himself.

And so it was, a couple weeks later, Luke, Macy and Travis were sitting in Luke's truck while they waited in the Booneslick Mall parking lot for the other two guys to show up for the road trip to Georgia.

"I hate this, Luke. I don't want to be alone."

"I know, Macy. I promise I'll do all I can to get you and Travis and the baby there as soon as possible. I'll call you all the time. I'm going to miss you so much," he said, rubbing her neck while they rested on each other's foreheads.

"I'm going to miss you."

The two hugged and kissed. Macy did all she could to hold back the tears—especially for Travis. She didn't want him to see her upset or scared.

"I love you, Travis. You're going to take good care of Mommy and the baby for me while I'm away, right?"

Travis just smiled.

"I'll see you real soon. I love you so much."

"I wuv you, Da Da." Travis said as he went back to playing with his Legos.

"I love you, Luke."

"I love you so much, Macy."

And just like that, Luke was gone.

Macy cried in secret the whole way home, worrying about the little baby growing in her belly and the sweet little boy sitting next to her.

It was extremely stressful living under Peter and Leanne's roof, especially since she was not working. She left the marketing company when Luke moved to Georgia. Her boss hated her and she was too emotional to handle the feeling of never being able to please her. Plus, she didn't have the extra help getting Travis to and from the sitter and or the money to pay for it anyway.

Macy always worried about what the next thing would be that might set her parents off, which could be just about anything at any time. She tried to keep things clean around the house, but it just wasn't ever good enough. Peter was always yelling at Travis with that 'I'm the boss' voice of his—which ultimately just scared him. Macy also missed Luke like crazy. Without him there, Peter and Leanne's disappointment in him was a constant and obvious truth that she couldn't ignore. There was no Luke for her to escape with.

On top of the pressure from living with her parents, this pregnancy was going so differently than her first. Macy hardly put on any weight and only craved pizza and junk food. She was still seeing Dr. Charlie and he confirmed that the baby was healthy but was going to most definitely be tinier than Travis was. He thought Macy could put on a little extra weight but didn't hassle her about it.

The baby was constantly active. "I swear this kid is doing somersaults in there." Macy would tell her sisters. The baby would press it's little foot against her rib and then slide it off as if he or she was trying to stretch, and Macy's darn ribs would get in the way. He or she had hiccups all the time. *I'm sure my stress level is only adding to this child's constant activity,* Macy would think to herself. As soon as Macy would feel like she could rest or fall asleep, the baby would start the fetus Olympics, taking the gold every time; rest was not something Macy would get much of.

Luke called as often as he could. He'd share stories of the huge swells they'd get caught in when the boat would head out to sea. So many people would get seasick from the boat being bounced around, including him. This boat wasn't like the riverboats back home. It was more like a cruise ship and they had to sail so many miles out to sea before gaming could begin.

"I'm sorry I haven't sent any money yet. I had to help with the deposit on our apartment and chip in for some food and toiletries." Luke apologized to Macy.

"Luke, I have bills here too. Dad is always mad at me, at us. I need to give him some money. I can't keep sponging off of them."

"I know, Macy. I feel awful. The casino's getting a lot of heat from the community. It's a huge bible belt down here—Southern Baptists—and they don't want gambling going on in their town. Even though we go out to sea, they're still complaining. They protest and try to stop customers from boarding the boat. So when there isn't that many people gambling, it means less tip money for me, I mean us. I'll send you some money once I get my next paycheck in a couple of weeks."

It had been almost two months that had gone by and still no money. *The baby will be here soon and I have NO money, NO insurance, and NO place of our own to live!* It was almost too much for Macy to think about.

Peter had gotten home from work one day and went straight to Macy. "So, when are you going to see some money from that husband of yours," he asked with heavy sarcasm—shutting the refrigerator door and popping open his beer.

"He said in a week he should be able to send some," Macy replied as she continued to feed Travis—not turning to make eye contact.

"Yeah, right! Macy. This is just getting absolutely ridiculous. What the hell is he doing down there. There is no reason for this, and frankly, I'm getting completely sick of doing his job. I'm sick of giving you a free place to live and free food. He's an idiot. We're already out the money from the deposits on your wedding; and now you are racking up phone bills and grocery bills. Why should I have to keep paying for you?" Peter yelled.

"I don't know Dad. We'll just leave. I'm so tired of being a burden to you and mom. This is not how it's supposed to be and I just can't live like this—with you." Macy yelled back, picking Travis up from his high chair and heading downstairs.

That evening, Macy started having contractions. She was so angry from the argument she had with her dad earlier, and she was certain these contractions were a direct result of that. "I am so stressed out, this poor baby!" Macy cried tears of anger.

Macy's sister got home from work. "Kyle, I need you to drive me to the hospital."

"Oh my gosh, Macy. Are you having contractions? Should I call Luke?" Kyle asked frantically.

"Let' just get to the hospital and decide there. We need to go now!"

The contractions were coming faster and harder.

"Kyle, put your foot on the gas and don't let up. I don't care if we pass a cop. Just go!"

Sure enough, a police officer pulled them over.

"Just let me talk," Macy instructed her.

Kyle rolled down her window, and as the officer leaned down to ask for "license and —"

"I'm in labor," Macy blurted out.

"How far apart are the contractions?" he asked.

"Two and a half minutes," Macy said as she took constant breaths.

"What hospital?"

"St. John's."

"Follow me," he said.

The officer got in his car, turned on his lights, and led Macy and Kyle to St. John's. Kyle was smiling, "Holy crap, Macy. You just got a police escort to the hospital." They both snickered and Macy gripped the door handle in pain.

Kyle and Macy checked in with Labor and Delivery. There she was again...witnessing the quick transformation from wheel chair to hospital gown, bed, monitors, vitals, etc. The nurses confirmed contractions were coming hard and fast, but no dilation was taking place at all. This went on throughout the night and since her doctor wouldn't be coming in until the morning, they gave Macy shots to slow down her contractions.

Kyle called Luke. "Macy's in the hospital, can you get home? She really needs you here."

"Absolutely! Is the baby coming?"

"She's been contracting all night but not dilating. So they keep giving her shots to stop the contractions. She's so tired and miserable. The doctor will be in around seven tomorrow morning, so we'll know more then." Kyle shared all she knew with Luke.

"Okay, okay, I'm leaving now. I'll be there as soon as I can." Luke was frantic.

It was seven the next morning when Dr. Charlie, came in to check on Macy. "How are you doing, my dear?" he asked Macy, holding her knee as he took a seat on the bed.

"Miserable. The contractions were coming and coming but the nurses said I wasn't dilating so they've been pumping me full of shots to slow down my contractions." Macy had tears in her eyes. She was stressed, exhausted, worried and Luke wasn't there.

"Alright, well let me check things out and see what we've got. You're about a three. And, why have they been giving you shots all night?" Dr. Charlie asked, agitated. "You should have been in surgery hours ago."

Dr. Charlie talked with the nurses. Macy overheard him saying, "Why are we pumping her full of shots when she's obviously not progressing? It's not necessary to put her through that. Let's get her prepped for a C-section right away."

The nurses came in and relayed the news about the C-section. At this point, Macy was so exhausted that she was okay with his decision. "So, we'll have the anesthesiologist in soon to give you an epidural. That way you'll be awake for the surgery but won't feel any pain," the nurse shared.

Luke was on his way home but they weren't sure he'd make it in time for the surgery. "Luke, please get here," Macy would whisper into her pillow as tears fell down her cheek.

By ten o'clock, Macy had gotten her epidural and was changing beds to head into the operating room. They wheeled her into the room and put twice as many devices on her as she had before. Dr. Charlie walked in with his hands in the air to keep his scrubbing efforts from being contaminated. The nurse put more gloves on him. Macy was covered with blue sterile sheets and there was another light blue sheet drawn up to keep Macy from seeing Dr. Charlie's work.

"How are you doing, Macy?" Dr. Charlie asked.

"I'm okay I guess. I just wish my husband was here." Macy replied.

"Well, I hear he's on his way, so let's hope for the best."

Dr. Charlie was washing down Macy's belly with iodine. She could feel the brushing of the sponge but it was an odd sensation; the medicine was doing its job. He then made little pokes with the scalpel, "Can you feel that, Macy?" He asked. You should be able to feel it but with absolutely no pain.

Macy confirmed, "Yes, that's what I feel."

"Okay, I am going to make the incision and then you are going to feel a lot of tugging and pulling."

"Yep, I feel it."

"I see your baby, Macy."

A nurse stormed in. "Macy, your husband's here. We're getting him changed now so he can be with you."

"Oh, thank God!" Macy exclaimed as Dr. Charlie continued to pull and tug.

"I'm here, lil' mama." Luke grabbed Macy's hand. "Oh my gosh, you should see this, Macy!" he was peering over the sheet.

Dr. Charlie was pulling their little baby out just as Luke came in. "It's a girl!" he shared.

"A girl? Oh my God, I knew it was going to be a girl," a tear fell down Macy's cheek.

"And, she's been busy," Dr. Charlie added. "Not only was the cord around her neck, it has a knot in it."

"Really? Well, that doesn't surprise me at all," Macy chuckled. "That kid was constantly doing somersaults in there."

"And it shows!"

The nurses cleaned her off, swaddled her and gave her to Luke.

"Oh, honey, look at her...our little Avery. She's so tiny and beautiful! I'm so very proud of you." Luke held her down by Macy's face so she could kiss Avery's face as he kissed Macy's forehead.

"I'm so glad you made it in time," Macy whispered to Luke, touching his face.

"Me too, baby."

Macy was extremely sore from the surgery. She couldn't just sit up in bed. She had to roll to her side and then swing her legs off the bed and push herself up with her arm. It hurt to cough or laugh. A nurse from the nursery wheeled little Avery into Macy's room. But when Avery started choking and coughing up bubbles, Macy struggled to get up and then still couldn't reach her. She called for the nurse. "I can't reach my baby!" Macy sneered.

The nurse sneered back, "Well, get out of your bed!"

"Uh, I just had surgery four hours ago, I'm a tad sore." Macy said with pain and sarcasm.

It was time to leave the hospital and take baby Avery home. Macy put one of the new outfits Leanne had bought for her on Avery, but she was so tiny she swam in the zero to three-month onesie. Avery weighed only five pounds, eleven ounces when she left the hospital. She was like a tiny little bird.

This time around, being a mom came much more naturally to Macy, and right from the start too. Even with breastfeeding. Avery latched on right away and Macy loved the natural sensation and healing process that was taking place with her belly and incision. Nursing Avery was a natural pain reliever and perfect healing remedy.

Avery was completely different from her older brother, however. She had colic and required extra special treatment to get her to sleep. The poor baby just never seemed to settle down or relax. Macy and Luke would take turns hovering over her crib patting her on the butt for what seemed like forever. Just when they'd think she was asleep, they would stop and slowly and quietly head back to bed, only to have Avery start crying again. Both had their methods to try to comfort her; they would rock Avery, sing to her, walk with her but not much helped. Many times, Macy would fall asleep with her little Avery on her chest.

The stressful situation of Luke and Macy living with her parents with their two babies only got worse now that there seemed to always be a crying baby or someone up at all hours making bottles, taking showers, giving baths, etc. The tension grew thicker and thicker as the days went by. And, worse yet, they had no money.

"Peter, would you be able to loan us twenty bucks? Macy's out of meds and we don't have enough to get it refilled for her."

Peter said nothing. He just sighed and rolled his eyes as he pulled some cash out of his wallet.

"Thanks. And, I'm sorry." Luke hung his head as he thought more to himself. *We can't even afford medication. What are we going to do about the hospital bill? Her surgery alone was like ten thousand dollars.*

Christmas came and went so fast that year. With Avery being born just a couple weeks before, there wasn't much time for shopping. In fact, there was just no money for shopping either. This Christmas was just not the joyous holiday it had been all the years prior.

CHAPTER 6

"Loser"
1994

Just like the past three years, the New Year brought new scenery for Luke and Macy: new homes, new jobs and new problems. Luke landed a job dealing black jack on the Alton Belle. This new job gave Macy and Luke the chance to follow through with the promise to move out that Macy had made a month ago to her dad. They found an old two-story home with very high ceilings, a long staircase and Victorian moldings just up the street from the Belle. It had been converted into a duplex by the cement wall that ran smack dab down the middle of it. It was more than enough space for Luke and Macy's little family. With three bedrooms, one bathroom, a small kitchen and nice-sized dining room and living room, they' had all they needed.

Macy packed all of their clothes and other belongings while Luke rented a moving truck and found some friends to pack up their stuff and get the other furniture out of storage. The next day they said good-bye to Leanne and Peter before heading off to their new home. On her way out the door, Macy took down the "Luke and Macy Owe" note that her mom and dad posted and updated regularly. It had been on display for all—neatly pinned on the bulletin board above the phone in the kitchen. She quickly stuffed it into her purse, hoping to hide some of the guilt and shame it represented.

A friend helped Luke move the furniture while Macy kept the kids occupied and put kitchen items away. It felt so good to get back into a place of their own. No more stressing over whether or not the babies would keep up Macy's mom and dad or if they were eating more than their share of the food. And there's no doubt Peter and Leanne were relieved with Luke, Macy and the kids being out of the house again.

They still struggled with how they would pay the bills and make ends meet; but they'd worry about that later...or at least do whatever they could to pretend all was just fine and well.

Luke started his job with the Belle a few days later. He worked random shifts and had no set schedule. Macy did not care for this inconsistent schedule but was glad he had a job. Most times, Luke would have to work the late shift which wouldn't get him home until three or four o'clock in the morning. Macy took a part-time job with the boat working in the office as a Customer Service Rep handling reservation requests. However, it was short lived, as her position was eliminated just a month after she had started.

There was a park a few blocks away from their house. Macy would take the kids to the park at times just to get out of the house. With Luke working more late nights than any other shift, he'd sleep during the day, so heading out to the park kept the house quiet for Luke.

In the midst of toddlers and late night shifts came some really good news. The Sisters of Mercy had written a letter to Macy and Luke that read, "Through the generous donations of our caring donors, your surgery and hospital stay has been fully paid for and there will be no financial responsibility on your part." Macy gasped in amazement and gratitude. Nothing like this had ever been given to her. It truly was the most amazing gift she had ever received.

Not too long after losing her job at the boat, Macy found another job. She accepted a part-time waitressing job with Show-Mes. There weren't a lot of job opportunities in the small town they were now living in—that's what Macy told herself to justify the new job and the awful revealing uniform. She hated waitressing and felt degraded when she was 'approved of' for the job, if you could even call it waitressing. But she made decent money that they sorely needed. Macy just didn't let herself think too much about the type of job she was taking on, for she knew if she did, she would back out of it. Money was the main priority at this point; the main priority for both of them.

As Luke continued to deal black jack, he witnessed enormous amounts of cash exchanging customer's hands. He believed more and more that he knew how to play; that he had the skills necessary to make big winnings. Since he had been taught how to deal, he also understood the strategy behind winning the game—so he told himself. So he frequently tried out his 'skills and strategies' at other casinos (policy being that employees couldn't gamble at the casino they were employed with).

"Luke, did you get your paycheck? We need to get that in the bank to pay bills," Macy asked Luke.

"I got it but I don't have all of it." He confessed.

"What do you mean you don't have all of it?"

"Some of us went over to the Casino Queen and I ended up losing four hundred dollars. So, I only have four hundred left."

"What? Are you kidding me? How could you do such a thing, Luke?"

"I can win it back, Macy!"

"So, wait...you cashed your paycheck from the Alton Belle and then lost money at another casino? How do you even do that? What are we supposed to pay bills with now?"

"I don't know what you want to hear. It's gone, but I'm going to win it back."

Macy felt like she just got the wind kicked out of her. *What is happening? Why is he doing this to us?* She cried alone in their bedroom.

Luke came into the room and sat down on the bed next to Macy. "Honey, I'm sorry. Please don't be mad. It's no big deal. I just gotta win it back for us. I was up almost seven hundred dollars. I just got greedy with my betting. I know what to do next time."

"Luke, we have got to get caught up on bills. We're behind on the car payment; rent will be due next week. How do you possibly think we're going to take care of this?"

"I'll figure it out, Macy. I told you I was sorry. I feel bad, okay?"

Luke kissed Macy and pulled her closer to him. They spent the rest of the night making up. Macy loved him and, even more, she needed to feel him and that he needed to feel her too. Luke loved her and he did need to feel her as well. They both just longed to feel loved and wanted.

Macy played the game when she worked her waitress job. Making conversation with the UPS guys or the college students who came in for lunch. She knew they were lurking and commenting when she turned away from the table to go put in their order. She would come back with a big ol' smile on her face—pretending she thoroughly enjoyed being gawked at. As payment for her "show," they always tipped her well.

Macy and Luke had made some friends with people they had worked with. They all would go out dancing or hang out at a bar. Sometimes they would grill out at each other's houses. But despite doing all of these normal couple things, anger and guilt seemed to burn stronger in each of them as the days went on. The overwhelming frustration would cause them to act out more and more.

"Nope. I'm staying." Macy slurred to Luke as he grabbed her hand and led her off of the dance floor.

"It's time to go, Macy. We've had enough. YOU'VE had enough." Luke was telling Macy what to do for a change.

"NO! I'm staying. I haven't had enough and I'm staying."

Luke's friend Cooper said, "Luke, I'll get her home. I'll be leaving in a bit anyways."

Cooper fulfilled his promise and drove Macy home but Macy was too mad and drunk to go inside. So she got in the driver's seat of their car and just sat there in their driveway. She wanted to start the car and leave but knew she couldn't.

Macy woke up two hours later with the urge to throw up. She was freezing. As quietly as she could, she went in the house and upstairs to the bathroom. She cleaned herself up, left her clothes in the bathroom, and slid into bed and close to Luke—just enough to feel his warmth but not wake him up.

Luke was getting ready for work putting on his black dress pants and light yellow uniform shirt when Macy began to rouse.

"You have fun last night?" Luke asked with heavy sarcasm.

Macy was still hung over and her head was pounding. "Yeah," she sneered back. "Up until when I got sick."

"Maybe it was from those damn cigarettes you were smoking."

"Yeah, maybe."

Luke walked out and left for work. Macy lay in bed feeling sick and helpless.

And so it began...again. The unresolved frustration brewing between Macy and Luke was at a constant simmer—and the lid was ready to blow.

Later that day, Macy was startled by a knock on her door. It was her dad. "Dad, what are you doing here?" Macy asked as she opened the door, somewhat scared to let him in.

Peter was pissed. He had come straight from work, still in his Parts Manager uniform shirt and steel-toed boots.

"Oh, I just thought I'd stop by. Check in. You know..."

"Okay," Macy said apprehensively. Something was up, and frankly, she was scared. Luke wasn't home and as had happened many times before, she had no idea what was coming.

"So, I got a call from Ford Credit this afternoon," Peter said as he took a seat on the couch.

Oh shit. Here it comes. Macy could feel her temperature rise as she heard her heart beating in her ears.

"You haven't been making your payments."

Macy sunk further into the couch cushions—feeling like she was 7 years old all over again.

"Macy, what are you doing?"

"I accidently let Pudgy out. I was walking out of the gate and he squeezed through." Macy was getting her bike so she could go chase after their dog.

"Dammit, why is it so difficult to keep that dog where he belongs? You better go find him. You have ten minutes, then he's on his own."

Macy rode her bike franticly yelling, "Pudgy, Pudgy, come here puppy." By the time she made it around the block, Pudgy was in their neighbor's yard. She picked him up and returned him to the safety of their backyard.

"So you know what happens now, right. If I don't pay, my credit's screwed. What did you promise me when I co-signed again?"

"I know, Dad. I'm sorry. Obviously, I don't mean for this to happen. We just don't have any money right now."

Travis and Avery were playing in their rooms when Peter had arrived. Travis made his way downstairs, and when he saw his grandpa he ran in the living room, "Papa!"

Peter's personality changed immediately. "Well hello, Travis!" he said as he scooped him up and plopped him on his lap. "What were you doing up there?"

"Playing with tee-tee" (that's what he called his little sister). Travis showed Papa his Lego sculpture proudly.

"Very nice. Well, why don't you go check on your sister while Mommy and I talk?"

"Okay!" And Travis was off.

"I expect this to get taken care of immediately, Macy! No more jacking around. Don't you two care about your credit? Or mine? This is not what I signed up for."

"Alright, Dad. I got it."

After Macy's dad left, she saw the mailman through the front window. She tried to take a couple deep breaths, but the sight of the mailman just created more anxiety for her. She put the kids down for their naps.

Why do I even care to see what's in the mail, of course it's only bills, she thought to herself.

Macy got the mail from the box attached to the front door. She glanced through the envelopes as she walked through the living room to the kitchen.

"Bills, bills and more bills. Cable bill, electric bill and phone bill—go ahead and turn it all off!" Macy sighed.

"What the...?" As she filed through the envelopes, the phone bill felt unusually thick. She opened it only to find pages and pages of charges for calls to 900 numbers at three and four o'clock in the morning. Macy grabbed the phone, a box of cigarettes she had stashed in her purse, and headed out to the back door.

When Macy and Luke first met, she smoked on occasion. If Luke found cigarettes in her car or purse, he'd throw them out. She sat down on the back step, lit a cigarette and dialed the first 900 number on the bill. A voice recording of a girl comes on, *"What do you want to talk about? I'll do anything you'd like! Want me to talk hot to you?"* Macy's stomach turned as she listened. She hung up the phone and threw it across the backyard. She felt like she was going to vomit.

How could he do this to me? she thought to herself.

She quickly grabbed the cable bill and ripped it open. It had charges for adult movies too.

"I hate him! I cannot believe this. I'm asleep in bed and he's watching porn and calling slutty answering services right below me. Why God? Why is he doing this to me? What have I done to deserve this? I want out of here so damn bad I can't stand it." Macy screamed.

Macy sat there in seething silence smoking her cigarette crying tears of sickness and rage. Luke absolutely could not stand those disgusting cancer sticks, but Macy had no other outlet. She couldn't leave the babies and go for a drive or go to a bar.

How much more of this can I take? I just don't think I can do this anymore. Macy sobbed with her head in her hands.

Luke didn't get home from work until late, but Macy waited up for him. She had planned on confronting him, and she wasn't backing down. She was on the couch waiting for him in the dark.

"Well, there's the son-of-a-bitch," Macy said as Luke made his way in the house, not even waiting for him to change out of his ashtray smelling work uniform.

"Excuse me?" Luke said, startled by the voice coming from the dark living room.

She turned on the light, "You heard me, you son-of-a-bitch."

"What is your problem? Don't talk to me that way!"

Macy's anger took over. "How could you, Luke? How could you do this to me? You sick asshole."

She threw the bill at his face; papers flew everywhere as Luke flinched.

"You've been calling 900 numbers and watching porn while I'm right above you sleeping. You're acting like some desperate loser. And, now we have to pay for it with money we don't have, Luke!!" Macy screamed.

"Oh, give me a break, Macy! You're sleeping. What do you care?"

Macy was shaking and got in his face pointing, "You asshole. You're such a selfish asshole."

Luke's blasé attitude pissed Macy off even more. He showed no remorse and he didn't even try to come up with an excuse or apology. Macy's heart felt like it was about to explode. Her stomach was in her throat and she wanted to scream loud enough for the entire world to hear her pain. But nothing would come out. Luke acted as though he didn't give a shit.

Macy pushed Luke. "Why are you doing this to me, Luke? Why? What have I done to you?"

"Macy, if I want to watch porn, I'll watch it. This is my house and my TV."

"Really, Luke? And you don't care how I might feel about it? You know how I feel about that crap." Macy's tears turned into deep sadness.

"That's your problem."

"I hate you Luke! I hate you for doing this to me."

Macy began hitting Luke in the chest and pushing him, her arms flailing. Luke was trying to grab Macy's hands and pushed her. Macy just swung right back at him. Neither of them saw that little Avery had made her way down the stairs and was now standing between them crying.

"Mommy...Daddy..." Avery's wails became louder as her initial attempts didn't seem to get noticed.

Luke pushed Macy away and scooped up his baby girl, immediately changing his demeanor to that of a happy, caring father.

"Avery, what are you doing out of bed? You need to be asleep. Don't cry sweetie. It's okay!" as he gave Macy his 'you bitch' scowl.

Macy sunk down onto the floor crying. *Why? How? What are we going to do?*

Luke took Avery back to bed and Macy sat there on the floor crying with her head in her knees. She woke up an hour later, curled up in a ball on the hardwood floor and went up to bed. Luke turned towards her as she lay down.

"Macy, I'm sorry. I don't know why I did that. We'll be okay, I promise." Luke said and kissed her neck. "I love you so much."

"Luke, what are we going to do? My Dad was here today too. We owe everybody."

"I know. I get paid in a couple days. I promise I'll make some payments to everyone we owe." He continued to kiss Macy. She moved closer and kissed him back.

"I love you so much, Luke."

"I want you, Macy."

"I want you too, Luke."

Macy woke up later that night; she couldn't sleep. She went through a box that hadn't yet been unpacked. It contained some photo albums, birthday and anniversary cards and other items that carried fond memories and sweet notes. And, then she found the little green notebook she and Luke had exchanged notes to each other in. She found a pen and captured her thoughts and feelings.

9/12/94

Dear God,

Well here it is, 4 years later. Luke and I are married now and have two children. We have no money. We have no religion. We're just here.

So much has happened in these past four years. I never thought anything would go the way it has. We eloped - no ceremony - and had a cheesy reception at my folk's house. We are always fighting. I don't know what I want to do with my life, neither does Luke. He knows he wants to be rich but that's about it. Sure it'd be great if we had money, but who's to say we wouldn't be fighting then? Even still, Luke's ways of getting rich aren't very logical.

I'm so pissed off. Why did I have to fall in love with him? Why did he have to become my best friend? Why?? We look at each other in two totally different lights. I am almost always angry with him. I hate this life of mine. I hate it. I have no way of changing it either or even to make it better.

I'm beginning to suffocate. I can't breathe. I need some major space but I have two children that come before me always. So what am I to do? No money for counseling, no babysitters, no time to myself, nothing. I don't know what else to do. Someone please help me.

Things continued down this path for a while. Although the 900 number phone calls eventually stopped, the gambling didn't. Luke continued to create greater debt for he and Macy; every day it seemed they plunged deeper and deeper into financial trouble.

They did whatever they could to get by and pay what they could when they had money. But it always took two and three requests from the landlord, phone company, electric company or others before payment would ever get made. And nothing was ever paid in full; it would always be twenty dollars now and twenty dollars next week. It became a constant negotiation attempt.

There were some happy moments while Macy and Luke lived in their home in Alton sprinkled in with the bad. One of them was being in Kyle and David's wedding. Macy was the matron of honor and Luke was an usher. They found a little tux for Travis and a beautiful dress for little Avery. Leanne made her a hair bow to match. They all four looked beautiful all dressed up and coordinating. Leanne paid for Macy's bridesmaid's dress and manicure (fake nails) to match the other bridesmaids.

A few months later, they had a decent Christmas with their families despite not having much for gifts. This was always a good time for them. They put on their 'everything was okay' faces and enjoyed the holidays with both of their parents and siblings. Watching their baby's faces as they opened new toys and games was the best part of all; they just weren't from Macy and Luke. They could only afford two small gifts for each of the kids. Little Travis and Avery were sweet children that the entire family adored. They were spoiled by their grandparents and aunts and uncles. Both with their big blue eyes and sweet smiles and perfect frames, what wasn't to love?

CHAPTER 7

"Crazy"
1995

"Macy, some of the guys are moving up to Elgin, Illinois, to work on a really nice casino. I think we need to go too. They're paying dealers a lot more, and the tips are better," Luke said. Finding other places to gamble nearby intrigued him even more. As well as the fact that they would be further away from the majority of people they owed money to.

Macy knew they needed the money and was of course excited by the hope of bills getting paid, so she ignored the little voice in her head reminding her that they had nowhere to stay and said, "Alright, Luke let's go."

The drive to Elgin was a long one. Four hours north from their duplex with two toddlers in the backseat. Their trunk was overflowing with clothes, toys, and all the bare necessities that they could fit in their little black Escort. All the other items stayed back at the duplex in Alton. They would go back and get things on visits (which Macy hoped to do as often as possible).

"Let's just check in here," Luke said as they found a motel not far from the casino. The kids were getting restless and wanted to get out of their car seats. Luke came back with the key to a room with two double beds, complete with crummy bathroom and a safe for all of their valuables. Macy chuckled when she saw it.

Luke's intent was similar to past plans. "We'll just stay here until we find a place to rent." Luke almost immediately started at the casino dealing craps—a new and exhilarating game to deal. He always would bring in a lot of tips, not to mention, catch a glimpse of a celebrity here and there. One evening, he dealt to Richard Gere. Luke always loved feeling like a star. His job was to perform after all. To keep the game moving and exciting while encouraging the players by cheering them on and telling them how well they're playing. The more they won, the more he was acknowledged and tipped.

Macy got a job as a cocktail waitress in the casino's main lobby bar. It was a big bar and was always busy. Luke and Macy took turns staying with the kids at the hotel room while the other would work.

Living in the hotel room was awful. They were always right on top of each other. Travis and Avery would take turns getting in bed with Luke and Macy throughout the night. The bathroom sink was the closest thing they had to kitchen. Macy would make oatmeal with hot tap water, well as hot as it would get. Kool-Aid was also made in the sink even though the damn pitcher wouldn't fit under the faucet. Having no kitchen forced them to eat out all of the time. Between paying hotel room charges and eating out, the money never seemed to accumulate into savings or anything for that matter. Luke and Macy didn't have much of a social life either. They knew no one else except for a couple other dealers who also moved from the Alton Belle. There was, of course, no family to help with the kids.

"Luke, what are we going to do about another vehicle? I want to go back home for a visit soon. And, you're going to need a car." Macy asked one day.

"Yeah, I know. I guess we should go look around. Don't know how we're going to pay for it. Guess we need to pray that someone will give us a loan."

They found a used car lot in town and sat down with a salesman. He put them in a Taurus wagon and got them financed with a ridiculous interest rate. They had bad credit and were high-risk applicants after all. The car wasn't the nicest looking car, but it fit the four of them with plenty of room to spare.

Macy made plans to make a trip back home for Easter. Luke would stay back since he couldn't get a couple days off, and besides, they needed the money.

Luke and Macy filed their tax return with H&R Block prior to Macy leaving.

"Yes! A twelve hundred and fifty dollar refund. We so need that!" Luke said, as he began listing what they would do with the money. "That's enough for a place to live, the car payment, and we can even pay some back to your dad."

"Agreed. Good plan, Luke!" Macy smiled.

She packed up the kids, kissed Luke good-bye, and Macy, Travis and Avery headed home to see their families and a quick stop at the duplex to pick up some things.

Macy called Luke to let him know they arrived safely. "Hey, baby, how are you doing?"

"Pretty good. Miss you though! How's the family?"

"They're all good. They say hello! I miss you and wish you could've come home too!"

"Me too. Work left a message for you. They said they need you to call them...something about a problem with the schedule."

"Oh? Okay. I'll call them when we hang up."

"I love you, Luke! "

"I love you too! See you soon!"

"Hi, Steve! This is Macy. I had a message that you wanted me to call you."

"Uh yeah, hold on one second. Okay, so we had you scheduled to work on Saturday, but you didn't show." Steve explained.

"What? No, I had switched with Susan. She was working for me."

"Well, Susan wasn't here either. If that's something you two had worked out, we didn't know about it. Since you were the one on the schedule and you didn't come into work, that's grounds for termination." Steve said matter-of-factly.

"What? Are you serious?"

"Yes, I'm very serious. We're going to have to let you go, Macy. You can turn in your uniform and card pass to the Supervisor's office."

"Well, that's just not fair at all." Macy said, trying to hold the tears back. *Are you freaking kidding me?* Macy said to herself almost laughing with rage.

And just like that, Macy was out of a job… again.

She put the phone down and went into the bathroom. She sat down on the toilet and cried.

"Why does this keep happening to me—to us?" Why can't we just pay our bills? How much more can we take? My poor babies deserve so much better than this!"

"Luke?"

"Oh, hey! What's up, sweetie?"

"The Lounge fired me."

"They what?! Why?"

"Because I was a no-show on Saturday."

"But you said you found someone to work for you."

"I did…but she didn't show up, so I'm the one getting fired."

"Oh, what the hell! How ridiculous. I'm so sorry, honey."

"Luke, I don't think I can go back to that hotel. It's just not fair to the kids to be cooped up in that room all the time."

"I agree. But what do you suggest we do?"

"I'm going to see if I can stay here until you find us a place. I'll clean out the duplex and we can go from there. We've got that refund coming, so that should hold us over for a bit."

"Okay, I'll try to find a roommate to move in with. I know a couple of guys that have an apartment."

Macy sighed a heavy sigh.

"Once again, here we are—apart! Why Luke? Why must this keep happening?"

"I know, honey. I'm so sorry! I hate moving us around like this! I love you and truly want to take care of you and Travis and Avery. Do you believe me, Macy?"

Macy didn't reply.

"Macy?"

"Yes, Luke! I believe you. I love you too. I better go, I'll talk to you soon."

"Please enter your 9-digit social security number followed by the pound sign. Please enter the amount of your refund."

Macy entered the numbers on the keypad.

"Your refund has been issued," the automated voice responded.

Then why hasn't H&R Block called us yet? Macy thought to herself. She called them a couple times to check on the status of their refund check but had to leave messages each time. It was tax season after all and it was difficult to ever get a live person on the phone.

Macy called Luke. "Luke, have you heard from H&R Block regarding our refund?"

"Um, no. Why?"

"Because per the IRS, our refund has been issued but we haven't heard from H&R Block that they have it. I've left them a couple of messages but haven't heard back."

"I'm sure it's just in the mass of work they have going on with tax season."

"Yeah, probably so. How's work?"

"It's going okay. Nothing new."

"How's living with Ryan?"

"Pretty good. We tend to work opposite shifts, so I don't see him that often."

"Alright, baby. I'll talk to you more later. I love and miss you lots!"

"You too, honey!"

The next day, H&R Block returned Macy's call.

"Mrs. Hawthorn? This is Jane from H&R Block.

"Oh, hello! You got my message?"

"Yes we're sorry for the delay getting back with you but it's quite crazy around here this time of year. So, you called inquiring about your refund, correct?"

"Yes, per the IRS automated refund system, our refund has been issued?"

"That's correct, it has been issued. And, I see that your husband, Luke, picked it up. In fact, the check has already cleared."

"Um, what?" Macy felt the like the wind just got knocked out of her. "I'm sorry, how is that possible? Both of our names were on the check, and both of our signatures were required to pick up the check."

"Well, it looks like your husband signed for the both of you."

"You've got to be kidding me," the devastation became more and more crippling.

"There's a note here that says, 'husband said it's okay to sign for his wife since she is out of town visiting family.'"

"I'm not sure how you can let him do that."

Oh my God, I can't believe he forged my name. He lied to me. Macy was shaking and having an anxiety attack. *Not now, not again. Please tell me he didn't gamble away this money. Please, he couldn't have.*

Macy already knew in her heart the money was gone. The shame began to take over and control her emotions. Abandoned and alone, she felt left to the wolves. How would she survive another attack? She'd been beaten down over and over. One thing remained constant between Luke and Macy: they argued about money and Luke's inability to keep a dime in his pocket.

"You lying son-of-a-bitch! You lied to me again!"

"Macy, I didn't know how to tell you!"

"Where is it, Luke. Where's our refund check?"

"I lost it."

"What do you mean, you lost it?" She knew full well what he meant, but she wanted to hear it. She wanted him to have to say it.

"I gambled it and lost it." Luke said matter-of-factly, disguising his extreme guilt and shame as best he could.

There it was again...that kick in the gut. She couldn't breathe, she could only scream. "I hate you! I hate what you are doing to our family and me. How do you do it? How do you decide to forge my name, cash our check, and take it to a casino? I don't understand. Please, Luke, please help me understand!"

"Macy, I don't know how. It just happened. I don't know what you want me to say." Luke began to cry. "I'm so very sorry. I am. Please don't say you hate me."

"What do you expect me to do now, Luke?"

"You don't have to do anything. I'll fix it. I promise."

"Yep, I've heard that one before."

Macy thought a lot about what she should do. She felt she couldn't rely on Luke anymore. Still at home with Luke five hours away, Macy did the best she could to use those anxiety-producing events as fuel to do what she needed to do.

Meanwhile, Luke stayed busy. If he wasn't working, he was out with friends playing darts or pool or gambling.

Macy got a job at Western Union as a call service rep handling wire transfers. She also signed up for a couple of classes at the community college thanks to financial aid. Macy had desired to fulfill her childhood dream of being a nurse. *I need to take care of me*, she would attempt to encourage herself. It felt good to take charge of what she wanted to do again. She had to do more for her and Travis and Avery.

Some time passed since Luke and Macy had seen each other. They weren't talking as often either. Macy was afraid to hear what Luke was doing, and he didn't want to hear from Macy how he was a bad husband and dad. Macy could feel herself separating emotionally from Luke. She was still so angry with him for lying to her, but worse, for not keeping his word. *He's just not living up to his promises—the promises he made to me over and over. If you say you're going to do something, freaking do it.*

"Good afternoon, Mrs. Hawthorn. It's nice to meet you."

"Hi, Mr. Broscoe. You too."

"Please have a seat."

"Thanks."

"So what brings you in today?"

"I need help. I need to get a divorce."

"Okay, tell me a little bit about what's going on."

"I love him. But, I just don't believe he loves me. He has developed a serious gambling problem and we are so behind on bills, our credit is destroyed. So I'm the one paying the bills. And we're living apart...he's in Elgin working at a casino there."

"So wait...he works for a casino *and* he has a gambling problem?"

"Yeah, I know. Just like an alcoholic working as a bartender. I just don't know how we can keep on living like this. He's promised he'd fix it all but I don't think he's ever going to change."

"Well, I can help you. It's a fairly simple process granted he doesn't contest anything. We just need some tax records, employment info, socials, etc. and we can begin the filing process. You have kids?"

"Yes, we have two. Travis, our son, is almost three and our daughter, Avery, will be two in December."

"Okay, we can file the standard custody agreement of every other weekend with their father and there are government guidelines we'll use to determine child support amounts. I'm going give you this packet as well. There's a list of documents I will need to create the file. If you can gather those, I will have my assistant write up some papers. Let's schedule a time to meet in a couple weeks to review."

"Okay, I will. Thank you."

Macy felt awful leaving Mr. Broscoe's office. While pulling out of the parking lot, she thought to herself, *What have I done? What is happening? How did we get to this point?* The thoughts filled her heart and tears flooded her eyes. *Why is this happening? It's not supposed to be this way!* She thought of the kids and how they don't deserve this. *I love Luke so much. Why does he have to be this way? He just isn't the man I fell in love with any more. I don't understand how he can keep stealing from us. How are we not important enough to him? Why doesn't he want to fight for me, for us?*

Macy didn't tell anyone about her meeting with the lawyer. Their lives had been on constant display for so long, Macy did what she could to protect those most private areas—mainly the areas she didn't care to get anyone's unsolicited opinions on.

"Hi, Luke."

"Hey baby," sounding a bit shocked as he was always surprised that Macy still wanted to talk to him. "How are you? How's school going? I sure miss you like crazy!"

"It's going well. I'm enjoying it so far. It's hard, but I like it."
Silence filled the air.

"What's wrong, Macy? Everything okay?"

"Well, not exactly. We need to talk."

"Oh, okay. What is it?" Luke asked tentatively.

"Luke, I talked to a lawyer the other day."

"About?" Luke's voice cracked as he hesitated.

"About filing for divorce." More silence. "We just can't live like this anymore. It's not fair to me or the kids, to any of us."

"Oh my God, are you serious, Macy?"

"Luke, I wouldn't joke about something like this. I'm hurting, you have no idea. The stress of our debt is just too much to bear. And living with Mom and Dad and your Mom is too much.

Besides, you haven't mailed any money home like you promised. It's been almost five months..."

"But, Macy—wait!" Luke cut her off.

"Luke, you're there. You have no idea what we're going through, nor do I think you care."

"Macy we can work this out, can't we? I love you, baby. I don't want it to end like this. I don't want us to end, period."

"How are things going to possibly get any better or be any different?"

"I don't know. I know I've made things very hard for you, for all of us. But give me a chance to fix it."

"Luke, you've had a ton of chances. We've been down this road too many times. I'm sorry. I've got to go." She couldn't hold back the tears any longer. The sobbing began as soon as she hung up the phone.

One week later, Luke called. "Macy, I'm coming home. I haven't slept at all the past couple of days. If you'll let me, I'd love to meet with you when I get back. I've already quit the casino and I've got all my things together. I'll be home tomorrow afternoon. We can work this out. I know we can."

Macy was speechless...again feeling that desperate hope for their marriage and relationship to work out, for Luke to get over his addiction. Macy sat down gripping the phone to her chest and started to cry.

The next afternoon, Macy got a message from Judy that the Taurus had broken down and he was getting a ride but he'd be home later than he planned. Luke had to leave the car on the side of the highway. Stupid Taurus. That freaking car salesman sold them a lemon—and probably knew it. Four days after they bought the car, the serpentine belt fell off as they were pulling into the parking lot of the local super market. It cost Luke and Macy five hundred dollars to have it fixed. It was always something—stalling, oil leaks, battery, etc. And, now they had to pay for the heap of junk thanks to the high interest loan they had on it that was now abandoned along Highway 70.

Luke finally made it into town and immediately called Macy.

"I'm here, Macy. What a mess, but I'm finally here."

"Hi. I heard about the Taurus breaking down."

"Yeah, freaking piece of junk. Not sure how we can get out of that loan. They sold us a complete lemon." There was a long pause. "So, enough about that. It's a beautiful day. Would you like to go to the park with me?"

Macy hesitated, "Um, I guess so. But it'll have to be later—around 6 okay?"

"Okay. I'll see you then. Can't wait to see your face!"

Macy was nervous to meet Luke. It had been a while since they had seen each other. She's been so mad and hurt and she didn't want Luke to patronize her instead of addressing all the wrong that had gone on. But she also knew how she felt about him. She knew what to expect when she'd see him—all the emotion would overwhelm her and cloud her memory. There was no one else that made her feel this way. And it was the very same for Luke. Macy was the only woman that had a hold on his heart the way she did.

Stick to the issues, Macy, she told herself. *Don't let him sweet talk his way out of what's most important to you. He can't just say he loves you anymore. He's going to have to show you—actions speak louder than words, right? Right!* She continued her pep talk as she drove to the park. She reminded herself of the 900 numbers, her Dad's visit, the porn, how he forged her name on their refund check that he squandered at the casino, not sending money, etc. to keep her emotions and desires for him below the surface.

There he is. She saw him as she put the car in park. He met her at the car door.

"Hey!" Luke said, as he reached out for her hand.

"Hi Luke!" She smiled a cautious smile and accepted his hand.

"Oh my God. I've missed you so much. You smell so good!" Luke squeezed her tight.

"What do I smell like?" Macy asked.

"My Macy," Luke smiled.

The two walked and caught up. Macy shared how school was going and a little about her job. It was a beautiful warm evening and she loved this time with Luke. She felt normal and momentarily forgot about all of the pain and troubles they were enduring. Luke was all she wanted. Why couldn't he fix this for her—for Travis and Avery?

"Macy, I don't want a divorce. Please! I want to make this work. I want us to work."

"Do you think I want this, Luke? Because I don't, really. But it's the same thing over and over again. You make promises, break them, apologize and then it starts all over."

"You have every right to be mad at me. *I'm* mad at me. I'm completely disgusted with myself. But, I just know we can make this work! I do." Luke said, peering into Macy's sad and lonely eyes. He nodded his head in an effort to convince her that he was committed and meant it this time. And that's when he leaned closer and asked, "Can I please kiss you?"

Macy didn't pull away.

"Hi. May I speak with John?"

"Hello. This is John."

"Hi, John. I need to talk to you about the divorce papers."

"Yeah, okay. What is it?"

"Well, I'm not going to file after all. I'm going to give him another chance."

Macy wanted nothing more than to believe Luke's promise. She wanted to believe they could work this out and get through all of the crap they were going through and make it right.

They moved back in with Judy while they waited for a place of their own. Luke got a job at the new casino. It was all the way downtown so he would car pool with some other guys that worked there. Macy would drop him off at the commuter lot where they'd all meet. Macy was just a month into school and she was enjoying it a lot. She loved having textbooks and notebooks and doing well—getting good grades made her feel so good for a change. The job at Western Union was decent pay and flexible enough to work around her class schedule. But sometimes the callers she'd have to deal with scared her. They wanted their money right then and there, and if it wasn't available, they would threaten her.

Macy had also enrolled Travis and Avery in the Mother's Day Out program at Judy's church so she could study, do homework, and occasionally have some alone time. The kids loved all the new friends they made and the teachers were so wonderful to them and so very nice to Macy. Soon after they were getting all settled once again, Macy began feeling run down and exhausted.

"I think I'm coming down with the flu or something," Macy told Luke as they got in bed one night."

"You don't feel good, baby?"

"No, not at all. Just so tired and sick to my stomach. Maybe I picked something up from the kids?"

"You need me to get you anything?"

"I'll be fine. I took a couple of aspirin before I laid down."

"Just get some sleep and we'll see how you feel in the morning." Luke said, as he pulled the covers up under Macy's chin and kissed her forehead.

The next morning as Macy went to use the bathroom, it took one look as she went to flush to notice something all too familiar. *Oh dear, God—not again!* She thought to herself. Cloudy urine, not feeling well, exhausted all of the time...I'm pregnant. This time

Macy said nothing right away, thinking maybe she was wrong. She did whatever she could not to think about it. Macy spent the next couple of days in serious denial. She'd cry in secret. She hid from everyone making excuses to have to go to the library or store. She'd sit in her car crying, dreaming up ways for this to not be real. The night she spent with Luke talking in the park, they were together. Their third child conceived. Macy tried to desperately see this new life as a blessing, but the overwhelming fear left her feeling hopeless and depressed.

Things with Macy and Luke weren't all good yet either. They still had a lot to do, like find a place to live and pay their bills. Now an even greater financial burden would be here in just nine short months. And the best part was that they had no health insurance. No money to pay for the family they already had. *How could you let this happen?* Macy was so disgusted with herself.

Luke and Macy went to Luke's aunt and uncle's house to visit with his cousin, Shane.

"Remember our auditions at Six Flags?" Luke asked Shane. "I bombed so bad."

"Dude, I felt horrible. It was your idea for us to audition, and then I made it."

"I know bro. Not like I would've expected you not to accept the part. I just went completely blank when I was singing. And on a song like *New York, New York*...a song I've sung, crap, I don't know how many times. Just would've been cool to sing with you."

"I know?!" Shane replied.

"Hey Luke, would you come up here for a second?" Macy called from upstairs.

"Okay, where are you?" Luke was coming up the stairs.

"In the kitchen."

"Yeah, what's up lil' mama?" Luke asked as he found her standing against the counter.

"I have something for you in the oven." Macy's level of denial was now being masked by her sense of humor, as dry as it was. She was looking for a snack to eat when she saw something that gave her the idea on how to tell Luke.

"In the oven? But it's not even on," he said as he turned around to look behind him. He opened the oven door and there was a hot dog bun. He picked it up and, confused, he turned to Macy.

"I don't get it?"

"Well, what is it?" Macy asked.

"A hot dog bun?" Luke answered.

"And, where'd you find it?"

"In the oven."

"And, what is it again?"

"A bun...in the oven?" Luke said still not understanding the joke. "You left a bun in the oven?" His eyes got wide as a light bulb went off. "Oh my God! Do you have a bun in the oven? You're pregnant?!"

Macy just smiled a half smile and said, "Yes, there's a bun in the oven," as she held her belly.

"Um, okay...wow! So that's why you're not feeling well."

"Yep!"

"Oh no! Scary stuff we keep getting ourselves into, huh?"

"You think?" Macy wanted to cry. Luke wanted to run out the front door but they both laughed and hugged each other hoping something good would come their way soon.

Macy realized she had to rearrange her plans, her life, once again. She was experiencing depression and a lot of shame and guilt. She withdrew from school and kept working at Western Union.

How humiliating—I feel like such a complete waste, Macy would often think to herself.

Luke's going out and gambling returned and with a vengeance. He seemed to become 'good' friends with the ones who would join him in late night dart and pool games and gambling. Many nights Macy would page Luke in the casino in order to get him home. One night, she showed up at the bar down the street where he was and got in his face.

"Don't you think you should be at home? You have babies too. They're not just mine to take care of. And, some friend you are! Asshole." Macy wasn't afraid to address Luke and his 'friends' either. "You obviously don't care that he has a wife and babies at home."

"Oh, no one is holding a gun to his head, Macy. Give the guy a break." One 'friend' said sarcastically.

"Give *me* a break, Brad!" Luke never had a comment.

She turned around and left. Luke crawled into their bed an hour later. Macy turned to face the wall, pretending to sleep but mostly to make sure he knew he wasn't welcomed there.

Some good news finally made its way around to Luke and Macy when Kyle shared that she and David were moving out of their apartment. They had just purchased a lot and were going to build a new home. Kyle called Macy to let her know that their landlord asked if they knew anyone that would be interested in the apartment since they were moving out. "Of course, I thought of you," Kyle told Macy.

"Yes, that would be awesome, Kyle. We'd love to talk to them." Luke and Macy met with the landlord and the apartment was theirs. Two bedrooms, one bathroom, a basement for their washer and dryer, a driveway and a storage shed. Finally they would have a place all to themselves again. It had been so long. They could sleep together, shower together, be themselves together—scream and yell and argue—in their own space.

Kyle left the couch as well as a handful of other things for them. Luke and Macy got the kid's beds and the rest of their stuff out of storage and moved in. Their place was small, all six hundred square feet of it, but they didn't have much to fill it with anyway. Macy and Luke's bed—a queen size mattress and box spring—sat on the floor. They had one dresser—a hand-me-down from Leanne and Peter—one of their wedding gifts. Travis and Avery would share the other tiny bedroom. Their little racecar and princess beds and matching toy boxes would fill the room. But it was theirs, all theirs.

With Macy being pregnant, every emotion was magnified by what seemed like a hundred times. Especially when Luke wasn't there for her to help her with the kids.

I've given up so much for this guy and he could just plain give a crap, Macy would often feel.

Macy left her job at Western Union. She was too tired and stressed all the time from callers that threatened her and were just plain ignorant all of the time. The supervisors were never there for the staff to take the hostile calls, so Macy would end up saying, "I don't have to listen to your hostility. I'm ending the call." Just for another angry caller to be waiting in the queue.

The weather was growing colder and the holidays would be here before they knew it. Macy and Luke continued to struggle making ends meet. Rent, utilities—the apartment had so many leaks; it took a lot of heat to keep the place warm—groceries, cars, etc.

Macy had always been a saver. She never spent her money. She would save up for things she wanted and never bought anything for the kids or the house and especially for herself, without first analyzing the need versus the want. One of Macy's shopping habits was to go into a store, grab a cart and start browsing. She would gather items she liked, as she'd go from shoes, to purses, clothes, etc. Her process was so picky; the price had to be under a certain limit and she'd have to come up with a legitimate need. She'd go try on and start confirming her selections. Then she'd go back into the store all the while deciding she didn't need a certain item, and leave it behind. When she'd check out, it would be maybe two or three things and most times nothing for her but something for Luke or the kids. She had to force herself to buy something for her and especially when it was just because.

Obviously money was still a constant struggle. They couldn't pay their bills. When they did have money, Luke would lose it gambling. And, so many times, Macy would pay a bill and then Luke would drain the bank account. So not only were they out money, they'd have bounced check fees due to insufficient funds when the check would attempt to clear. Macy's depression grew deeper and deeper. She was consumed with worry, fear and anxiety. She constantly felt trapped and out of control. Luke was feeling the same way and wanted to run—which is all he really knew how to do; so he buried himself by staying out drinking and gambling.

Macy was on her way to pick up the kids and just up ahead at the end of the street was a telephone pole. She told herself to slam on the gas and don't let up. *Just end it. Slam into that pole and end it!* She cried. She pressed her foot down on the gas, but she couldn't do it. She had nowhere to go. Her family had bailed her and Luke out too many times and she was too embarrassed to admit how horrible things were becoming. She couldn't sit at a bar and drink, she was pregnant, and what about little Travis and Avery. She couldn't run away. She had no way out. Macy contacted a behavioral health center in a desperate cry for help.

"Macy?" A young black woman called from the office door. Macy got up and headed in her direction.

"Are you Macy?" She was tall and thin. Macy thought she was pretty.

"Yes, ma'am."

"Come on in. You can have a seat here." She pointed to the chair in her office. "So, what brings you here today?" She asked.

Macy swallowed hard and fidgeted in her chair some as she tried to get the words to come to her lips. "Um, well... I'm 24 years old and pregnant with my third baby. My husband has a serious gambling problem and I'm finding it very difficult to live. I've thought about ending it—my life—but can't. I just don't know what to do any more." Macy talked more with the counselor about the financial situation and her constant anxious emotional state. "And, it's all my fault."

"I'm sorry? What exactly do you mean by that?" the counselor asked.

"Well, if it wasn't for me telling him about the lady I worked with and how she suggested that I be a black jack dealer, we would have never even visited that casino. He would have never gotten addicted."

"Macy, how would you have known that gambling would have become a problem for him?"

"It's not like he's cheating on me, he just has a gambling problem." Macy's tone changed quickly.

"Macy, this is not your fault. And, based on what I'm hearing you say, he's spending his time somewhere else—it's still cheating. His time, energy and thoughts are consumed with gambling, his new love, and not with you or the kids," the counselor responded.

"Well, I guess you're right." Macy had never thought about it like that.

"I'd like to suggest you take part in some of our group therapy sessions. Do you think you could manage making it here two nights a week? There will be some homework too."

"Yes, I can do that." Macy felt ashamed but somewhat relieved. Someone listened and offered help. More importantly, she hated talking negatively about Luke and she felt guilty for it. He was the most loving and tender man she had ever known. His gambling turned him into someone Macy didn't know. She just couldn't understand how he could lose their money or take that risk so easily without any thought or consideration of the potential outcome. She longed for the answers that Luke absolutely NEVER had. How could he possibly?

Macy soon joined others going through similar problems in an outpatient therapy group. Among the group were a couple people dealing with drug addiction, others wanting to hurt themselves and some just trying to overcome depression. Macy was given homework which consisted of writing assignments and reading a couple of books that would help her understand the cognitive therapy that they practiced there as well as the destructive cycle of co-dependency. She learned to understand her role as a co-dependent spouse and then how to 'reprogram' the way she thought; therefore, manipulate a negative thought into a positive one—searching for the rational outcome. For example, "I can't get out of bed," isn't rational; however, "I can get out of bed, I'm not crippled," is.

Macy listened to the others in the group. It was somewhat fulfilling for her to be there for them and respond with encouraging ideas to their concerns. She often felt when leaving the group that things were going to be okay. Especially since she saw what the others were going through. She didn't think her struggles were as bad as theirs—after all, it could be so much worse.

When hearing Macy speak of her anxiety regarding her family's money issues, her social worker encouraged her to apply for government assistance. This was a thought that absolutely never crossed her mind. While they were struggling so much financially, she still felt great humiliation, unworthiness, and shame and she hated asking her family for money. They never had food in the fridge or in the cabinets, except maybe some hotdogs, a couple eggs and Kool-Aid. And there is just no way they could cover the doctor and hospital bills for a third baby. There was no question Macy and Luke needed help; but was it right to take advantage of government assistance?

Macy had mentioned the suggestion to her mom one afternoon. "So, my counselor suggests that we apply for government aid. I'm not sure that's the right thing to do, though."

"What do you mean you don't think it's the right thing to do? Macy, if you need help which I'm certain you do after seeing what's in—or not in—your fridge last weekend, then you should get it. Besides, it's my tax dollars and I'd feel a lot better knowing it's going to someone that I care about and does in fact need it."

When she called to make an appointment with her OB, Dr. Charlie, she was told that he didn't accept Medicaid. "I'm so sorry. We're not an approved provider in the Medicaid plan," the office clerk told Macy.

"So... that means I can't see Dr. Charlie?"

"No, I'm so sorry."

"But he was my doctor with my other two pregnancies. Now what am I supposed to do?"

"I'm afraid you'll have to check with the Medicaid office for an in-network doctor."

"Yep, okay." Macy hung up the phone frustrated and scared.

Macy was referred to wonderful doctor, a sweet British man, to help care for her with this third baby. She had in her mind that no one would ever compare to Dr. Charles. He was the next-best, though. He was an older man who was extremely kind and old-fashioned, which was just what Macy needed.

That first time Macy pulled the vouchers from the mailbox, she put her head down and closed her eyes, afraid to open the envelope. She wondered if anyone else had seen the dark yellow envelope in her mailbox. She was overcome with relief, even if it did come with a giant shot of guilt. It was an awful reminder of what they didn't have nor could provide to their babies that might as well been stamped in big red letters across the envelope— IRRESPONSIBLE, LAZY, DELINQUENTS.

She did what she could to find light in the situation and took the kids to the grocery store to shower them with a cart full of food. Macy and the kids had a great time at the store loading the cart—burying Travis and Avery with milk, cereal, bread, cheese, hamburger, and so much more. But, when it came time to check out, Macy stalled. She didn't want anyone to come in the lane behind her. She didn't want anyone to see her paying with food stamps and WIC vouchers. She didn't want anyone to judge her or believe they didn't deserve the government assistance that they were in fact approved for. Macy already believed she didn't deserve it, she didn't need any more judgment. More so, she didn't want to be reminded of their secret; the secret that they were all living with addiction and in poverty.

Macy left outpatient therapy once the holidays arrived. She wasn't sure how they'd scrounge up enough money for Christmas.

About that time, Macy got a call from Leanne.

"Hi Mom."

"Hi Macy. How you and the kids doing?"

"We're okay – hanging in there."

"Well that's good. I'm glad. So Aunt Jackie called me just a little while ago. She was wondering if you would be interested in babysitting Jed and Lindsay for her for a couple of weeks. She said you could bring Travis and Avery too. Since you could use the money, I thought you'd be interested."

"Really? Wow, of course. That'd be great! I'll give her a call."

"Okay, sounds good, Macy."

"Thanks, Mom!"

Macy took Travis and Avery to Jackie's house the following Monday. Jed and Lindsay were the same ages, so they all played together pretty well. Macy made lunches and they would have picnics in the living room while watching movies—it was too cold to go outside. The money Macy earned from babysitting her cousins allowed them to buy Christmas gifts for the kids. Which made Christmas that much more enjoyable to spend with family.

Luke had picked up a second job with a carpet cleaning company. A couple times a week, he would go to the office to pick up carbon copy appointment slips with the customer's address and room requests. Luke would load up the massive equipment into their tiny Escort and clean people's carpets. The extra cash would go towards rent and pulling various items out of pawn and an occasional bet.

Luke and Macy would spend the Christmas holiday going to Macy's grandma's house on Christmas Eve and then Luke's mom's and Macy's other grandma's house on Christmas day. They celebrated with Peter and Leanne on a day close to Christmas. Macy loved sitting around the dinner table sharing a wonderful meal and conversation the most! Sitting on her parent's hard wood dining room chairs got to be very uncomfortable after just a short while, though. Macy had developed a sciatic nerve problem mainly due to all the stress she was carrying during the pregnancy. Her OB told her that the baby could be sitting on a nerve but more likely things of this nature are caused by stress and anxiety. She agreed she had definitely been under a *little* stress.

Luke was great at putting on the right face—a poker face— for whatever occasion, even though he was embarrassed and full of shame. He especially had to put on a 'happy' front whenever he was around Macy's family—mister jokester and 'nothing can get me down' attitude. If he wasn't busy putting on a face, his eyes were glued to the TV in a football coma, which would always turn into intense fear and desperation.

"How much did you lose on that game?" Peter asked Luke with that 'you-son-of-a-bitch, who do you think you are, you're not fit to take care of my daughter or grandchildren' tone of his.

While at Judy's, Luke opened his gift from her. "What's this?" Luke held a piece of paper in his hands. Macy leaned over to get a closer look. "It's an invitation... to the "Weekend with Your Spouse" marriage conference hosted by Family Life Ministries. It's at the DoubleTree Hotel, and I'll watch the kids."

Luke and Macy didn't spend too much time deliberating. "What do you think, Macy?" Luke asked.

"I'm not sure I want to leave the kids all weekend."

Luke sneered, "Can you not ever find anything positive to say?"

Macy rolled her eyes.

"Come on. Let's go. If anything, to get away just the two of us. We could reminisce from when you used to work there," he grabbed her hand to kiss her ring. Luke always did whatever he could to get Macy to smile. It was the one thing that gave him the affirmation and hope that she still loved him.

"Yes, Luke. Okay. I want to go away too."

CHAPTER 8

"You Oughta Know"
1996

The conference started on a Friday evening. There were so many couples at the conference. Macy and Luke were undoubtedly the youngest couple there. The facilitator introduced the agenda and itinerary for the weekend and then took the audience through a list of the wife's needs and the husband's needs and how to say what to each other. "Now for your assignment this evening, go on a date. Be sure to remember each other's needs and enjoy your evening together. We have a lot to cover tomorrow. We'll see you bright and early in the AM." The facilitator closed the session.

Luke and Macy went to a nearby restaurant. All of the discussion was still fresh in their minds. Macy was feeling the frustration and anger stirring in her gut that their marriage was on the rocks in the worst way, that she truly believed that Luke loved gambling more than he loved her and the kids. And, that her love for Luke couldn't fix all of the problems they had gotten themselves into. Luke did all he could to keep the conversation light, doing what he could to make Macy laugh and smile. And, he was so good at it.

"Remember our first night in our apartment? We sat up all night listening to Slaughter and Johnny Gill. Or, late ice cream runs, or when I got you Nyquil in the middle of the night?" Luke asked Macy.

Macy smiled, "Of course. I overslept the next morning and Mark reamed me a new one for being late to work."

"Yeah, but you got the sleep you needed and felt better, right?" Luke smiled looking for that affirmation he so longed for.

They finished their dinner and went back to the hotel room. They watched a movie and spent the rest of their night entangled in each other's arms and legs. The passion between them had never been impacted by all of the anger and frustration. If anything, both Luke and Macy felt like it was the one thing that was right between them, and their babies of course. They felt intimately connected and deeply lost all at the same time when they were together.

The next day of the conference was filled with recaps and volunteers sharing some of their experiences from their date nights. "Is there anyone else that feels comfortable enough to share what you got from practicing the techniques we went over yesterday?" the facilitator asked the group.

Macy reluctantly raised her hand as she looked at Luke. He looked at Macy's hand and while raising his eyebrows and with wide eyes, he mouthed, "Really?" He was surprised she was willing to share. But deep down Macy was dying to be heard.

"Macy and Luke, great. Come on up here and take a seat so we can all see you." The facilitator grabbed two chairs for them. "So using the techniques we talked about, take us through what you would like to work on."

Macy and Luke sat down. Luke said a few things and then the anger brewing in Macy's gut began bubbling up to the surface. She felt that desire to scream but could feel her voice weakening and had already convinced herself that no one would hear her. But when she opened her mouth, there were words and volume. "Your gambling has gotten out of control. I don't feel as though I am a priority for you or our babies. You make me so very angry when you take money away from us. The one thing we don't have and need you lose at other casinos and you work in a casino. I'm not sure how much longer I can live like this."

Luke's face instantly went red and he had tears in his eyes while Macy thought to herself, *Macy, what did you just do? You just called him out in front of all of these people.* The anger was still spewing from her eyes, but now her heart panged with guilt for hurting him. Her heart was now in her throat so she tried to keep anger to the surface instead of tears.

You could feel the entire room sit in awe and shock. You could have cut the silence with a knife. There was so much more going on in Macy and Luke's relationship, marriage and lives than this room was prepared for. This raw emotion and honesty took every single one of them by surprise. Many of the couples thought about nudging their spouse, "That's you." Some of them could totally relate and were relieved when Macy was brave enough to speak up.

The facilitator was also somewhat speechless but agreed there was definitely a lot more that needed to be worked out in Macy and Luke's marriage. He whispered to them both, "We'll have you meet with Mr. Cane after this session."

It was a difficult ride home from the conference. Both Macy and Luke were feeling so much, and anger was the most prevalent feeling of all. Luke was clearly pissed off. They stopped at Judy's to pick up the kids. After they got home, Luke left. He gambled and lost even more money than usual that night.

A couple that was touched by Luke and Macy's story stopped by to visit with them a few times and always came bearing gifts. Their first visit they brought a basket filled with bibles, devotional books and stuffed animals for the kids. Macy picked up the book on codependency and as she read the first few pages began to feel a little bit understood.

In February, Macy went to Kelly Services to seek employment.

"Yes, I'd like to submit my resume and see what opportunities you may have available."

"Great. What type of work are you looking for?"

"Any sort of administrative work. I'm an excellent customer service advocate and am very skilled in computers and Microsoft Office."

Macy felt intimidated and embarrassed. She was six months pregnant, dressed in a maternity dress seeking employment. *Who wants to hire a pregnant chick?* But then her cognitive therapy reminded her to turn that around… *You're pregnant, you're not stupid.*

Macy filled out an application and then headed back home. Later that same afternoon, the recruiter she had met with called her.

"Hi, Macy?"

"Yes, this is she."

"This is Jenny from Kelly Services. We have an assignment we thought you would be a good fit for."

"Seriously?"

"It's in the office of Senior Management at MasterCard. It's only a one week assignment at the moment, but there is a possibility it will be extended."

Macy immediately thought, *Um, senior management? I've never worked for anyone at that level before. But then again, what could go wrong in a week?*

"Sure, I'd love to take on this assignment." She got the details from the recruiter and on Monday she'd report to the Senior Offices at MasterCard.

Macy was so excited to get a paycheck again. And to do something she was good at, and more importantly, getting out of the house would be just what she needed. With Luke having the evening shift at work, he would stay with the kids while Macy worked during the day.

When Macy showed up to the MasterCard office, she was impressed with how high-tech everything was and it was so nicely decorated too. The HR department had her set up with a badge with her picture. She was on her way up to the fifth floor. She used her badge and entered the Office of Executive Management (OEM). This area was even nicer than what she had seen so far.

"Hi, Macy?" a voice came from a desk to her left.

"Yes, Hi!"

An older woman with short whitish-blonde hair came out from behind the desk to greet Macy. She reached out to shake her hand, "Hi, I'm Joy. Welcome."

She walked Macy over to the desk on the other end of the office, "This is where you will be sitting, so why don't you put your things down and I'll introduce you to everyone and show you around."

Macy put her coat and purse in her beautiful cherry wood desk.

Joy led her into the office right next to her desk. "Aaron, this is Macy."

A man with glasses turned from his computer and stood up. His shirt was pressed with heavy starch. He was about five foot seven and a tad on the plump side.

"Well, hello Macy. It's a pleasure to meet you. Welcome!"

"Aaron is who you will be supporting this week. He's our VP of Special Projects."

"Great! It's very nice to meet you, Aaron."

Joy led Macy on the rest of the tour. "This is where all of our office machines are; copier, fax, printer. Darla and I have our own printers and so do all of the guys, but you will use this one."

Joy introduced Macy to Darla, the other admin in the office. She also met Matt the VP of Finance and Jack the President of Global Ops, the division Macy was now a part of, well temporarily.

The week flew by and Macy loved being there every day. Working for Aaron was refreshing. And they all liked Macy a lot. They extended her assignment another two weeks and then another two weeks. After that first month, they told Macy, "If you're up to it, we'd like to keep you on until you have the baby."

"Really? Absolutely, I would love that. Thank you so much." Macy replied.

Aaron was not only an amazing boss; he was just an all-around genuine person. It was just the kind of relationship Macy needed and one that would be completely uncommon to her. He trusted Macy not only with his professional tasks but also with some of his personal needs. On one occasion, he was going to be stuck in meetings the entire day, so he called Macy from the phone outside the conference room and asked that she search for some family-friendly jokes that he could use at his son's boy scouts banquet that evening. "Just log onto my computer and do a search. Print out whatever you can find and I'll pick them up on my way out tonight." He instructed Macy.

At times, Aaron's wife, Katie, would call and before Macy could transfer her to Aaron, she would ask how Macy was doing and how little Travis and Avery were, how she was feeling, "How's that little baby treating you?" she'd ask.

Macy's confidence grew every day as she built these wonderful new relationships with her co-workers. Aaron was a teacher first and foremost and he loved that Macy loved to learn, so he'd teach her new things on the computer—she picked up quickly and always found ways to apply Aaron's new lessons in her daily tasks. She watched Darla and became a PowerPoint expert in very little time. And the best part of all, Macy's paychecks were helping her and Luke get back on track with their bills.

April arrived before she knew it. Macy turned twenty-five. The girls took Macy out to lunch for her birthday. Joy asked Macy, "What are your plans after you have the baby?"

"To continue working...here if at all possible," Macy replied.

"Well, that's great to hear because we want you to come back after the baby is born."

"Really?!" Macy beamed.

"Yes. You've done a wonderful job and we'd like to keep you as long as we can."

"Well, of course. I'd be honored."

"Will you help us find someone to sit in for you while you're out with the baby?"

"Certainly!"

Macy shared the good news with Luke. He was excited for her and perhaps a little jealous. He was now working for Ameristar Casino just ten minutes from their apartment. Although it was close to home, he was back to the crazy, inconsistent schedule he had dodged for a while.

May came in an instant. It wasn't quite summer yet but the heat outside made it sure feel like summer. Luke celebrated his twenty-sixth birthday. The day after Luke's birthday, Macy called into Dr. Walters' office. "I've been spotting this morning and thought I better call to check in with the doctor." A few minutes later the nurse called back to confirm they wanted Macy to get to the office to have an ultrasound.

"You want me to go with you?" Luke asked.

"No, I should be fine. Just stay with Avery and Travis and I'll let you know what the doc says after I've met with him."

They were ready for Macy as soon as she arrived at the doctor's office. During the ultrasound, Macy watched the screen as the tech moved the wand around her belly. "Is that what I think it is?" Macy asked.

"Did you not want to know the sex?"

"No. But I've been pretty sure I knew what I was having."

"Well, then yes. That's what you think it is."

Macy's doctor came in to check her as well. "The ultrasound confirmed no scares for us, so it's just that you're progressing. And, you're about a two so that would explain your spotting."

"Really? I'm two centimeters?" Macy said excitedly.

"You sure are, my dear." He said in his endearing British accent.

Macy went home and shared the good news with Luke.

"Everything okay, sweetie?" Luke asked.

"Yes, no worries. I've started progressing." Doc checked me and I'm already at a two.

"Really? Wow! So, it could be soon then."

"Yes, most likely. I can't wait to not be pregnant anymore." Macy didn't tell Luke what she saw on the ultrasound. She wanted him to be surprised.

That night as she and Luke slept, Macy woke up to a contraction, and then another. She lay there timing them by the bedside alarm clock. She got up to get some water, gulped a big glass down, and went back to bed. The contractions died off a bit as she lay on her side.

The next morning, the contractions started back up. Being her third pregnancy, Macy felt like a pro. She knew what she needed to do and remained calm throughout the morning. She showered and breathed through the contractions as they came. It was late morning that she and Luke dropped off the kids with Judy and then headed to the hospital. This time they'd check into a different hospital—again, thanks to Medicaid.

It was very quiet on this Labor and Delivery floor, which was so different from the extremely busy floor where Avery and Travis were born just a few short years ago. The nurses here took their time getting Macy prepped and responding to calls. But Macy did well with her breathing and focusing through every stage of her labor. She felt good with her ability to work through the pain with each contraction. Luke held her hand and kissed her forehead between TV watching and napping.

It was around seven o'clock the next morning when shift changed occurred that Macy got the go-ahead to get her epidural. "YES!" This time she was ready.

"I've worked hard for this. I deserve it." She said to the anesthesiologist. But here, Luke was not allowed to get anywhere near Macy during the epidural process like he could at the other hospital. Macy sat on the edge of the bed, hunched over, trying not to move nervously while the anesthesiologist threaded tubing into her spinal cord.

Macy was finally comfortable and ready to get this baby out of her. As they prepped her for delivery she was asked if she'd like to be able to see the delivery. A little puzzled, she just looked at the nurse. The nurse came around the curtain with a mirror for Macy to watch the delivery. What an absolutely amazing miracle, she thought to herself the entire time.

"It's a boy!" Dr. Walters called out.

"Oh my gosh, baby, a boy!" Luke was so excited. "It's exactly like we dreamed." Luke kissed Macy. She thought back to that time in Chicago where she and Luke were discussing their hopes and dreams for their future together—*we'll have three babies, boy, girl, boy, two dogs and a cat and then we'll be a family.*

"I know, honey!" Macy smiled thinking about how she thought the very same thing during the ultrasound and a tear ran down her cheek.

Luke cut the umbilical cord right after a nurse got about two tablespoons of cord blood for the donor program. "How amazing was that?" She asked Luke.

"Pretty cool!" He smiled back.

They named him Noah.

And, now they were five. Luke and Macy were twenty-six and twenty-five and had three babies under the age of three.

Noah was such a sweet baby, calm-mannered and peaceful. Travis and Avery adored their new little brother. Macy and Luke had been working on getting Avery potty trained before the baby came.

I really do not want two kids in diapers, Macy would think as she bribed and pleaded with Avery. But she was a girl and just like her mother, determined to make up her own mind—she would use the potty only when she wanted to use it, certainly not when anyone asked her to.

Macy kept telling Avery during her pleading sessions that babies wear diapers but big girls wear panties. "You don't want to be a baby too when Mommy brings home your little baby brother or sister, do you? You can't be a big girl if you have baby diapers on."

The first morning that Noah was home, Macy peeked around the corner to see Avery sitting on her potty chair. "You did it! You used the big potty all by yourself! What a big girl you are. Mommy's so proud of you!" Macy hugged and kissed little Avery. Avery just beamed with pride. "You better go tell Daddy what you did." And that was it; Avery was officially the big sister—no more diapers.

Those six weeks flew by. Macy returned to work at MasterCard, which was a huge relief. Macy told herself that she was a better mother going to work eight hours a day despite the hurt and guilt she felt leaving her babies.

Luke returned to his life in the casinos and bars—not that he had ever really left. The nights of arguing and hating on one another became more and more constant. That fear was always looming in the back of Macy's mind—Luke's too—*I don't want to become another statistic. I don't want our marriage to end, I don't want a divorce. I love him so much. I love her so much. It doesn't have to be that way. Why can't he change, for us, for him? Why God? Why! Why can't I stop, for us, for me? Why God, Why?* They now had three babies, and yet, couldn't take care of themselves and certainly couldn't take care of their emotions. They were emotionally unavailable for one another and the kids.

Macy found the papers on compulsive gambling that the therapist had given to her when she went in for that first consultation visit. She had been reading a book on co-dependency and began to relate more and more with her place in their relationship. Luke's addiction gave her a dependency that she grew to believe is what she had to fix or deal with or be a part of to feel normal. And the compulsive gambling addiction and constant loss was Luke's normal. Chaos equated to normal in their minds. When all would seem to be going decent—or what some would call uneventful or even-keeled—is when they would somehow bring in the destruction to bring back the chaos...the normal.

One of the papers Macy read was titled, "Are you a compulsive gambler?" Thinking about her Luke, she answered the twenty questions:

1.) Did you ever lose time from work or school due to gambling? *Yes.*

2.) Has gambling ever made your home life unhappy? *Yes.*

3.) Did gambling affect your reputation? *Yes.*

4.) Have you ever felt remorse after gambling? *He says he does.*

5.) Did you ever gamble to get money with which to pay debts or otherwise solve financial difficulties? *YES.*

6.) Did gambling cause a decrease in your ambition or efficiency? *Yes.*

7.) After losing did you feel you must return as soon as possible and win back your losses? *Yes.*

8.) After a win did you have a strong urge to return and win more? *Yes.*

Macy stopped reading. There was no point in reading any more. She knew—and so did Luke.

"Luke, I need to ask you a very important favor." Macy asked one evening after Luke came into bed from being out late. They both lay facing the wall with their backs to one another.

"And, what would that be, Macy?" He expected to hear one of Macy's rub-his-nose-in-it sarcasms.

"I've been reading up on compulsive gambling and found a group that I'd like us, that I'd like you, to get help from."

"Okay..."

"You've admitted that you have a problem, Luke, but you're not doing anything to correct it. Gamblers Anonymous has weekly meetings at the hospital on Thursday nights. I'd like you to go. And I'll go to the Gam-anon meetings for family members. They meet the same night just in a different room."

Luke didn't say anything.

"Luke?"

"I heard you, Macy. I'll think about it."

The following evening, Luke agreed to go. Macy arranged for her sister to come sit with the kids while she and Luke took the short drive to the local hospital. The meeting took place on the main floor in a couple of the conference rooms. They signed in and went to their separate rooms.

Macy sat and listened to children and wives and husbands discuss the extreme financial burdens they were under due to their parent or spouse's gambling addiction. One husband had taken a second mortgage out on their home and had lost it all. A mother had racked up almost thirty thousand dollars in credit card debt from cash advances that she would use to gamble with.

Macy felt a bit guilty for her rage with Luke. *My gosh, we don't have that kind of debt. I guess it's somewhat of a good thing that we have bad credit. I guess it could be a lot worse.* Her mind tried to downplay their situation by comparing it to the other family's amount of loss. What she didn't factor in was the amount of income they had compared to what they had lost.

They would attend just a couple more meetings—mainly to appease Macy—never really gaining any insight or tools to rid their lives of this destruction. If anything, it confirmed in Luke's mind that he could manage it all just fine and in Macy's that they weren't as bad off as she thought.

Luke checked to see who just paged him. It was Macy; she had paged their phone number. He deleted it and clipped it back on his belt.

Where the hell is he? Macy was crying mad. She was in the kid's room getting their pajamas ready as little Travis and Avery were splashing and laughing in the tub and Baby Noah was in his pumpkin seat already snoozing.

Luke never called Macy. She was furious. *How does he just ignore me like that? He knows why I'm paging him. He should be here helping with the kids. How is it okay for him to go out drinking all night long? Screw this; I'm going to go find him.* Macy put the kids to bed and as soon as she knew they were out, she grabbed her keys and got in the car.

Crying, hands shaking, heart racing, she knew exactly where she needed to go. Macy drove a few blocks into town and pulled into the parking lot of a small strip mall. On the corner was John's Tavern. She parked the car and walked in. The smoke hit her in the face like a brick wall so thick and nasty. The place was a dive. Luke wasn't at the bar, just two older men that seemed to be permanent fixtures. She walked towards a room in the back that had pool tables. He didn't see her walk in. "There's the asshole."

Luke stood up instead of taking the shot, pool cue in hand. "What are you doing here?" he asked.

"What the hell are you doing here?" Macy replied.

Luke's friend chimed in, "You need to let Luke get out, Macy."

"Shut up, Bill. Maybe when you have three babies at home, I'll be interested in your opinion."

Luke replied, "You shut up, Macy. I'll go out if I want to go out. And I'll be home when I'm ready to go home."

"Oh, no you won't. You don't have a home anymore. Get the hell out of my life. I want you out!"

Macy turned around and left. She slammed her fist on the steering wheel, furious and enraged with Luke. She hurried home. Although she was a little worried that the kids would be awake and crying for Mommy, she mainly wanted to beat Luke home. She was done. Her attempts to control their home, their finances, and especially Luke and his gambling and drinking had all failed and this would be the last time she'd let a failed attempt define her.

Back home the kids were still asleep, "Thank God!" she whispered to herself, kissing them all on their foreheads. Macy's anger grew into rage and fury as she closed their bedroom door behind her. She pulled a duffle bag out of the closet and started to pack all of Luke's stuff. Luke would be coming home soon and she wanted him to feel all the pain that she had been feeling. *He can't be with us anymore. He's made his choice all too often. Now he can go out whenever he wants, drink and gamble all he wants and not hurt me anymore.* She was saying to herself through the tears and sobbing. *I don't deserve this bullshit!*

Luke came home to a locked bedroom door and his duffle bag of clothes left in the living room. He pounded on the bedroom door, looking for the little screwdriver to make his way in. They hollered back and forth through the door.

"Who the hell do you think you are, Macy?"

"Leave me alone, Luke. Get out of my life! And don't come back. LEAVE!"

"Fine, but not until I get the rest of my stuff."

He unlocked the door and started pulling stuff off of the dresser and from the closet. Macy tried to push him out of the room. "Get out of here, asshole! I hate you!"

"Fine, I'm out of here, bitch. I'm sick of never being able to satisfy you—it's always what *you* want."

Luke went out into the living room to call one of his friends. "Hey man, I need a place to stay. Yeah, tonight. It's bad."

Macy put her finger on the receiver. "Why the hell are you doing this to me?" Macy screamed. "How can you just forget about us, you bastard. I hate you so much." She picked up one of the kids toys and threw it at him. "You selfish piece of shit. You have screwed me over too many times. Leave!" She threw a pillow, desperately wanting him to stay. After all, that was the very reason she was so hurt in the first place. *Why do you always leave me?*

"What the hell's wrong with you?" Luke said. "You're freaking psycho. I'm leaving."

Luke turned for the door; Macy swung and hit Luke in the chest. "I hate you," she screamed at him.

Luke pushed Macy up against the wall. "Don't you touch me! Is this what you want me to do to you?"

Macy punched and flailed. "You're doing this to me. You make me hate you." Macy said, scared of Luke's force.

The punches and pushing continued. Macy grabbed the phone. "I'm calling the cops."

"Go right ahead. You punched me, remember."

Macy dialed 911 but then hung up as soon as the operator came on.

"Mommy, Daddy?!" Little Avery and Travis had made their way in the kitchen to see Mommy crying, hair disheveled and Daddy's t-shirt torn at the collar.

Luke immediately consoled them. "What are you two doing up? You need to get back to bed."

Just then, a loud knock, knock was on the front door. Macy opened it. There were two police officers standing in her doorway. *Oh my God,* she thought. "It was just a misunderstanding, sir."

"What's going on here?" Both police officers were now standing in their living room eyeing all of them and the duffle bag and clothes. "It's obvious there's been a struggle here."

"Sir, why don't you come outside and talk to me for a minute," the officer led Luke outside onto the front porch.

Macy gathered around Travis and Avery—whose big eyes were riddled with fear and confusion. "It's okay! I promise. Everything's going to be just fine," she said to them as she squatted down to face them on their level.

"Ma'am can we talk out here?"

"Let me get the kids back to bed, please."

She carried them both back to their room. "I love you both so much," Macy said kissing them on the forehead and tucking them in, trying not to cry. "I will be back in just a little bit."

Macy sat down with the police officer.

"Ma'am, did he hit you?"

"Yes, but—"

"What went on here tonight?"

"He has a gambling problem, officer, and we have three babies and tonight he went out to the bar and I just, well, I can't take living like this anymore. So I packed up his stuff and words were exchanged and the fight started."

"Sir, tell me what's going on here tonight." The other officer was out on the porch with Luke.

"Well, I had gone out with a buddy for a little bit tonight, and when I got home I found all of my clothes packed up."

"Have you been drinking?"

"Yes, I've had a couple beers earlier."

"Did you hit her?"

"We both were punching and pushing."

"Do you have somewhere to stay tonight?"

"Yes. Yes, I do." Luke said with his head down.

The officer and Luke came back into the apartment.

"Okay, well I understand there has been some pushing and arguing," the officer that was with Luke said as he confirmed with the officer that talked with Macy. "And maybe a little more that we're not aware of. At this time, Luke's going to gather his things and stay at a friend's until you can all cool down and get this figured out. Ma'am you wait with me here until he gets his things."

Both officers stayed until Luke left.

"Now you get in there and take care of those babies," the officer said as he walked out the door.

"Yes, sir. Absolutely." Macy replied.

She locked the door behind him, slid down the door, and sobbed as she realized that she was now really alone and someone of authority now knew about their fighting and their secret. The knot in her throat got bigger and made it hard to breathe. She walked to the bathroom to wash her face. She stared in the mirror ashamed and embarrassed at what just happened. She continued to cry as she splashed water on her face.

Luke drove to his buddy's house—crying with rage and anger the whole way. *I can't believe this just happened. Why did I let that happen? How am I going to live like this? I don't want to be alone.*

Macy went into the kid's room to check on them. *Poor babies,* she thought. They were sleeping but not the peaceful sleep they should be. Macy laid down on the floor between Avery and Travis's beds and fell asleep.

Macy had a seat in the lobby of Mr. Broscoe's office, which consisted of two chairs and a table with Money and Time magazines strewn about.

"Macy Hawthorn is here to see you," Macy heard the receptionist say over the phone as she thumbed through one of the magazines. Shortly after, John came down to meet Macy.

"Hi Macy. It's good to see you again."

"You too."

"Come on upstairs to my office and you can catch me up."

Macy followed John up the narrow staircase to the upper level. The walls of his office were lined with shelves filled with books. There were stacks of files all over the floor surrounding his desk. He was a nice man and obviously very busy with cases.

"So how are those little babies?" he asked as he looked for his pen.

"They're doing well—keeping me very busy. We have three now, by the way."

"Wow, well congratulations. I guess you *are* busy. So, what's going on? What brings you back to the office?"

"Well, it's time—time to move forward with the divorce filing. Luke is still gambling, drinking, and out all of the time. I...we just can't live like this anymore. I don't deserve it, and more importantly, our kids don't deserve it."

"Let me pull your file. I saved some notes from last time we met. We can review them together and make the necessary updates." John said.

After he left his office for a minute, he returned with a manila folder. "Okay, let's see." John sat back down and opened the file.

"I guess we have another baby to add to the file! What is his full name, birthday and social security number?"

Macy gave it to him.

"Where is Luke working now? I'm assuming he's not at the Elgin Casino anymore."

"No, since we moved back to St. Charles, he's working at Ameristar Casino."

"Okay, do you know how much he's making there?"

"Yeah, I believe it's somewhere close to the thirty thousand range...that's with tips."

"And you're working, yes?"

"Yes, I'm a full-time employee at MasterCard."

"Okay, you're salary is?"

"Nineteen thousand."

"Alright. I think I have everything I need. I will edit the documents and look up state recommendations for child support to be included. I'll let you know when I have it completed. Probably a week at the most. Okay?"

"Okay."

Macy headed to work after her meeting with John. She had told the office that she'd be in late because of a doctor appointment. She didn't want to tell them exactly what was going on just yet because she just wasn't sure how they would react or if their perception of her would change. She prayed this new status—single mom—wouldn't change how they felt about her. Macy cared a lot for Aaron and the others in the office. She had never met such generous and genuine adults who truly cared for her and her well-being. She really hated lying to them. *How am I going to be able to keep this from them?*

She thought about her meeting with John all day and she thought about what everyone there at the office was going to think of her. The last thing that Macy wanted or needed was for these new relationships that she cherished to be tarnished by her failed marriage.

Toward the end of the day, Macy stepped into Aaron's office.

"Excuse me Aaron, do you have a second? I need to make you aware of something."

"Oh? What is it, Macy?"

Macy sat down. "Well, I may be in need of a few days off here and there during the next month or so. I'm filing for divorce."

Aaron sat back in his chair, stunned by Macy's comment and carefully thinking about how to reply. "Oh. Okay. I'm so sorry to hear that, Macy. But take whatever time you need. Is there anything I can do to help?"

Macy smiled, wanting to cry again being reminded of his kind and generous nature. "No, this is something that's gone on for a while now and I've tried everything I can think of but it's just not getting any better. I really appreciate your offer."

The next day was a fairly normal day at work. Aaron called Macy into his office.

"Sit down for a second, Macy. Katie and I were talking about your situation last night and we just wanted to let you know that we support your decision. I know it took a lot to share this with me and I appreciate your honesty and vulnerability."

Macy's eyes grew wide as she was not expecting that. She did all she could to hold back the tears.

"I'm sure this is not something you decided to do overnight and I can tell it is very difficult for you. You do what you need to do to take care of those little babies and we'll be here if you need us."

"Wow, thank you so much, Aaron! I can't tell you what that means to me. I greatly appreciate your concern and support. Please give my gratitude to Katie!"

Macy drove home that evening, crying thinking about just how hard this is and is going to be—a life without Luke in it. *What will it be like? Are we going to hate each other? How is he going to take it? Is he going to be okay? What about our kids? How are they going to get through all of this? God, I just love him so much. I don't want to lose him. Why does he have to be like this? Why doesn't he care enough to stop throwing our money away? Our lives away? His life away?*

"Hey, baby!" Luke was home before Macy. A couple nights after their last big fight, Luke had come back to the apartment for a few things and ended up staying the night and then just never went back to his friends. They were out of control—in love with one another but unable to figure out how to live together all at the same time.

Luke grabbed Macy's shoulder to pull her close and kissed her. Macy wanted so badly to kiss him back but she turned away. He had no idea that she had met with John and shared with Aaron her intentions. He was going to be the last to know. She hated that but knew it couldn't be any other way.

"Let's go do something. Want to go see a movie and get something to eat?"

"I don't even know what's playing. And what about the kids? Who's going to stay with them?"

"I'll see if my mom will come over."

Macy just shrugged her shoulders.

Judy came over to sit with the kids.

"Thanks so much, Ma. We'll be back around midnight, okay?"

"Please no chocolate for any of them. They're eating dinner now and can have a Gogurt or fruit snacks before bed. Don't worry about giving them baths. I'll do that tomorrow," Macy instructed on their way out.

"Okay, kids. Have fun!"

"Thanks!"

Luke and Macy enjoyed their evening out. It had been a long time since they laughed and had a good time. But Macy's meeting with John wasn't far from her mind. And she wondered where Luke got the money to pay for everything tonight. *He must've actually won for once.*

When they got back home, Judy was asleep on the couch as were the kids. Macy dropped her stuff to go check on them.

"Ma, wake up. We're home."

"Oh right, okay. The babies were angels. You are truly blessed, my son!"

He locked up behind her and shut off the lights.

Macy went to the bathroom to brush her teeth. Luke was now behind her, kissing her. Divorce or no divorce; nothing could change the love that Macy felt for Luke and Luke for Macy. She knew that he loved her and not just a physical love, but something that touched them both so deep, they were connected no matter how they tried not to be. Problem being they just did not know how to be a husband and wife or father and mother together.

They made love that night. "I love you, baby." Luke whispered as he drifted off to sleep. "I love you too, Luke." Macy began to cry silently. *Why God? Why?!*

"Hi, Macy?"

"Yes."

"Hi. This is John Broscoe."

"Oh, hi John. How are you?"

"Doing well. How are you?"

"Hanging in there, I guess."

"Well, listen. I believe I have everything in order for you to review. Would you be able to come in sometime tomorrow for me to show you what we have?"

"I'd have to check with work, but it should be fine. I'll call you back to confirm."

The next day, Macy went to Mr. Broscoe's office on her lunch hour. She was so anxious, as all of this was becoming more and more of a reality. Thoughts of their recent date night flew through Macy's mind, at times making her heart skip. She had no doubt divorce was the only thing left to do, but that didn't mean it was what she wanted. She wanted the love of her life, the father of her children, to just stop and admit there was a problem and get out. But he wouldn't. *This was the only way out.*

"Okay, here is the actual divorce decree which states you are the plaintiff and Luke is the defendant. It also lists the three children with their ages and birthdates. Here is the visitation section, which I have indicated joint custody as you asked. It states that you will both split holidays and birthdays as well as Luke having the kids every other weekend."

Macy chuckled, "Not sure how that's going to happen with his work schedule, he always works weekends. But okay, that all makes sense. I agree."

"Now this is the section that addresses child support. When we take into consideration your salary, Luke's salary, and the kids' ages and daycare, health care, food and clothing costs, the state of Missouri indicates Luke is responsible for this amount in child support per month."

"Twelve hundred dollars?" Macy gasped. "Oh my God! How is he supposed to come up with that and still live?"

"I don't make up the amounts; this comes directly from our Missouri Child Support criteria and calculator tables. Now the judge may very well decide a different amount, but this is what we're suggesting per the guidelines provided."

He's going to...Oh my God, what's he going to do? Macy thought to herself, fearing the worst.

"Well, I guess it's set. I know that dollar amount is not going to go over well at all and I don't expect to get that every month; but everything else I'm in agreement with."

"Okay. Then I will get these officially filed with the court and get a court date set. If Luke doesn't contest anything in the decree, you both sign and it's done."

"Wow, that's it, huh?"

"Yes, granted he doesn't contest and based on the conversations we've had, I really don't see him doing that. Once the papers are filed, Luke will be served."

"Oh wait. Is there a way that doesn't have to happen? Could I give the papers to him myself?"

"Um, well, I don't suggest that; but I suppose I will allow it."

"Okay, thank you. This is going to be extremely difficult for him to accept. I have to believe me delivering the news will help ease the blow some." *Yeah right, what am I thinking?* She thought to herself.

"I will give you a call when I have everything. You can come by the office to pick up the papers."

"Sounds good. Thank you, John."

"You're very welcome, Macy. I wish the best for you."

Macy's favorite time of the year was here. It was the middle of October now and the leaves were changing; there was a chill in the air but the sun still produced warmth that meant she could get by with just a sweater. Travis just had his fourth birthday and the holidays were right around the corner. Macy had thought differently about special occasions now that a divorce was quickly approaching. *I'm going to have to split holidays and not have my kids—we won't all be together,* she thought to herself. Everything began to appear different as she looked through new eyes—the scared eyes of a single mother.

Macy had a voicemail message when she arrived to work. It was John. "Hi Macy. It's John Broscoe. I have the documents ready for you. You can pick them up whenever you're free. I'll have them waiting with my secretary. Take care, and I'll talk to you soon."

Oh boy. Here we go, Macy thought to herself. *This is going to be ugly, I just know it!*

She stopped by Mr. Broscoe's office on the way home. She left the envelope in the car. After putting the kids to bed, she got the package from her car, sat down on the couch, and thought about her plans and how she would deliver the news to Luke.

The next day she asked Kyle to pick up the kids so she could talk to Luke. He was off that night and she didn't want to put it off any longer. Kyle agreed and got the kids from pre-school and took them to her house for the evening.

"Hey there!" Luke got up from watching TV to greet Macy.

"Hi.

"Where are the kids?"

"Kyle wanted to have them over for a little while so she picked them up from pre-school."

"Wow. Okay." Luke scrunched his eyebrows, thinking that was kind of weird.

Macy put her stuff down, thumbed through the mail and grabbed a drink. After going to the bathroom, she talked to herself in the mirror for one last reminder, *this is for the best, Macy—it's what you have to do.*

She took a deep breath and sat down in the living room with Luke. She turned off the TV and as Luke said, "Hey! What the—"

"We need to talk" Macy said with immense fear while trying to sound strong and capable.

"What? What do you mean?"

Macy handed the big manila envelope to Luke.

"What is this, Macy?" Luke pulled out the papers. "Divorce Decree? Oh my God. Seriously?! You're divorcing me?" He looked up at her. His heart started to race and he felt like he had just been slapped in the face and kicked in the gut.

Macy just sat there with tears in her eyes staring at the floor.

"This is what this is, right?" his volume increased.

Luke was getting angrier and scared with each page he turned. His voice was shaking, "I can't believe you want a divorce, Macy. You really want me out?"

Macy looked at him and nodded.

He looked down at the papers again, still flipping. "Oh great, every other weekend. I can't go that long without seeing my kids. What? What the hell is this? Twelve hundred dollars in child support?" His voice shrilled. "Do you not want me to not survive? Divorce me, take my kids from me, and rob me of every dime I make? This is absolutely ridiculous!"

"Luke, this isn't set in stone. It's just the generic divorce arrangement and the child support amount comes directly from the State of Missouri suggested amounts based on the kids' ages and financial status. You can take it to any attorney yourself if you disagree or choose to contest it."

"You know there's no way I could possibly pay you that and be able to survive on my own."

"Again, I didn't come up with the amount, Luke." *Don't the kids and I deserve some pay back from all that you and your gambling have taken from us?* Macy thought to herself.

"So that's it? You want me to move out?"

"Well, yes. I understand that it's not going to happen tonight, but its best for you to find a place of your own. You'll need a place where the kids can stay with you."

"I really can't believe this, Macy. I've never felt like this; you have completely stabbed me in the heart. You're literally killing me!" Luke did all he could not to lose it, to stay tough and not let Macy see the breakdown that was occurring inside of him at that very moment.

"This isn't easy for me Luke. Nothing's changing. You know how much I've been hurt from your gambling and drinking. I can't live this way anymore. I don't deserve to be lied to and walked all over."

"You're right, Macy. You deserve some rich asshole that can buy you all you want and meet all of your financial dreams and expectations."

"Luke, you know that's a lie."

"I hate you for this, Macy. I hope you're happy to finally getting what *you* want. Don't worry, I'll be out tomorrow."

"I'm sorry, Luke. I truly am."

"Yeah, whatever. Go to hell, Macy!"

Macy sat and cried knowing full well that this was how it was going to go down...but more so she was overwhelmed with sadness that she was officially losing Luke—the love of her life, the father of her children. He was going to live a life without her in it...someone was going to take her place someday. That thought made her gag. She ran into the bathroom and threw up.

The next day when Macy and the kids got home, Luke was gone. She looked in the bedroom, his half of the closet was cleaned out and his pillow too. No note...nothing. Luke no longer lived there, and they all knew it.

Macy did all she could to focus on the normal evening routines of getting dinner made and kids fed. Watch a little TV before bath time, and once the kids were all in their PJs, Macy let them all pick out a book. They all squeezed in Travis' little car bed and read stories. She squeezed them all tight, gave them kisses, and tucked them in for bed. Macy switched off the light, "Sweet dreams—sleep tight!"

"Love you, Mommy," Travis called out. "I love you too, Mommy," Avery followed.

"I love you all so much!" Macy replied.

Macy sat down on her bed not sure what to do next. Luke was really gone and not coming home. It was just she and the kids. She got into her pajamas and laid down on the couch to watch TV for a little while.

The phone rang. It was Luke.

"Hello?"

"I just wanted you to know that I'm okay and I have a place to stay for a little while. I'll pick up the kids on Saturday after work. You can reach me on my pager if you need to."

"Um, okay."

"Okay, I'll talk to you later. Bye." He hung up.

Macy cried herself to sleep on the couch.

When Luke dropped off the kids the following Monday night, he dropped an envelope on the kitchen table. It was the signed divorce papers along with a note:

> Although I believe this to be against my 'better' judgment, I'm signing this document. Mostly so you stop saying I always have to have things my way.
> I hope this eases your stress and tension a little
> Talk to you whenever!

"Wonderwall"
DISSOLVED

November 8th. Macy was at the courthouse by nine thirty in the morning, right after she dropped the kids off at pre-school. Mr. Broscoe was already there.

"Good morning, Macy. How are you?"

"Hi, John. I'm doing okay, I guess." Macy sighed.

"Well, granted we have no surprises, this should go fairly quickly. The judge will ask if either of you contest the divorce decree and if not, you will both sign the filing and he will submit his judgment for the dissolution of marriage."

John led the way into the courtroom. Luke was already there and he had a lawyer. "I didn't know he had a lawyer," Macy whispered to John. "I'm sure he's just looking out for himself," John replied.

Within fifteen minutes the session was over. Luke did not contest anything in the decree and they both signed the filings. *That was it. A judge and a couple of signatures and we've become a statistic,* Macy thought to herself. *One in every two marriages ends in divorce,* kept streaming through Macy's head like a CD stuck on repeat.

They left the courtroom.

Macy turned to John, "So, that's it? We're done?"

"Yes, that's it, Macy. You are now legally divorced."

"Well that was fast. Okay, well, thank you so much for all of your help." Macy stammered.

"Don't mention it. Take care of yourself!" Mr. Broscoe said with compassion as he placed his hand on Macy's shoulder.

When Macy got to her car, Luke was there waiting for her.

"Hey!"

"Hey."

"I was wondering if you would want to get a bite to eat with me—I'm starving!"

Macy was confused. *Is he really asking me to go to lunch with him?*

"Just lunch, Macy." Luke could see by the look on Macy's face that she was a bit put off.

"Well... Okay...I'm pretty hungry too. I didn't have any breakfast."

"Yeah me either. So what sounds good?"

"I don't know...whatever you want," Macy replied.

"How about Pizza Hut?"

"Okay, I'll meet you over there."

It felt odd to Macy to be having lunch with her ex as of just forty-five minutes ago; but then again, *perhaps we can create a civil relationship through all of this,* she thought.

They shared their favorite—jalapeno and pepperoni pizza—and a little conversation. Nothing too deep, just random chatter. They split the bill and Luke walked Macy to her car. He gave her a hug, "I do love you and want you to be happy, Macy. I'm just sorry this has happened."

"Yeah, me too, Luke. Me too!"

As the finality of the divorce began to settle in, the kids began to pick up on what was going on. Macy had to admit to them that Daddy did, in fact, not live with them anymore. "But Mommy, why doesn't Daddy want to live here with us?" Travis asked.

"Oh, he loves us very much, but Mommy and Daddy just—"

"Is it because you are always fighting?" he interrupted.

"Well, yes, Travis honey, that's a big part of it. It's not fair to you or your brother and sister to see us fighting all the time. But Daddy's getting a place of his own where you can stay with him when you go to visit. And, you'll get to see Grandma Judy and Grandma Leanne just as much as before. Okay?"

"Okay. But I miss him." Travis said with a sad face...one that Macy had never seen before.

Avery echoed, "Me too, Mommy."

"Me too!" Macy said. "I'm so sorry. I didn't want it to be this way."

The divorce continued to take a great toll on the kids and Macy. One morning after Macy got settled in at work, Ms. Tracy from preschool called.

"Ms. Hawthorn, I have Travis here with me. He's not well. He's thrown up a couple of times. He's not running a fever, but we still need to send him home."

"Oh my goodness. Okay, I'll be there in a few minutes."

Macy explained the situation to Aaron and the others in the office and took the rest of the day off. She got to preschool and took all of the kids home. She spent some time with Travis telling him it's okay to be upset and that she was there for him.

Macy told Luke about Travis' sadness and his throwing up at school. "Just so you know, I want you to be aware that he's hurting and we need to do all we can to comfort him."

"Oh no. Poor guy. Of course, Macy!" Luke agreed.

Travis seemed to be doing better, but then it was Avery's turn to go through her sadness. When Macy dropped them off at preschool, Avery would cling to her and not let go. This was not normal for her. She was usually the first to find a toy and join in on the fun with the other kids.

Macy would walk to the play kitchen sets and attempt to help Avery settle in.

"Mommy has to go to work now, sweetheart. Will you make me something good to eat so I can have it when I pick you up?"

"Okay, Mommy. I'll make you some cupcakes."

"Mmmm, that sounds wonderful! I can't wait."

"Well you help, Mommy?" Avery grabbed Macy's sleeve.

"I have to go to work, honey. But I'll be back to get you in just a little bit." Macy headed for the door but before walking out, she turned to blow kisses to her sad-faced little Avery. "Will you wave bye to me?" Macy tried so hard to hide her broken heart. Avery nodded and turned to go to the window. "I love you, sweetie!" Macy called out to her.

As she drove past the front window, Avery was standing up on the sill of the giant front window with her arms spread wide, she was trying so hard not to cry, but she did. "Bye, bye Mommy," she mouthed and waved.

Macy blew kisses and waved back, "I love you, baby!" and drove off but continued to watch Avery in the rear view mirror. She saw Avery crying harder as one of the teachers tried persuading her to come down and play with the others. Macy cried the rest of the way to work.

Seeing her little girl so sad reminded Macy of her very own sad days at Happy Time preschool. Clinging to the chain link fence in the play area, bawling her eyes out screaming for her mommy, "Don't leave, Mommy!" It was all too familiar. But now it was her baby girl doing the bawling. As hard as it was to watch her little Avery cry for her, it was harder to acknowledge that it was all due to the fact that her mommy and daddy didn't live together anymore. Besides, from her little point of view, *if Daddy moved out, what if Mommy does too?*

Avery turned three that December. Macy and her family celebrated at Peter and Leanne's house with cake and presents. Avery was still such a little bitty thing. Thirty-six months and 3T clothes were still too big for her. She was infatuated with soft things, especially Macy's silk nightgowns and underwear. She was always getting into Mommy's dresser drawers. Avery would come waddling into the living room with Macy's satin panties around her neck and nightgowns tied around her shoulders like a cape.

"Here, this should keep you out of my drawers." Macy cut up one of her nightgowns in to three small 'blankies'—one for bed, one for the diaper bag, and one for the car. Avery carried her satin blankie and her little baby doll, Molly, which was already a permanent fixture with Avery everywhere she went. Macy kneeled in front of Avery and rubbed one of the blankies on her face, "so soft, so soft." Avery smiled and did the same thing. Macy hugged Avery, giving her a huge squeeze and big kiss on the neck. "Mommy loves you so very much, little Avery!" Avery grabbed her mommy's face and with their foreheads touching said, "I love you too, Mommy."

By Christmas, Division of Child Services filed "Notice of Income Withholding" with the casino Luke worked for since Macy hadn't received any child support payments. It didn't take long for Luke to call Macy, furious. "They're garnishing my wages, Macy. Did you know that? Well, I'm sure you probably put them up to it. Just how in the hell am I supposed to live?"

"Luke, I'm not in control of that. It's up to the state to make that happen. It's the law, remember?" Macy yelled back over the phone.

"Macy, I have nothing left to pay MY bills. What am I supposed to do?"

"Maybe you'll just have to not spend your money the way you have been. Quit going out and wasting it on alcohol or the boats or bookies."

"Whatever, Macy. You're always right. It's always got to be *your* way. Whatever makes *you* happy."

"You really think this is what makes me happy, Luke? You think I wake up and wonder how the hell I can ruin your day, week, or month? You're out of your flipping mind. I have a million other things I need to worry about. How the hell am I supposed to take care of these three babies on my own?"

"You make more than I do, Macy!"

"And how do you figure that, Luke? Just because you blow your paychecks at the boat and in the bar doesn't mean I make more than you. I don't know why you are doing this to me...to us...to our kids! Just live up to your responsibilities for once."

"God, you're such a bitch, Macy!"

"Yep, what I do best!"

For the kid's sake, Luke and Macy decided to spend Christmas together—well, under the same roof anyway. Macy went to Luke's Uncle Bob's to celebrate with their family. Luke also came over on Christmas morning while the kids opened their gifts. It was awkward to say the least.

Luke always turned on his "everything's awesome and I'm overly happy" face. He was so enraged with Macy for divorcing him, making him move out and having his wages garnished and not being able to see the kids; but he never let his kids see any of that.

Macy really hated that about him. Her kids saw her as the angry, sad disciplinarian while Dad was always the life of the party and doing nothing but fun things. She wanted her kids to understand why Mommy was so angry and emotionally unavailable, because Daddy left her—and them—for gambling and partying and wanting a life that didn't involve responsibility. But they never saw it. Macy worked hard to keep up the cold walls to hide her true feelings of hurt and sadness from Luke. But none of that mattered...none of the laughter and goofiness mattered, really. Their hearts were breaking...all of their hearts.

CHAPTER 9

"The Freshman"
1997

The New Year brought some much-needed relief to Macy. She could for the first time in a very long time count on a certain amount of money to be deposited into her bank account and remain there until she spent it. She could pay the bills and she loved being caught up with the rent. Her current landlords were the most patient landlords they had ever had. Even though there was never enough money at the end of the month, it was her money and no one else was touching it. Fear and worry didn't consume her 24 x 7 as they had just a short time ago.

Macy had finally gained back some of the control she had longed for. No more pawning the TV or VCR or stereo for money to buy groceries or pay a bill.

"We'll just pawn it for some money and then buy it back as soon as I get paid," Luke would say. Sometimes this would happen, sometimes not. The kids learned how to not whine or get upset when they couldn't watch their movies. Despite the arguing they did with one another, this is when the kid's creativity came out the most; they had no other choice, really.

The engagement ring that Macy's dad co-signed on was pawned and never bought back. That pear-shaped solitaire would be gone forever, but not the debt. Once again, Luke and Macy owed on something they no longer had in their possession. *No more!* Macy said to herself. *I know what I make, and I know what I can and can't afford.*

Luke, however, was moving from place to place—living with different friends out of a couple duffle bags. He hated always being on the move, but then again, it was a part of him that was all too familiar and normal.

More relief came Macy's way when she got her tax refund. She actually got the check and deposited it into *her* savings account and nothing happened to it. It didn't get cashed and lost without her knowing it. Sitting in the drive through window at the bank, Macy realized she was breathing and was no longer feeling anxious. She looked in the mirror and saw light in her eyes, something she hadn't seen in a long time. Macy missed Luke so much, but knowing that she could take care of things on her own was somehow comforting. Gambling wasn't impacting her finances and stability anymore. She was in control.

That's when a random idea entered Macy's mind for the first time in a long time. *"I need a vacation!* Macy thought.

"Is there anything else I can do for you today?" the teller asked over the intercom.

"No, thank you," Macy replied and quickly resumed her thoughts of vacation as she pulled out of the drive through. *I could go to Florida maybe. Get a hotel room and lay on the beach. Oh that would be amazing! It will be my birthday gift to myself.* Macy couldn't remember the last time she had done something just for herself. It would prove to be the most freeing opportunity of her life.

The following April, Macy was at the airport awaiting her early morning flight out to Ft. Lauderdale. The wait to board the plane was exhilarating yet peaceful. And the anticipation of the beach and the ocean and, more importantly, to be alone for five days was so forthcoming she could practically taste the Florida air. Macy flipped through a magazine someone had left behind, thinking of the comments thrown back and forth between she and Luke prior to her leave.

"You can stay here if it's easier for you. I just need you to take care of the kids. I don't want to leave them with Mom or Dad or your mom all week."

"Well that's fine, but I'm going to have to get some help from them throughout the week. I've got a life too you know? Who you going with anyway?"

"Who am I going with?" Macy asked. "Where?"

"Give me a break, Macy. I know you're not going to Florida all by yourself."

"I most certainly am." Macy laughed, "Even if there were someone else, I'd still not take them on this trip."

"Oh, so you're just meeting him down there?"

"What? Luke, not that it's any of your business, but I really am going alone. No one is meeting me there either."

"Yeah, whatever, Macy!"

Macy put the magazine down in her lap and laughed quietly to herself.

"Flight 812 to Fort Lauderdale is now boarding." The announcement she had been waiting for finally came.

The very first thing Macy noticed as she got off of the plane was the warm, humid air. *Yes, I'm here!* Macy waited for her bags to make their way down the carousel then headed down to the car rental counter.

"Your car is ready Ms. Hawthorn. Just take the shuttle to aisle 4B, there you'll find the gold Buick LaSabre."

"Thank you so much!" Macy said.

The gold sedan was right there just as the rep had promised. The shuttle driver helped Macy with her bags. Macy threw her carry on in the back seat and then got out her CD player and CDs. It took her a few minutes to get oriented with the map the rental car agent gave her. She decided to take Hwy 95 north until she could get off at Hwy 1 to drive along the coast. Macy was amazed at all of the palm trees and how she could taste the ocean's saltwater in the air.

She made the forty-five minute drive to her hotel with the windows down and her music playing and the biggest smile on her face. One that she had worried might never reappear again. She watched the ocean outside the passenger window; people were jogging, flying kites, walking their dogs, roller-blading and all taking advantage of this glorious place. Macy was convinced this was where heaven and earth met.

Macy made a stop at the supermarket near the hotel. She got herself some snacks and a bottle of wine. *Oh Yes! You're all mine!* She said to herself smiling at the pretty bottle of Riesling. Macy checked in and signed the room slip, *Macy Hawthorn*. Getting the key to her hotel room made Macy beam. The room was all hers and for very little cost too. Macy's sister Kyle still worked for the hotel so she was able to get the room for the thirty-five dollar employee rate.

"Oh my gosh. This is so wonderful!" Macy said as she dropped her stuff on the bed. She went to open every drawer and closet door. The front room had a small living area with a couch and chair; through the hallway was a nice sized bathroom. "Yeah, that tub will do just fine!" she said. In the back was the bedroom with queen sized bed, TV and desk area. She put all of her clothes away and put her CDs and CD player on the nightstand.

"Hi, Luke. I made it in okay. How are the kids?"

"Oh hi. You're there? You're flight went okay?" Luke said, making small talk.

"Yeah, it was good."

"Kids are doing well. They're eating dinner right now. Yes, it's Mommy. They want to talk to you."

"Okay. Oh, hi Avery! How's my baby girl?"

"Hi Mommy! I'm good. You in Flowida? Travis hit me at school today."

"Oh, honey, I need you two to get a long and be nice to each other while I'm gone okay? I love you, baby."

"I love you too, Mommy."

"Let me talk to your brother now."

"Travis, Mommy wants you."

"Hi Mom!"

"Hey little man, you doing alright?"

"Yes, Mom. How is Florida? Is it hot there?"

"Yes, it's pretty warm. Listen, Travis, I need you to watch out for your little sister and brother? Be a good example for me, okay?"

"Okay, Mommy, I will."

"I love you soooo much!"

"I love you too!" Travis handed the phone back to Luke.

"Can you put the phone up to Noah? I want to say something to him."

"Sure. Noah, Mommy wants to talk to you."

"Hi Noah! It's Mommy." She heard him smile through the phone. "I love you so much."

"I yuv you Mama. Bye bye."

"Thank you, Luke, for being there with them! I really do appreciate it."

"You don't have to thank me!"

"I know, but, well I'm in room 306 if you need me. The number to the hotel is on the paper I left for you. Take care and I'll talk to you later."

"Okay, Macy."

"Good bye, Luke."

Macy put on some shorts and a t-shirt, grabbed her sweater and drove to the TGIF she passed on the way in. She ordered a burger and a beer. If anyone looked at her because she was alone, she didn't even notice. That was the best tasting beer and burger Macy had in a long time. She thought to herself, *I can't remember the last time I've heard this sort of silence – exquisite peace.* There were many people there all having conversations, but she didn't hear a thing. Macy felt hope again...a peace, she realized, still existed within her.

After paying her bill, Macy decided to go for another drive further up the coast. She found an open area to park the car and got out and just walked for a while. A park bench spoke to her as she approached it, *Sit here and enjoy the scenery.* So she sat and just watched the people passing by as they smiled and nodded at her. The hour quickly passed by as the sun began to set. It was time to head back to the hotel.

Macy spent the rest of the evening soaking in a hot bubble bath while enjoying her Riesling and music. It felt so good to be able to relax in the tub without the kids banging on the door wanting to come in. But in that same moment, she was overcome by sadness and a tear fell down Macy's cheek. *My marriage failed. The one man I love so much abandoned me. And, I abandoned him. Oh dear God, I don't want to raise my babies alone. This is not what I dreamed of. This is not how it's supposed to be. We're supposed to be married and raising our babies together and we're supposed to be in love with each other. I can't believe we've let this happen. We're just another statistic now!* Macy sobbed. She was overcome with how sad and alone she was. *All alone.* "But, I still love him!" Macy cried herself to sleep that night...which was nothing new.

While Macy was away in Florida, Luke was doing everything he could to not have to stay in that empty apartment.

"Mom, I need to meet with Alex later to practice some techniques they're asking us to do at the casino now. Can you watch the kids for a bit?" Luke asked his mom.

"Well, when do you think you'll be home?" she asked.

"I don't know, midnight?"

"I guess so, Luke. But you can't be later than that. I have work in the morning."

"Yeah, Mom. I know. Thanks a lot!"

He hung up and called Alex.

"Dude, we're hitting it tonight." Luke said to Alex.

"Oh yeah? See you at the usual spot?"

"You know it. Just gotta wait for my mom to get here to sit with the kids and then I'll be there."

Luke met Alex at a bar on the riverfront not far from their apartments. Buckets of beer, shots and hustling some pool and darts and then singing karaoke. Luke was an amazing singer; but tonight he wasn't singing for the love of his talent, but instead to pick up girls. He was known to work the crowd by taking the microphone around the room and singing to a particular girl or two.

He was pulled over on his way home. *Oh shit!* Luke said to himself. *Just stay calm.* He tried to maintain his composure even though his heart was in his throat. He found a piece of spearmint gum in his change compartment and tossed it into his mouth.

"You know why I'm pulling you over?" the officer asked.

"Probably my damn tail light. It's the wiring. It'll work and then it doesn't." Luke explained, hoping it was working.

"Where are you heading tonight?"

"Home. Its right down that street, Officer," Luke pointed up the road.

"Alright, just sit tight a minute."

"Oh great, he's gonna give me a ticket."

The officer came back with a ticket, "Now get that fixed," he said as he handed Luke the ticket.

"Alright, I will." Luke promptly stuck it in his glove box and forgot about it as he pulled into the driveway. He told his mom to go home and he crashed on the couch.

The next morning, determined to enjoy her vacation, Macy packed her bag for the beach. A book, some magazines, her towel and sun tan lotion, "I'm going to get some sun while I'm in

Florida!" She hopped in the car and made it to a wonderfully quiet spot on the beach. Macy lie there reading and watching the occasional jogger go by. There was a chill in the air, so getting her toes wet was as much ocean water she could stand. Macy even dozed off for a bit. Waking up, it took her a few minutes to remember where she was. She brushed the sand from her cheek and reminded herself, *you're on vacation, dork.*

That evening she brought dinner back to her hotel room and watched a movie. She thought about what she would do with her remaining days. After crashing on the bed, she'd have to figure it out in the morning.

Macy enjoyed the rest of her stay by being the typical tourist—driving around town stopping off at the beach and looking for little shops, etc. But she wanted to plan just one more final extravaganza before her departure. She stopped at the ATM and pulled out some cash and went to the closest mall to enjoy a shopping spree—all for her. She bought two new suits, a simple black dress, shoes, and a couple swimsuits. It was the perfect ending to a vacation just for her—a time to just be herself and breathe.

It was so good to see the kids when she returned. Macy had missed them so much. And in an odd way, it was good to see Luke too. It always made her heart beat fast to see him after being apart for a while. It did his too. The fact that he still did this to her only reminded her of how much she still loved him and probably always would. But no one could know that secret. No one.

"Hey sweetie!" Macy kneeled down, dropping her bags as she walked in the door.

"Mommy!" Macy and Avery hugged.

"Oh, I missed you so much," Macy spoke into Avery's neck, smelling her hair. "Were you good while I was away?"

"Uh huh!"

Luke watched Macy with their babies and then thought to himself, *God, I miss her. Wonder who she was with down there?*

Travis ran over and wrapped his arm around Macy's neck and kissed her cheek.

"How's my little man doing?" She turned and asked. "You did a great job looking after Noah and Avery! I missed you so much!"

"I love you Mommy," Travis laid his head on her shoulder.

"Did you bring me a prize, Mommy?" Avery asked as she quickly sat down on the floor to go through Macy's purse.

"In just a minute, okay Avery."

"How's my baby, Noah." Macy asked and she and Noah both reached out for each other. Noah just smiled back with that enormous grin of his. "I can't believe my little man will be one year old next month. How old will you be?" Macy asked him. He just stared at her hair and earrings. She smiled as she thought, *It's me. Your mommy came back.*

Luke grabbed his bag. "Okay, so I guess I'll talk to you later," he said as he reached for the door.

Macy turned and grabbed Luke's arm so he'd face her. "Thank you so much, Luke. It means so much to me that you were here with them."

"Yeah, sure no problem, but you don't have to thank me!" It was hard for Luke to turn away and leave this. His family. Macy divorced him and he had to just leave. The wound opened all over again. *She is so angry with me. I've failed my marriage. I've failed my kids.* He looked in the rearview mirror, first at the apartment disappearing in the background and then at himself, *she's the only person that knows you; she's the only woman that you've loved with everything you are and she's probably the only woman that will love you the way she has. No one will ever compare. And, now she's gone.* A tear rolled down his cheek. As he pulled into the parking lot, he turned off the engine and sat there a minute with his head on the steering wheel.

But then started the car again. Just down the street was the bar. Luke pulled in and sat down. "What can I get ya?" the bartender asked.

"Bud light," Luke said. "And, a shot of tequila." It didn't take long for Luke to get hammered and find someone to hustle pool with—perpetuating the way Luke had learned to cope with his pain and anger from the divorce. Which, when he was being honest with himself, really wasn't all that different from what had been taking place the past few years. The divorce only added another layer to his growing addiction.

Noah turned one the following month. Grandma Judy baked cupcakes and brought them over to the apartment with Aunt Rose while Macy was out. Luke had been sitting with them while Macy ran her errands. They sang 'Happy Birthday' and opened gifts. Luke was frustrated as he thought about not only he and Macy being separated but what it had done to their families as well. Their families were separated now too.

Meanwhile, Macy coordinated a first birthday party for Noah at Peter and Leanne's. She kept herself busy with the details and planning—cake, presents and side dishes—keeping her mind off of the fact that Luke wasn't with them and how he and his mom just had a party for Noah and she wasn't there. The constant reminders that they were no longer a couple were too much for her to accept at times.

Luke continued to move from place to place, staying with friends in their apartments or houses, as well as from casino to casino basically evading wage garnishments for child support. He didn't have a home nor did he have a family. He was reliving his past—never having a stable thing in his life since he lost his parents to divorce at the tender young age of 5. His 'friends' were made up of gamblers and single, childless musicians and drinkers. He'd hook up with various girls he'd meet in bars mainly out of anger towards Macy but also as a way to fill that hole in his heart. Luke longed for affection and affirmation more now than ever.

He also continued to have brush-ins with the law. Luke's license was suspended; and then he was caught driving with a suspended license. The tickets he owed piled up alongside of the child support, IOUs, lawyer fees and so much more. When Luke looked in the mirror, he didn't recognize the guy looking back at him. Worse yet, he hated that guy in the mirror.

Luke would also miss his scheduled time with the kids—often blaming work for not taking them. "I gotta work, Macy. You take so much from my check; I need to work more hours to have something to live on." He'd say. But when he was with his kids, they would never learn of any of that. They wouldn't have cared anyway. Travis, Avery and Noah couldn't wait to be with their daddy. And why wouldn't they? Their daddy was the most fun person they knew or ever wanted to be with. He always goofed around with them. He let them play games or bang on his drum set. He was always so affectionate with them, always kissing them and hugging on them. Just how he imagined a daddy should love on his kids. But the visits weren't long. He just couldn't keep the thoughts of winning it big and being able to pay everyone back far from his mind. It was just too overwhelming—it truly consumed him. Luke believed that he could truly beat the game, whatever game he was playing at the time. After all, he was a dealer. He knew every little trick to the game(s). But what Luke refused to accept was that he was never going to win. That desperation wasn't a means of entertainment; it was a means of life and survival; A means that would never have an end.

It was the beginning of October, just after celebrating Travis' fifth birthday with a party at the skating rink, when Macy's other grandfather, Peter's dad, was losing his battle with cancer. His last days would be spent at his home surrounded by family. They all took turns sitting at his bedside. Macy and the kids had just gotten a picture taken with her grandpa—their great-grandpa—a month ago, and now here he was breathing his last breaths.

Macy took her turn to say her goodbyes at her grandpa's bedside. She placed her hand on top of his frail hand and whispered in his ear, "I love you, Grandpa! I think it's about time we start saying that around here, don't you?" She smiled. Macy saw his eyes move under his eyelids and he moved his thumb to touch her hand. Macy knew he had heard her. And, then, he was gone. Her grandpa was now at rest and at peace.

CHAPTER 10

"I'll Be"
1998

The past couple of months were so hard and very depressing. Macy had to deal with her grandpa's funeral and then turn around to "celebrate" the holidays with and without her babies and Luke and his family. It was a truth that she still had a difficult time dealing with. Her heart didn't want to accept it. Nor did Luke.

It was around this time that Macy started journaling again. It was her only constructive means to deal with her sadness, pain and anger. Perhaps someday someone would hear her and understand how alone she was. Often she would long to scream at the top of her lungs in hopes that the entire world would hear her pain; but all Macy would ever be capable of were those airy, silent screams. Besides, she was pretty certain that no one would really ever listen or understand anyway.

Macy was now in a new department at MasterCard, working as a Customer Support Rep. She had new work friends that she would spend most of her free time with. Two of the girls she spent a lot of time with bonded through their anger towards men. Often bashing the men they were with or not with, it gave them the support they needed—a sort of justification for the anger and sadness they often felt. Many nights were spent after the kids were asleep on Macy's front porch where she and Amber and Mary Ann would drink wine and smoke cigarettes, laughing and exchanging dating horror stories.

Even if they never admitted it, Luke and Macy were both obviously drowning in anger and loneliness. While they coped in completely different ways, they were destructive ways nonetheless. They believed nothing more than the fact that they deserved nothing and that things would just never work out. But through some indescribable force, they would subconsciously cling on to a bit of hope and kept it tucked away far beneath the surface. And yet, somehow they continued the push-pull relationship they had grown to resent and yet depend on.

While Luke continued his pattern of drinking and regularly losing bets, he was able to slowly move away from working for the casinos and into serving at a well-known restaurant right down the street from where he lived. The most fun for him became running karaoke at a couple bars two and three times a week. Sleeping during the day and living for the night, he surrounded himself with all the wrong people. People who wanted the same things as him: to drown themselves in liquor and hopelessness while making it look fun to live the party life.

Luke soon got himself an apartment a few miles down the street from Macy. Often on his way home, he'd drive past his house to take a quick pass by Macy's. One night there was another car in the driveway as he pulled up. Luke turned off his lights and quietly parked the car. He peeked in the windows to see who Macy was with. The anxiety was overwhelming as he felt like he was being choked. A rush of excitement from seeing Macy and the man on her couch kiss was extinguished with the reality that Luke couldn't have Macy.

Luke didn't know it, but Macy would often drive by his apartment as well. Looking up at the second floor window, trying to make out figures and shapes the light would cast onto the walls. It was gut wrenching and sickening to Macy to think that he was up there touching someone else. To think someone was touching him. The thought would make Macy gag as she sobbed.

After a night out with her girlfriends, Macy got in her car and the buzz she had from her two tequila sunrises drove her to the bar where Luke was doing karaoke. She walked in and sat at the bar for a bit just watching him. Luke hadn't seen her, and that's how she preferred it. Macy wanted to see him in action—what he was like now that he wasn't with her. Macy also longed for his hands and lips to be on hers.

"Excuse me, but would you mind giving this request to the karaoke guy?" Macy asked the guy sitting next to her at the bar.

"Uh sure," he replied, wondering why she couldn't just do it herself.

When Luke saw the request, Macy saw him take a quick glance at it but then go back to what he was doing, but only for a second. He picked it up and looked at it again before looking out to the crowd. Macy leaned back on her bar stool and the two made eye contact. Luke was excited to see her but also cautious. *What is she doing here?* he thought as he made his way to the bar where she was sitting.

"Macy, holy shit. What the hell you doing all the way out here?" Luke asked. "Hey Sally, this is Macy. Macy this is Sally. They take extra good care of me out here."

"Hi Sally, nice to meet you." Macy extended her hand across the bar for a shake.

"Well, nice to meet you darling." She shook Macy's hand and nodded her head.

"Sally, will you give my friend a Bud Light and put it on my tab, please."

"You don't have to do that, Luke."

"I got this one," Sally said.

"It's so crazy to see you here. You wanna do a shot?" Luke asked in that goofy, overly excited way of his. He was all kinds of nervous.

"Okay, sure."

"Sally, two tequila shots."

"You got it, honey."

Luke sang and so did Macy—not so well though. Luke was the singer, Macy was the wanna-be, but it was a known fact that she could dance. Luke repeated that to himself as he watched her on the dance floor.

Macy ended up following Luke home that night. Back at Luke's apartment they finished off more drinks and sang, danced and laughed. Macy went through his stuff; shuffling through the Modern Drummer magazines, TV Guide and cards on the coffee table. She got up to use the bathroom and looked through the medicine cabinet. He really didn't have much.

Luke was standing outside the bathroom door, waiting for Macy. She just stood there in the door as they stared at each other. Luke brushed some hair out of Macy's eye, pushing it behind her ear. She could smell his hand as it brushed by her face. Macy looked down but then back up at Luke as he leaned down to kiss her. That rush of longing overcame them both. They were in each other's arms and in Luke's bed before they knew it.

Macy left for home a couple hours later without Luke knowing it, quietly picking up her shoes and shutting the apartment door behind her. When Luke woke up, his bed—and heart—were empty again.

A couple weeks later as Macy was on her way to work, she was flipping radio stations when she stopped to hear a tune she had never heard before. She was completely lost in the southern, bluesy rock vocals coming through the speakers.

As soon as Macy could leave for her lunch break, she went to Best Buy to hopefully buy the new CD with the song she just heard. It had been playing in her head all morning. She had to buy it for Luke. It said everything she wanted to say, perfectly.

Luke was coming over the next day to visit with the kids while Macy got her hair cut and ran errands. As she was leaving, Macy said to Luke, "I got you something. It's on the kitchen table."

"Oh, Okay? I'll check it out." He got up to go to the kitchen.

There was the CD with a yellow post it that read,

> Listen to track 4.
> Love, Macy.

Luke unwrapped the case and popped out the CD. Macy's boom box was sitting on the kitchen table so he quickly dropped it in the player and listened. Avery came to join him and sat on his lap and listened too.

"Who is that, Daddy?"

"I don't know, Avery. Mommy left it for me to listen to."

"I like it," she said

"I like it, too," Luke smiled back.

Luke knew exactly why Macy wanted him to hear it. His eyes welled up with tears as he listened. She was his greatest fan and always had been and probably always would be.

Moments like these came occasionally between the two of them during the months that followed. And so did the arguments for non-payment, for missed child visits, for ruining each other's lives. Luke knew how to get into Macy's apartment without a key and helped himself often to the smell her pillow and a peek at her journal. And, some nights, he'd slip into her bed—careful to be gone before the kids awoke.

Macy enrolled Travis in soccer and t-ball and Avery in dance and Noah would be their little cheerleader, tagging along for every event. While Travis liked leading and strategizing, he was not a fan of sweating or the other kids stealing the ball from him. Avery excelled in dance. Every Saturday morning, Mommy would get her little Avery to dance class dressed in her pink-leotard-and-tights. Macy loved watching her with the other girls and how quickly she'd pick up the steps.

"They're really cute, aren't they?" Another dad said, making small talk during dance class one day.

"Oh my gosh, absolutely." Macy replied.

"Hi, I'm Adam." The young man reached out his hand to shake Macy's.

"Hi, I'm Macy. Macy was thanking herself for getting cleaned up and looking presentable this particular morning.

"You've got quite the cutie there," Adam was pointing to Avery through the observation window.

"Oh thanks. I sort of think so too," Macy smiled.

"Well, it's obvious she takes after her mommy," he smiled back.

"What's your daughter's name?" Macy asked, trying to redirect any notice to her cheeks blushing. This was the first attention she had gotten in a while. And it felt nice.

Adam and Macy shared coffee a few weeks in a row during dance class. Then he asked her for her phone number and if she'd like to go out sometime. "Maybe dinner and a movie?" he asked.

"Yeah, sure, that'd be nice." Macy responded.

Adam picked up Macy and bought her dinner at a nice local restaurant. They shared casual conversation about their kids, jobs, along with a handful of laughs over a couple cocktails. *He's a nice guy*, Macy thought to herself. *He has a nice car, a good job and a house, and he's pretty cute too.*

Adam held Macy's hand and kissed her neck a few times while in the movie. Macy was very much enjoying the affection so when Adam asked if she'd like to share a nightcap back at his place, she ignored her gut and quickly accepted.

It was the following week at dance class when Adam wasn't there to drop off his daughter that Macy accepted the fact that after no phone calls or email exchanges, what they had was merely a one-night-stand and nothing more. Macy spent the rest of the afternoon wallowing in her shame and guilt.

It was time for school to start and this meant that little Travis would be off to Kindergarten! It also meant it was time to find a new babysitter. Macy found a sitter not far from where she lived that had three children all the same ages as Travis, Avery and Noah. Travis would catch the bus with her oldest son. The first day, Luke and Macy would both be there to take pictures and see him off. It was a bittersweet moment seeing their little boy walking up the steps onto the bus and looking for a place to sit. He waved to them both and off he went. Avery and Noah would walk back with the sitter and stay there until Macy picked them up after work.

These times were so hard for Luke and Macy—not being able to really share in the experiences of their babies accomplishing an important event 'together.' It was a tension that they'd have to live with from now on.

Macy made attempts to have the social life she had put on hold for so many years. She spent nights out with girlfriends from work going to clubs and meeting new people. She had never been a fan of being on the lookout for guys nor did she care to be hit on. The single-life scene left Macy with much to be desired. Nonetheless, she went on dates, not a lot but a few. One blind date was all she'd need to not ever do that again. He was a friend of a friend from work. The whole experience was just awkward and didn't do it for Macy. And when it progressively didn't go well, it only made her think of Luke even more so.

"Hi Mom!" Macy called Leanne.

"Hi Macy! How are you?"

"Doing good," Macy smiled. "I have a date this Friday."

"Really?" Leanne smiled too.

"Yep, I met him a couple weeks ago and have talked a bit since and, well, he wants to take me to dinner. Would you mind watching the kids for me?"

"Well sure, Macy. I'd love to have them."

"Great! I really appreciate it, Mom!"

Macy met her date at the restaurant. It was a fancy restaurant and expensive too. He ordered a bottle of wine. They shared a nice meal and good conversation. After paying the bill, they'd sit in Macy's car until it was time to leave.

The whole way home, Macy was giddy from her date. The feeling of being pampered was a nice boost to her confidence, especially after the last (blind) date she had been on. While dancing and singing along to the radio, her giddiness was brought to a startling halt when the red and blue lights pulled up behind her. It was a little after 11 o'clock and she was just a couple miles from her mom and dad's house.

The female officer came up to her window and asked for her license and insurance.

"Is something wrong, ma'am," Macy asked.

"You were going 52 in a 40," she replied. "Just sit tight, I'll be right back."

"Awesome. Just what I need...a ticket." Macy said to herself.

The officer returned and asked Macy to get out of the car. "What do you mean, why?" Macy asked.

"Ma'am I have a warrant for your arrest for an unpaid ticket. I need you to put your hands behind your back."

Her fun evening and giddiness had completely vanished with the new fear and anger that overcame her in those five minutes. She was put into the back of the officer's car where she cried the entire way to the station. *My mom's going to kill me,* she thought to herself. *How am I going to get myself out of this?*

"Luke, it's Macy. I need some help."

"Oh yeah? What are you doing and why are you calling so late?"

"I just got arrested. I need some money to bail me out."

"And, you're calling *me?*"

"Yes, Luke. I didn't know who else to call. I'll pay you back. Can you please help me?"

Luke paid her bail and dropped her off at her mom and dad's house. Macy tried to be very quiet since it was now much later than she promised her mom she'd be home. Leanne was sleeping on the couch with the TV still on but woke up when Macy turned it off.

"Macy?"

"Sorry, Mom. I didn't mean to wake you."

"What time is it? Where have you been?"

"I got pulled over on my way home. And, they took me to jail for an unpaid speeding ticket."

"Why didn't you call me?"

"I was too embarrassed. I called Luke."

"Really, Macy? Why in the hell would you do that? You call me if something like that happens again." Leanne reprimanded, as if Macy were still a teenager.

Macy spent the night at her mom and dad's. She laid in bed thinking about her recent dates and although she had some moments of feeling happy and confident again, no one could ever take the place of Luke.

This Christmas was Luke's turn to have the kids. Peter, Leanne and Miriam were taking a trip to Atlanta to celebrate Christmas with Kyle and David and little Carson, Macy's new nephew. Macy decided to go with. After all, she would've been celebrating Christmas alone otherwise. They always had a pretty good time together and Macy loved playing and snuggling with baby Carson. But while Macy's parents and sisters would share in the meal preparation or organizing gifts, Macy would take occasional trips to the bathroom to cry. It was excruciating to watch Kyle and David with their new baby. She was so happy for them and loved her little nephew, but it was sucking the air out of her at times knowing that she wasn't with her babies because she and Luke were divorced. Divorced: it was such an ugly word and made Macy dislike herself in ways that a bad haircut or an old scar would never compare to.

Macy wouldn't sleep much while in Atlanta. Instead she'd lie wide-awake thinking about what she was doing with her life and what she wanted. If she couldn't have Luke, she didn't want to fill that space with just anyone or anything. She knew in her heart she needed to completely let go of everything and find a safe place—for her and the kids—to rebuild her life in a way that she'd be proud of.

CHAPTER 11

"I Will Remember You"
1999

It was Luke's turn to sing. He was running his karaoke gig and liked to get the crowd going in between singers when he could. He stood behind the stand in the middle of the floor and got all the ladies looking his way as he sang those familiar lyrics, "The strands in your eyes, they color them wonderful..."

Luke took the microphone off the stand and headed over in the direction of a young lady he had been checking out all night long. "And, I'll be your crying shoulder; I'll be love suicide... I'll be the greatest fan of your life." He was singing to her. The charm was practically oozing out of him and nearly impossible to ignore.

"Hi, I'm Luke," he introduced himself, still talking in the mic.

"Yeah, I heard you say that earlier," she replied. "You're the karaoke guy."

"You're correct, that'd be me." He flashed a coy smile.

She held out her hand, "I'm Susan. It's nice to meet you."

Susan was in school, studying to be a teacher and had two daughters. She was living with her parents as she was recently divorced and trying to save money while she was in school.

"I'd like to take you out some time," Luke said. "Can I call you?"

And so it began. Luke and Susan went to the movies and out to dinner. They'd spend time at the bars listening to music and having laughs. He'd call her baby and hottie and make her CDs.

"Macy, what do you think about getting the group together to go on a float trip this weekend?" Amber, Macy's friend from work, asked.

"Oh my gosh, that sounds awesome! This week has totally sucked and I haven't been on a float trip in so long."

"Okay, I'll send out an email to Patty, Chris, Randy, Jared and the rest of the group to join us. We'll just make a day of it."

"Yeah, I'm not down with the camping thing. Weather should be perfect, though. Sounds perfect!"

Macy met Amber, Amber's husband, Leo and Jared at the commuter lot. They all chipped in and brought drinks, snacks and ice. The four would meet the others at the river. The weather was beautiful, sunny and hot, perfect floating weather. And none of that really mattered since the water felt perfect and the beer was ice cold. It was a fun day full of laughter, canoe tipping, and sunbathing.

"Do you guys want to do anything later on tonight," Leo asked.

Jared looked at Macy, "Do you want to do anything later, Macy?"

"Sure. What were you all thinking?"

"Well, let's go back to our house to make some dinner. We can BBQ and finish off these drinks. Then we can just play it by ear," Amber suggested.

"Sounds like a plan to me." Macy agreed. "But I need to go home and shower first."

"Okay, so we'll just meet back at our house in an hour or so."

"You got it."

"See you there."

They spent the rest of the night sitting on the patio eating, drinking and chatting after playing a fun game of wiffle ball.

"Guys, I think I'm gonna get going. I have to pick up the kids pretty early in the morning."

"Okay, Macy. Thanks for hanging with us all day. It was such a blast!" Amber said.

"It was, no doubt!"

"Yeah, I'm gonna get going too," Jared said.

Jared and Macy walked out to their cars.

The two had been flirting off and on all day. They were already good friends from working together and having spent a fair amount of time together. Jared had three kids of his own. He and their mom never married and weren't together very long. He was also a recovering alcoholic so he didn't drink but instead smoked cigarettes and pot. But what Macy noticed was that he was a hard worker and he was always so kind to her.

"So you really going to go home and go to bed?" Jared asked.

"Well, I'll probably watch a movie or something, I don't know. Why do you care?" Macy smiled, replying sarcastically.

"I don't know. I was just curious."

"What are you going to do?"

"Nothing. Probably sit on my patio and eavesdrop on my neighbors."

"Oh, now that sounds exciting."

"You haven't been to my house, have you?" Jared asked—or rather, suggested.

"Well... do you want to come over to my place? We could watch a movie." Macy suggested.

After a month or so of this, Jared and Macy were officially dating. They were keeping it under their hats though; they weren't ready for the whole office to know and really didn't want any rumors flying around; nor did they want their kids to know. But eventually it became a known fact that Jared and Macy were in fact dating. Macy had made the announcement after a staff meeting when she noticed Beth whispering to Sharon while glancing at Macy.

Occasionally throughout the workweek, Jared would drive the two back to his house and make Macy lunch. They'd go to the movies and out to dinner. They also played cards a lot with another couple—Jared's best friends. They'd laugh and drink while Jared drank his Mountain Dew and got high. Macy had a boyfriend.

"Macy? Hey it's Luke."

"Hi. What's up?"

"Do you have a minute? I need to talk to you about something."

"Yeah. I guess so." Macy replied as she rolled her eyes.

"I wanted to give you a call to tell you that I'm dating someone. I want to be the one to tell you, and at some point I'd like you to meet her." Just like Luke to do everything quickly like there was some fire somewhere.

"Well, that's good for you, Luke, but I have no desire to meet who it is you're spending your time with. I know it's really none of my business, but I'd really like us to adhere to our agreement that our kids are to not be involved in our extracurricular affairs unless someone has a ring on their finger. I don't want the kids in the middle of any more relationship issues."

"I totally agree, Macy."

The hurt was turning in Macy's gut like acid. It stimulated the defensive wall that immediately went up as she decided to tell Luke that she was dating someone as well.

"Hello? You still there?"

"Yeah, Luke. I'm still here. I guess I should tell you that I'm seeing someone too."

"Really? Who?"

"No one you know, Luke."

"Well then who? He better not be sleeping over there."

"Really, Luke? I just told you that I don't want our kids anywhere near our boyfriends and girlfriends."

There was silence for a bit; neither knowing what to say as the strong emotions distracted their every thought. Even if they were divorced and single, it didn't make it any less painful to hear that the other had fallen into the arms of someone else. But even worse, that it was important enough to share with one another.

"Well, guess there's nothing more to say," Luke was the first to speak up.

"Yep, guess not."

"Well enjoy your life, Macy." Luke said with hurt and anger in his voice.

"You too, Luke."

Macy clicked the phone off and slammed it back in the holster.

"Mommy! Daddy took us to the pool yesterday. It was so much fun." Travis gave Macy a big hug around her waist and then threw his backpack on the living room floor. Travis loved telling Macy all he had done and where he'd been.

"He did. Well that's really great, Travis. I'm glad you had a good time." Macy was holding Noah, checking him over, smelling his neck and kissing him as she always did when the kids returned from Luke's.

"Yeah, they had this giant slide and Julie was too little to go down it, but Avery and I weren't."

"Julie? " Macy continued kissing on Noah, tickling his neck.

"You know, Mommy, Julie...Susan's girl." Macy sat Noah down on the couch next to Travis who was now flipping through channels to find Nickelodeon.

"Oh right, Okay. So Susan and her girls were there too."

Avery came out of her room with Noah's blankie and hers and joined the boys on the couch and she chimed in, "Yeah, we went swimming and then stayed with them last night watching movies and playing video games."

"Wow. Was Daddy there too?"

"Yeah, he and Susan were watching movies in the other room."

"So where did you sleep?" Macy was now unpacking the kid's bags sorting piles for the laundry.

Travis, now fixated on the Real Monsters show, replied, "Noah and I slept on the floor while Avery slept in the girl's bed with them."

"Well, I'm glad you had fun sweetheart."

"Yeah it was." Travis said as he went back to playing with Noah and watching his show.

Macy sat down at the kitchen table, shaking with rage and disgust. This is really happening. My kids are with her kids. She wanted to scream. She wanted the whole world to hear how angry she was that this was her life. A life she didn't choose and certainly not the one she signed up for; that her husband left her for gambling and drinking and now was in the arms of another woman as were her babies. But, then again, she was with another man. What could she do? Absolutely nothing.

"Jared, would you want to go to Aruba with me?" Macy asked Jared as they lay face to face on his bed. He kept it so dark in his room, she wasn't sure if he was sleeping or not.

"What? Huh? Aruba?"

"Yeah, you know my parents go every year in November and they had asked if I wanted to go with them this year to get away with all that's been going on. So I'm wondering if you'd like to go with me. It's not for a couple months yet, but we probably need to get flights booked."

"Wow, that'd be awesome. What do you think they'd have to say about that?"

"Oh, I'm quite certain they'd be totally down with it. I'll talk to Mom about it tomorrow. That is...if you want to go?"

"Sure, Macy. I'd like that." Jared kissed her on her forehead.

Macy lay there not believing what she had just asked him. She couldn't take it back now.

Luke's car pulled up out front. "Daddy's here," Avery ran to open the front door. She ran right out and jumped into Luke's arms.

"How's my little princess?" he asked her.

"I'm good, Daddy. Are we still going to the zoo today?"

"We sure are."

"Yes! See Travis, I told you we were still going."

"I knew we were going," Travis said as he walked out to put his bag in Luke's car.

Macy stood in the door watching all of the love unfold right in front of her in the front yard.

"Hi, Macy," Luke said.

Macy waved as she walked down the front steps to hang out in the yard with the kids.

And, then it stopped. Like being hit by a freight train, the joy was stolen from the moment... the moment Susan got out of the car to let the kids get in the back seat. The other woman was right there in front of Macy. Despite how awkward a moment it was, Susan attempted to offer a smile. Macy maintained the scowl on her face. She wanted to yell, *don't you smile at me!*

"Macy, this is Susan," Luke said.

Macy said nothing.

"Kids be good and take care of each other. I love you so much!" Macy said to them through the passenger window.

"We will, Mommy! Love you too." They all blew kisses.

Macy stood up and turned away from the car—not making any contact with Susan—and said to Luke, "I'm going to Aruba next month. And Jared's going with me. Just thought you should know. And by the way, I don't want *my* kids spending the night with her." *Now go f- yourself,* she added in her mind.

Luke just stood there, wanting to rip her head off for the way she had just ripped his heart out. The anger and sadness was crippling. Macy just walked back to the house and closed the door behind her without looking back. Instead she peaked through the front window making sure they couldn't see her.

Susan took Luke's arm in a way to console him. He just turned around and got in the car and they drove off. Macy stood in that front window staring at nothing but an empty front yard and street as tears filled her eyes and eventually blurred her vision. In an instant, she felt like that little girl standing behind the chain link fence as her mom drove off, the pregnant girl watching Luke leave her behind as he went out with his buddy, and watching little Avery standing in the window crying as she drove off.

Macy and Jared's relationship continued to grow more and more serious. Jared was now working in a different department so it was now much easier to separate their professional lives from their personal lives. Their relationship was so serious, in fact, Macy showed up at the dealership where her dad worked with the intent to trade in her Taurus for a minivan. She and Jared and their six kids could never go anywhere together since they didn't have a vehicle big enough to haul them all around.

"Hey, I'm on my way back to your place. I just left the dealership." Macy called Jared.

"Oh yeah. I'll have all the kids ready to go when you get here. I packed you a ham and cheese sandwich. Is that okay?"

"That sounds perfect. See you in a bit!"

Macy parked on the street in front of Jared's house. The front door to his house was open, and she could see all of the movement going on in the house through the glass storm door. She looked at herself in the rearview mirror and then back at the front door, clinging on to the steering wheel to keep her from falling. *Macy, what are you doing? What am I doing?* She asked herself. *Is this really what you want? Why are you really doing this?* Her contemplative thoughts were interrupted when Travis and Steven slid open the side door.

"Whoa, Mom, is this our new van?"

"Hey boys. Yep, it sure is! You guys ready to go see some monkeys?"

"Yeah!" They both yelled.

"Steven, does your dad need any help or is he all ready to go."

"No, he's ready. He's just helping Savannah get her shoes on."

The rest of the kids came piling in one by one. They all climbed in the van and immediately started arguing over who was going to sit where.

"No, Avery. *I* was going to sit next to Steven."

"Too bad I was here first and you didn't call it anyways."

"I did. Didn't I, Steven? Mom, Avery won't get up."

"Guys, there are plenty of seats. Now let's get along and work it out nicely."

"Hey gorgeous," Jared came by the driver's window to give Macy a kiss.

"Hey there. Got everything?"

"Yep, we're all set."

"Thanks for getting our lunches all packed!"

"No sweat. Now let's get on the road so the kids can enjoy this beautiful day and hopefully go to bed early," Jared smiled.

Macy was exhausted when they got back to Jared's house. She was happy to see that the kids had a lot of fun, but there was just too much running through Macy's mind. She witnessed her kids trying to get Jared's attention while he played with his kids and she also noticed how that annoyed him. She had mentioned it to him on the way home.

"Sorry, the kids were a little clingy today. I think it's just hard for them to see how much attention you're giving to Steven, Savannah and Josh. You know they just want to be included, right?"

"Macy, when I get to see my kids, I want to give them my full attention. It's not fair to them if I'm giving it to someone else." His voice was defensive and all Macy heard him say was that her kids weren't worthy of his time or attention—not when *his* kids were there.

She took the kids home, gave them all baths and got everyone in bed for a story. That night she laid in bed thinking about her future, since it was obvious that sleep was not coming any time soon. *You need to make a change, Macy. Your kids deserve so much more.*

The next afternoon, Macy called her grandma.

"Hi Grandma!! It's Macy."

"Macy, how are you?"

"I'm doing really well, Grandma. How are you?"

"I'm pretty good too."

With Macy's grandpa's passing the year prior, Grandma was now living all by herself in that big house of theirs.

"Listen Grandma, I wanted to talk to you about something....Well, actually ask you something. But I don't want you to answer now because I want you to think about it."

"Oh okay, what is Macy?"

"Well, I'm really thinking about moving back to Wentzville. I'd like to look into enrolling the kids in St. Patrick's."

"Really? That would be good for them I think, Macy. For all of you."

"Yeah, I agree." Macy paused. "And, so I was wondering how you might feel about having some roommates?" Macy smiled across the phone. "If you'd be at all interested in having us live with you? I'd like to save up for a house of our own. I'd pay rent and my portion of the utilities and what not. But, like I said, I want you to think about it. Don't answer now."

"Okay Macy, I will think about it."

Macy contacted St. Patrick's to see about enrolling the kids. Travis would be in first grade and Avery would be in Kindergarten. They had spots open and the tuition would actually be less expensive than the before and after daycare that Macy was currently paying. It all just seemed like the right thing to do. *Now if Grandma says yes, we'll be in good shape.*

Macy's grandma called her back the following evening. "Hi Macy! It's Grandma!"

"Oh, Hi Grandma!"

"Well, I thought about what you asked and, Macy, I would absolutely love for you and the kids to live here with me. I will help you get the kids to school and watch Noah too. I'll just need a little money for rent and any phone bills you may have."

"Grandma, you don't know how happy this makes me!" Macy was truly elated!

"I'm happy too, Macy. I'm very excited to have you here with me!"

Macy was thrilled; she was going to get some well-needed help and planned to purchase her own home for her and the kids in a year or so. The kids were pretty excited too. Travis and Avery were a little sad over starting a new school but didn't mind not having to get up early for daycare or hang out there to wait for Mom to get off of work.

Luke wasn't as thrilled with the distance that came with Macy and the kids moving 25 miles away. "Luke I promise, I will meet you in the middle when it's your time to be with the kids. You won't have to come all the way out there to pick them up."

"Well, gee, thanks Macy. That's so generous of you." Luke was upset and a bit jealous too.

"I don't want to live in this little apartment anymore. There's just not enough space for all of us." Macy tried to not rub it in his face. "I plan to purchase my own house and the money I'll save living with Grandma will help me do this."

"Okay, I get it. I'm sure your grandma will love having you all there." He tried to find the right words to say.

Macy's dad, David and Jared helped her move out of the apartment and into her grandma's house. It snowed that day, but they managed to get everything done in just a couple hours.

Macy, Grandma and the kids were all a family now. Travis and Avery were enjoying their new school—except the part of going to mass all the time—and Noah was thriving thanks to the one-on-one time he was getting with his great grandma.

Macy would stay up with her grandma after the kids went to bed and play cards or watch TV. She loved the stories her grandma shared with her. Mainly how much Grandpa was such a stubborn ass but she loved him and they had a good life together raising their eight sons. Macy was also amazed to see her grandma do all the things her grandpa used to do, like use the push mower on the parts of the lawn the riding mower couldn't get to. She raked leaves and took out the trash. A part of Macy thought she truly loved doing all of these things herself, she enjoyed the independence. She had never had that having been married at the very young age of sixteen.

Luke and Susan were pretty serious but so was Luke's drinking—which pushed him deeper and deeper into a silent depression. His nights running karaoke became more about getting wasted and not necessarily about singing. So many nights he'd follow up on the games he lost and bets gone bad via texts and calls from bookies all while drinking and maintaining his karaoke efforts. He stayed just drunk, lost and busy enough to forget about Macy and the kids and this new woman he was sharing somewhat of a life with...not to mention his legal issues, bills, and everything that wasn't going well. *Just maintaining the chaos factor—it's all I know dammit.* He'd slur to himself.

While in amazingly beautiful Aruba, Macy spent a few moments alone staring at herself in the mirror. *I should be here with Luke,* she'd whisper to herself. Luke would have been taking her out exploring the island, but Jared was content with just laying by the pool all day long. He liked the hot tub which Macy was not a fan of. Despite the sadness of not being there with Luke, Macy made the best of it and enjoyed as much as she could with her parents and the island and Jared. But the decision she made to invite Jared would be a constant regret and her mind would often go back to the recent afternoon she spent with him and the kids at the zoo after purchasing a new van for all of them, as if they were the Brady Bunch or something.

Macy came home with a nice dark tan and a very heavy heart. This was the first night she didn't get sleep in a long time. She did what she could to sort out all of the thoughts racing through her mind. She was feeling guilty and disappointed with so many of her decisions lately.

Macy, you can't continue like this. What are Jared's aspirations for the future? He's not giving up the pot smoking and he doesn't believe in God. And he's not willing to give himself fully to your kids, not while his kids are around anyways.

And, as it always was, Luke was also struggling with his decisions. After a very late night working karaoke and staying out, Luke woke up the next morning in his apartment on his bed still in his jeans. *Where am I and how'd the hell did I get here?* He thought, trying to adjust his vision through his pounding hangover and sickening nausea. He remembered leaving the bar and sideswiping the construction barrel as he got on the highway. He remembered the cop pulling him over...but that was it. He couldn't remember past that.

He made his way to the bathroom to get a couple aspirin. He sat down on the side of the tub with his head in his hands. *Luke, what the hell are you doing?* He asked himself. *You shouldn't be here right now; you shouldn't even be alive. You idiot, you could've killed someone or yourself.* He slammed his fists on his thighs. *You can't keep doing this. What about your kids? What about you? They need you. You've got to get out of this hellhole.* His depressed and angry emotions, mixed with the previous evening's liquor and second-hand smoke made their way up the surface, making the toilet his companion for the next hour. He'd lay on the cold floor crying his morning away.

CHAPTER 12

"My Redeemer Lives"
1999 (cont'd)

Now that the kids were attending a Catholic grade school, Macy decided it was important to take the kids to church on Sunday. For Macy, it was like riding a bike—kneel down, stand up, sit down, repeat. All the hymns and prayers came back to her like she hadn't missed the last ten years at all. There was something very comforting in the familiar tradition; it felt like home to her. She was home.

With Travis going into the second grade soon, First Communion was on the forefront of Macy's mind. *How will this work?* She wondered. *He hasn't been baptized."*

One night while on the phone with Jared, Macy was stuck on that memory from not so long ago sitting outside Jared's house in the minivan.

"What's the matter, Macy? You seem far away."

"Oh nothing really, just thinking. I've got a lot on my mind with this Baptism stuff."

"Yeah, I bet. Wanna talk about it?"

"Do you believe in God, Jared?"

"Do I believe in God? Gosh Macy, I don't know. I'm sure there's something out there that's above all of us...but I don't really know."

"Yeah." After a long pause, Macy added, "Jared, I'm returning the minivan."

"What? You are?"

"Yes. I shouldn't have bought it. It just doesn't feel right to me."

"Oh okay." Jared was hesitant and not sure of just how to respond, sensing Macy's distance.

Macy did in fact return the minivan. Back in the little sedan that fit only five. Driving home, she said to herself, *Yes, now this feels right,* as she squeezed the steering wheel, still feeling sad and ashamed for buying the minivan in the first place...for trying to conform to an idea that just didn't feel right to her.

Macy did all she could to take this time with her grandma to focus on herself and what she needed. What her kids needed. Often that was a very hard task to do when she worried about the kids tearing the place up, breaking something, or marking on the walls or something like that. Grandma kept a meticulous house. Macy and her kids were not meticulous.

But the worry took on a brand new meaning the night she dreamt of her grandpa. It wasn't until she got up out of bed and went to her window to take a look outside that she remembered the dream. Just as she raised the blind a bluebird flew down to the branch right in front of her. It seemed to be staring right at her. Macy was completely captured by the beautiful, tiny blue creature. And then the vision of her grandpa and her dream entered her mind. In the dream, Macy opened the door to the garage to go out to her car only to find Grandpa standing at his workbench in his white coveralls and fluorescent orange hat. Macy, shocked, said, "Grandpa, what are you doing here?"

He just looked at her and pointed, "You, my dear, need to quit worrying." And then he turned right back to what he was doing. That was him, a man of many words. But the few words he spoke were always pretty damn impactful.

Grandpa would visit Macy in her dreams just a couple more times. But as strange as it seemed, Macy believed he was behind the random bluebird appearances that she encountered. It always seemed to be a time that she was worrying about Grandma or money or Luke or the kids that a bluebird would appear right in her line of sight. Macy was certain that Grandpa was behind these timely appearances, that he was sending her a bluebird as a reminder of the hope that she had always, always clung onto; to never ever forget to hope...and more importantly stop worrying. These moments would be some of her most sacred times from that point forward living in her grandparent's house.

One morning while the kids were out playing and Grandma was at church, Macy went in the house to get a hat for Noah. She got a drink from the kitchen sink and as she drank, she began to cry. Thinking of how grateful she was for her babies, for her grandma and this house and the yard and fresh air, for being home; but also sad for what she didn't have—Luke—and the bills that were still hanging over her like a giant black cloud. The bill collectors still called regularly. *How can I ever get out of this hole? These kids deserve so much better than this?* She cried silently to herself.

Macy put her water down and walked to the kitchen table to get a napkin to wipe the tears from her eyes. As Macy wiped her eyes and turned to her left to look out the window, a bluebird landed right in front of her on the deck. The beautiful creature just sat and stared at her as she continued to cry. That's when she remembered, "You, my dear, need to quit worrying."

"Okay, Grandpa. I hear you," she said as she forced a smile to her face and wiped away the rest of her tears. The bluebirds always seemed to come just at the right time. She felt crazy at times trying to understand how these moments would happen. But then again, she believed and hoped that the impossible could happen, and most always, when you least expect it.

"Hey, Ma!"

"Oh, Hi Lukey! How's my handsome son doing?"

"I'm okay. I was wondering if you're doing anything for lunch. I'd like to take you to get a bite."

"Oh, that would be wonderful. I'd love that."

"So, how about we meet at Pasta House in an hour, say 11:30?"

"Sure, honey. I'll see you there."

Luke was already there when Judy arrived. He stood to greet her.

"Hi Ma," said Luke, as he reached out to give her a hug.

She squeezed back, "Oh, hello my Lukey. You okay? You don't look like you're getting enough sleep."

"No, I'm fine…Well, no not so much, Ma."

After the server took their order, Luke started to share his purpose for the lunch visit. "I am really tired, Ma. I quit my job at the casino and I'm thinking about giving up running karaoke. And, I'm cutting back my shifts at L&Cs."

"Wow, okay. What are you going to do for money?"

"Well, I had a couple interviews with UPS and I'm pretty sure I'm going to get the job. But I want out of my apartment and would like to ask if I could live with you until I can save up some money and get back on my feet."

Judy sighed and willingly took on the challenge to help—fix— Luke. "You know you're not going to be able to party at my house. And there will be no sleepovers with Susan or the girls."

"Oh my gosh, Ma, I know. Seriously! Besides Susan and I aren't doing so hot."

"Oh really, why not? I really like her, Luke." She said, insinuating he had done something wrong.

"We're just not, Ma. So can I move in or not?"

"Yes, of course but I'm going to be watching you."

"Alright, I got it."

Luke got the job at UPS. He was now a Shift Supervisor and helped unload and sort packages. There were a lot of tests involved with getting the job, which was not Luke's thing. But he indeed passed and this would be the first real manual labor job he'd ever had. It was hard work but worthwhile. He continued to work a couple shifts a week at L&Cs but stopped hanging out at the bar after his shift would end and eventually ended his career running karaoke (and driving home drunk). Luke was living life deliberately now—taking care of himself and being a better dad to Travis, Avery and Noah. His eyes were brighter and his head was clearer than it had been in a while.

Luke's lease on the apartment ended and he was now living with his mom. Something he wasn't proud of but knew would be a good transition for his new life and also a safer and healthier place for his babies, and obviously a familiar place. He was very close to work and would now save money on gas, food and utilities. Having some cash after paying bills and especially child support would be a very nice change for Luke.

Six months ago, Macy contacted Child Support Enforcement to request that the amount of child support be lowered from the originally suggested amount so it was a more reasonable for Luke. It was still a nice chunk of cash but a whole lot less than what was previously due.

"Grandma, what are your plans for the day? What can I help you with?"

"I had planned to do some work in the yard today. I need to rake and pull weeds."

"Okay, the kids and I will help you. It's so nice outside and all of us can get a lot done working together."

"Kids, come on! We're going to do some work outside and help Grandma."

"Doing what?" Travis asked.

"We're going to help Grandma rake and pick up some sticks in the yard."

It was a nice fall day for November, with the warm sun and cool breeze it was perfect for some yard work before the winter months set in.

"So, I guess I need to start thinking about Travis' Baptism." Macy started the conversation across the rows of rose bushes.

"Yeah, probably so. He's going to need to do that before he can receive First Communion."

"I guess I need to consider having all of the kids baptized. They're going to need to as well."

"You should speak to Father and let him know your situation and then he can most likely get you signed up for classes."

"Okay, I'll do that tomorrow after church."

Grandma and Macy continued on talking as they kneeled in front of the rose bushes that Grandpa had so meticulously planted and cared for, raking out leaves and weeds and pruning dead branches. Macy stood up to stretch her back and legs. She turned her face up to the sun and closed her eyes. She smiled as her mind was suddenly filled with the memories she had from this place— her grandparent's house. She remembered how Grandma babysat her when she was a toddler. And being excited as she stood on the couch looking out the front window to watch her uncles get off the 'goose-a-bus' (Macy couldn't pronounce school bus), playing with her uncle's Tonka truck and boy toys, and, oh, sticking that chain from one of the Tonka trucks into that electrical outlet in the kitchen. She flinched as she remembered the wall going up in flames, how she was thrown back and sitting on the counter, teeth chattering and sobbing, calling for her mommy as Grandma ran her charcoaled hand under the cool water from the faucet. Macy looked down at her left hand, staring in wonder—she was only 3 and a half but remembered it like it was yesterday. Then the thought jumped through her mind, *Oh, how I would love to have this house for my own. To have the opportunity to make it mine and keep it in the family would be absolutely wonderful.* She smiled to herself, put her glove back on her barely scarred hand, and finished her clean up in the garden.

The next day after church, Macy spoke with Father and he signed her up for Thursday evening classes to reacquaint her to receiving Baptismal rights. The classes were a tad boring, but she felt it was the right thing to do for her and the kids.

Travis and Avery were doing well at St. Patrick's. They liked their teachers and did well with their studies. And little Noah loved being home with Grandma. He looked forward to sitting with her as they waited in the van for Travis and Avery to get out of school. Noah was such an amazingly patient child, always taking his time with everything and everyone. Macy was certain he took to the older generation so well since they weren't in such a constant hurry like his mom and dad always were.

"Luke, man, it is so good to have you back with us on the worship team," said Kevin. He patted Luke on the back as he was taking his headphones off and getting up from the drum kit as they finished worship rehearsal. Kevin had been playing bass with the church worship band for years. He and Luke had played together in the past.

"Oh thanks, Kevin. It's really good to be back. Feels right, ya know?" Luke replied.

They walked backstage and made their way to the front seats of the auditorium. Everyone had cleared out so they stood around and talked for a bit.

"So, how are things going with you? How are Macy and the kids?"

"Well, Macy and I have been divorced for 3 years now."

"Oh man, I didn't know. I am so sorry." Kevin put his hand on Luke's shoulder.

"It's cool brother. How would you know? The kids are awesome. Just growing up way too quick. They're so fun to be with. I love 'em to pieces!"

"Aw, that's so awesome. You do have some good-looking kids! So, may I ask…you and Macy? What happened?"

"Man, it's a really long story. There's just so much but a really big part of it…well, I've had a problem with gambling for a while."

Kevin was stunned, a bit confused, and not completely sure how to respond. "Now you were working for the casino, weren't you?" Kevin asked.

Luke was shocked that he had just admitted to having a gambling addiction—out loud. "Yeah, I sure was." Luke nodded as he looked to the floor. "All of them at one point or another. But not anymore."

"But you can't gamble on the boat you work on, right?"

"Right, I would go to another casino." The questions were painful to answer.

"Man, I'm so sorry. So how is it affecting you today, your…addiction?"

"Well, I just take it one day at a time. It haunts me constantly but I just have no desire to let it destroy my life any more than it already has."

"Understood, brother. I'm proud of you. Did you know we have the Celebrate Recovery program here at the church now? Have you thought about participating?"

"No, I didn't know that." Luke put his head down, feeling somewhat ashamed and embarrassed but also wanting control back over his life—for himself and Macy and the kids.

"Well, they meet once a week and it's centered on the 12-step process and allowing God's grace to help release you from your addictive behaviors. You need to be experiencing authentic joy and everyone here can help you get there. We're here for you. Let me know if there is anything I can do. You've got my contact info."

"Yeah, I do. Thanks so much, Kevin. That means a lot!"

"Man, any time. Besides, we need you behind that kit. No one can bring that funk-styled rhythm like you do." Kevin said with his arm around Luke's neck as they headed toward the doors.

"Shut up, Bro!" Luke was smiling from ear to ear from the compliment—a genuine brotherly compliment that held such unconditional support and encouragement. Something he hadn't heard in a very, very long time. And, it couldn't have come at a better time.

"Hey, see you on Sunday?"

"You bet, Man."

Luke showed up out front of Susan's parent's house around 7:30am. "Kids, I'll be right back. I'm going to let Susan and the girls know we're here."

"Okay, Daddy." Avery said as she brushed her doll's hair.

Luke knocked on the door as Susan was opening it. "You ready?"

"Yeah, getting the girl's coats on now," she replied.

"Okay, I'll be in the car."

Susan and the girls got in their car and followed Luke to church.

"Guys, let's show Julie and Sarah where Children's Church is."

"Alright. C'mon...we'll show you." Travis and Avery took their hands and led them back to the youth rooms. Luke carried Noah while he and Susan walked further down the hall to the toddler area.

Noah's face lit up as he saw all the kids playing.

"Have fun, Noah. Daddy will be back in just a little bit." He said, as he lowered Noah over the gate.

"Bye, Daddy!" He blew him a kiss.

"Come on, Susan. Let's go grab our seats," Luke said as he put his arm around her shoulders.

"Luke Hawthorn! What's happening, Man? It's good to see your face." It was Mike...a blast from the past.

"Hey, Mike. You too, Man."

This happened a few more times as Luke and Susan made their way to the auditorium.

"How's this? I need to sit on the end so I can get to and from the stage." Luke pointed to a couple seats at the end of the row.

"Oh right. This is fine," Susan said as she took a seat. Susan sat alone as Luke played drums during the worship set. He was good; and she could see that it just came so naturally to him and that he loved it—immensely!

"What a great worship that was. Wouldn't you agree? Can I get an Amen?" Pastor Gabe said as he entered the stage and the musicians exited. "I am so glad that you are here with us today. We have a lot to discuss, especially about God's grace and what that means to you and your life at this very moment. Before we get into the message, turn around and say hello to the folks sitting near you."

Susan shook a couple folks' hands.

"Hi, I'm Mandy." The woman said to her.

"Oh, hi. Susan."

"It's nice to meet you. Are you new here?"

"Yes, today's my first time here."

"Hey there," Luke snuck in right as Susan finished her greeting.

"Good morning, Luke. I was just meeting your friend, Susan."

"Oh great. Good morning to you too, Mandy!"

Luke and Susan sat and listened to Pastor Gabe's message and it was as if he was speaking directly to Luke's heart. There was a lot there...and almost too much to contain. One thing he did hear, and was absolutely certain about, was that he was in the right place for once; a place where he was surrounded by supportive and encouraging Godly men and women. This was a safe place.

Jared never went to church with Macy. She only extended the invite a couple times.

Since Luke had the kids, Macy decided she should go looking around the area for houses. She wanted to live in the same town she grew up. The comfort of that constant stability was enticing to her and knew it was what she and the kids needed more than anything.

There was a new subdivision going up not far from where she grew up and even closer to the school and church. It was going to have soccer fields, baseball diamonds and swimming pools. This would be the perfect location. Macy began thinking through what she would need to buy her own house. She had a nice savings and wanted to keep it going. She was going to have some debt to pay off before she could even get a loan for a house, so she needed to get a plan in place for that. Macy hadn't even pulled her credit report in years. She had no credit cards, just her car payment. But there was also the fear that she wouldn't be able to even get a loan with her credit history and some of the debt (collections) that were inevitably lingering out there.

When Macy got home, her Grandma was coming in right behind her.

"Hi, Grandma!"

"Hi there, Macy."

"How was your day?"

"Oh, not bad! I got my grocery shopping done and had to run to the fabric store to get more batting for that quilt I'm making Uncle Tom and Aunt Kim. How was your day?"

"Good. I found a new subdivision on Highway Z that is under development. I love the location and the houses seem really cute too. It's called Meadow Oaks."

"Oh that sounds really nice. And, that's just a few miles away, too, so you'd still be close."

"Yep."

Macy and her Grandma sat down to the table as they both ate their dinner. Macy cleared their empty plates while her grandma warmed up her coffee and moved to her TV chair in the kitchen.

"Wheel of Fortune's on, Macy. You want to watch it with me?"

"Sure. Sounds fun."

They both took guesses as Vanna turned the random letters. Grandma was much better at it than Macy.

"So, Macy, I want to talk to you about something."

"Oh yeah? Okay."

"I've been doing a lot of thinking lately. Especially since that day we were all working in the rose garden. I've been thinking about selling this house. It's just too big for me and too much for me to take care of."

Macy understood why it would be too much for her. But then she started to feel anxious. *Is she telling me I have to move out? Does she not want me and the kids here anymore? It'd certainly be much easier to sell if we weren't all here.*

"I was thinking of selling it to your uncles, like Jonathan or Robert."

"Yeah that makes sense, Grandma."

"But, then I thought why not sell it to Macy?"

Macy's eyes grew wide and she needed to swallow but found it difficult as her mouth went instantly dry. She was waiting for the 'but.' Macy's grandma was smiling, a sly grin nonetheless.

"What? Me? Really, Grandma? I don't know. It should really go to the boys."

"Well, I've already talked to the boys and they are all completely okay and in agreement with selling the house to you."

"Oh my gosh, Grandma. I can't believe it. Seriously?! Do you know that day we were in the garden, I was thinking about this house too—how I would love to have the opportunity to keep it in the family. Although I could never do the job that you and Grandpa and the boys did. But, oh my gosh, I can't believe this!"

Macy jumped up and hugged her grandma feeling closer to her than ever. And at that same moment, she somehow felt as though her grandpa was there and feeling just as close.

"Oh, Macy, don't make such a fuss. I've already started looking for villas. So I'm just as excited to have something new built for me."

"Thank you so very much, Grandma! Thank you from the bottom of my heart."

The holidays were right around the corner and that meant...well, it meant a lot of things. It meant that undeniable sadness that came with sharing the kids over Thanksgiving and Christmas would make it's way through the door. This year even though Macy and Luke had Jared and Susan in their lives, the level of frustration and unhappiness was definitely higher than it had been years previously. There was the sadness and anger that came from the numerous conversations and arguments regarding the schedules Luke and Macy had. And then there was the coordinating of schedules with Susan and Jared—when would they have their kids and would they attend each other's extended family gatherings.

Macy typed up an e-mail to Luke. "I have the kids' letters to Santa. Here are the things they've asked for. Guess we need to figure out a time to talk about who should get what for them. The items in blue are what I'd like to get them. Give me a call later and we can talk more."

He replied just a few minutes later. "That's fine. I have a few things I'd like to get them that I had been thinking of too. I'll call you tonight after work."

It was supposed to be a happy time, but the heavy emotions were like a ton of bricks on both Macy and Luke's hearts. Things like divvying up the kids Christmas lists to alleviate duplicates (*Santa should know not to get two of the same thing*), pulling the kids from their playtime, family time or rest only to hop in the car and head of to another family event just wasn't the joyous time Luke and Macy would have preferred it to be; but it was the best compromise for all.

Amazingly, that Christmas came and went with only minor arguments between Luke and Macy. They both spent time with their families and their boyfriend's and girlfriend's families. And the kids were shuffled around in the mix. As kids usually are, they were in heaven with the abundance of gifts from all of the new families they were a part of. But they also were extremely crabby and bickered with one another—no doubt from the constant moving around and going from here to there and really never getting enough rest in between events. And, how could they really with so much stimulation in such a short period of time?

It was always hard to fully enjoy herself when Macy didn't have the kids. She was always pretty picky about what the kids ate. Chocolate was a rare treat and sweets were kept to a bare minimum. The kids didn't eat a lot as it was, so if they were going to eat she made sure it wasn't junk as often as possible. But she couldn't really monitor or enforce that rule when the kids were in other peoples' homes. One more worry that Macy lived with daily. Did they wash their hands; did they take a bath; did they brush their teeth; where did they sleep; what did they watch on TV; did they watch a movie that she wouldn't approve of? And the list went on and on.

But the worst part of all was the anticipation of what she'd hear from the kids when they'd return home—how much fun they were having with Daddy or Susan or her girls. Although that's all she longed for was for her babies to be happy, it was always so hard to hear them laughing in the background or how Daddy took them here or Susan gave them that. She was angry and jealous and, worse, she wanted to be with her ex-husband. She wanted him to want to get better and want to be with her.

Macy prayed that her heart would be healed. She prayed for Luke's heart and her babies...that they would all find peace and understanding somehow. Most importantly, she prayed for wisdom—wisdom on how to forgive and truly let go.

CHAPTER 13

"I Could Not Ask For More"
2000

As always, the New Year offered plenty of opportunity to celebrate with friends and ring in the year with new resolutions and beginnings; and perhaps endings. It was the year of Y2K, and despite all the fear and buzz that computer systems around the world would shut down and most likely put the world at a halt for who knows how long, they were merely that...plain old fears. Much testing, contingency planning and backup teams were put into action throughout the year to ensure we'd survive the turning of 1999 to 2000. Both Macy and Luke accepted the New Year as a time to reflect on the past hurts and move forward with plans to heal their hearts.

"Hey, Macy!"

"Hi, Jared. How are you?" Macy hesitated.

"Doing pretty good," he smiled over the phone. I was just thinking about you and wanted to call and tell you that.

"Well, that's nice of you." Macy grinned guiltily.

"I had a lot of fun at the New Year's Eve party, didn't you? Got a little crazy with those rounds of shots in the wee early hours. Did you feel okay the next day?" Jared had been her official date, picking her up and taking her home—the perfect gentleman.

"It was a lot of fun!" Macy laughed. "I wasn't feeling my best, but I managed. At least the kids let me sleep in some."

"Well, that's good. What are you doing today? Anything fun?"

"Nah. I think I'm going to help Grandma clean out some closets and then I'll probably go to Mass tonight so I can meet up with my family tomorrow. How about you?"

213

"I was thinking of taking the kids to see a movie. Not sure yet. I need to see what they're up to first."

"Alright. Sounds fun. I've got a date with Avery to play beauty shop in a few."

"C'mon, Mommy!" Avery called from the hall.

"I'm coming, Sweetie." Macy said to Avery pulling the phone below her chin.

"Jared, I better go. I'll call you later tonight."

"Okay, Macy! Talk to you then. Love you."

"Love you too." Macy hung up the phone but didn't let go of the receiver. *I don't love him. Why'd I say that? None of this is right.* She closed her eyes and hung her head as a teardrop fell.

"Mommy, let's go. I've got everything ready for our beauty shop," Avery pulled on Macy's belt.

"Oh okay, honey. I'm finished talking. Let's get beautiful." Macy wiped the tears from her eyes and let Avery lead her to the awaiting "salon."

Distance had found itself between Luke and Susan as well. Luke's focus and heart were just not in the relationship as it had been in the beginning. Isn't that the way it always goes? Those first weeks and months are filled with excitement and newness...new emotions and feelings come with a new set of lips to kiss, hands to hold, shoulders to hug, eyes to stare into, hair to comb fingers through, a new bed to share, terms of endearment to share, conversations and dates to have, memories to make and inevitably a new sense of loneliness and fear. But that all wears off. Especially when you realize it's just a void you're trying to fill.

"Hey Susan! What are you doing?"

"Nothing much. What are you doing?" Susan said, picking up Luke's call.

"I'm in the car...just dropped the kids off at my mom's. I'm going to join them in a little bit but had to run out to get a few things. I was wondering if you had a little time to chat with me. Are the girls with you or their dad?"

"Um, okay. Girls are with their dad, so I have some time. You coming here or do you want to meet somewhere?"

"Whatever you prefer. Not a big deal either way."

"Okay, well, just come on over then. The door's open when you get here."

Luke turned the corner and headed in Susan's direction. He pulled in the driveway and gave a giant sigh as he tried to swallow the knot in his throat.

"Hello?" Luke went on in.

Susan was at the kitchen table working on some homework.

"Hey there," Luke said, putting his hand on her shoulder. He leaned down to kiss her cheek.

"Well, hello." You could feel the tension; something was up.

"You doing homework?"

"Yeah, and it's not much fun either."

"Well, I don't mean to interrupt you. I just had some time and was thinking about... well, I thought I'd call and see if we could talk in person."

"Okay." Susan put her pencil down and straightened up in her chair.

"I'm curious...how are we?" Luke asked putting it—the 'distance' issue—right there on the table.

"How are we? What do you mean, Luke?"

Luke just raised his eyebrows and tilted his head. "Susan, you know what I mean. Things have been...*different* between us. Something's going on, and to be honest, I don't think it's just you. I have been trying to come to terms with a lot in my life lately and just want to figure it all out."

"I met someone, Luke." Susan just blurted it out.

"What? Um. Okay." Luke's eyebrows raised again, this time out of being completely taken off guard and with some disgust. "And, so, when did this happen?"

"A couple of weeks ago. At Walgreens."

"At Walgreens? You seriously met someone at Walgreens?"

"Yeah. We've been talking a lot and, well, I'm sorry I didn't say anything sooner. I just didn't know...well, I just didn't know what to say."

"Well, I guess that answers my questions. It's all good. I think it's time we called this off anyways. It's just not right. I guess it hasn't been for some time now. I didn't want to hurt you."

Luke stood up, pushed his chair in, and wished Susan well and walked out the door.

"Jared, what's up?" Macy asked as Jared picked up her call.

"Not a lot. What's up with you, Cutie?" Jared replied.

"Oh, just chillin' with the fam."

"How was your makeover?"

"Oh my gosh, Avery made me *so* beautiful." Macy laughed. "When I looked in the mirror, it was really hard to hold in my startled look."

"Haha, really? That scary, huh?"

"It was fun though. She's going to make a great artist someday!"

The silent pause was palpable.

"Macy, you there?"

"Oh yeah. Sorry. Just daydreaming." Macy was bored and wanted to be somewhere else. "Listen Jared, I need to talk to you about some stuff."

"Okay, what is it?"

Macy hesitated. "I need to be honest with you. My heart is somewhere else. As much as I care for you, I just don't feel as if this is right...if *we're* right anymore."

Jared was sitting on his deck, smoking a cigarette, silent. Macy heard him take a drag and exhale.

"I don't want to hurt you, Jared. You've been so good to me and I'm grateful for your friendship...something I don't want to lose. But, that's probably inevitable. I'm sorry."

"Why are you sorry?" Jared asked. "Macy, all I ever wanted was to make you happy. If that's not what I'm doing, then we shouldn't continue down this path."

"I know, Jared."

"I care about you, Macy."

"I have to go, Jared. I really am sorry!"

"Me too, Macy."

They hung up. Macy was sad but felt like she just dropped a one hundred pound weight off of her back. She cried that night out of guilt for getting into the relationship in the first place, for exposing the kids to something that came and went—one more example of instability and non-commitment.

"I Still Believe"
RECONNECTED

"Mommy, look at all that snow!" Travis yelled from the front window. Avery and Noah ran and jumped up on the couch alongside him.

Macy joined them. "It *is* a lot of snow! It's so pretty isn't it?"

Noah stared at his mommy. "Like you," he said with one those sweet grins of his.

"Oh, I love you my sweet Noah!!" Macy squeezed and kissed Noah's neck.

Noah beamed and chuckled from being ticklish.

"Come on, let's get to bed, kids."

After the kids were asleep, Macy got a call from Luke.

"Hello?"

"Hi Macy!" Luke melted a little when he heard her voice.

"Hi, Luke. How are you?"

"I'm really good, Macy. Really good."

"Well, that's awesome, Luke. I'm glad to hear that." Macy noticed something different in Luke's voice. "So what's going on? The kids are already asleep."

"Oh yeah, I figured they would be. I just wanted to call real quick and let you know that I was thinking of taking the kids sledding tomorrow at McClay Park. Would you be okay with that? I know it's your weekend, so I just wanted to check with you first before saying anything to the kids."

"Wow, really? Okay, well, that sounds like a lot of fun and I'm certain the kids would absolutely love it."

"Yeah, with all of this snow, they'll have a blast."

"Well, I'm not doing anything tomorrow, so I can bring them to you."

"Okay, that would be great. Thanks, Macy!"

"Sure. Thank you for asking."

"Okay, well, let's plan around noon at the park. Is that okay with you?"

"Yeah, that should work just fine."

"Well, I'll see you then."

"Okay...By the way, will Susan and the girls be there?"

Luke chuckled. "No, just me."

"Not that it matters if she was there or not but I thought if it was alright with you, I might hang around too. Sounds like a lot of fun. But I don't want to impose." Macy tried to not give away the real reason for asking if Susan would be there.

"Of course, Macy. That'd be great. I'm sure it will be awesome!"

The next morning, Macy couldn't wait to tell the kids what their daddy had planned for them that afternoon. She fed them breakfast and secretly pulled together snow clothes for them to wear. The kids had all been asking, "When can we play in the snow, Mommy? We want to make a snowman." Luke called and Macy got the kids in the circle and held the phone out so they could all hear Luke say, "We're going sledding this afternoon! There's a park nearby with a GIANT hill you can sled down!"

"Yes!" Travis yelled and ran to go get his coat and hat.

Avery jumped up and down laughing hysterically.

Noah jumped up and down with his sister.

"Alright, Luke, I'm getting them ready now. We'll see you in just a bit."

"Kids, listen. I already have all of your snow gear ready to go. So go into my room and find your things."

"Okay, Mommy!" They all screamed and laughed; a quick rush of little kid's feet ran across the room.

Macy and the kids pulled up and saw Luke waiting by the fire barrel. The kids ran in his direction as fast as they could in their puffy snowsuits and boots! "Hey kids!" Luke gave them all hugs.

"Look at those kids, Dad." Travis said, pointing across the way to all the kids sledding down the hill.

"I know, isn't that cool? I told you it was a giant hill."

"You weren't lying!" Travis said.

"Hi Macy," Luke gave her a smile and always wondered in times like these, *do I give her a hug or not?* He didn't.

"Hi, Luke. They are so dang excited. This is awesome."

"Good."

"Okay, kids, you ready? Let's head over to the other side so we can take on that giant hill."

"Yeah. Let's do it!" Travis exclaimed.

"Is your mom going to stay and watch?" Luke asked the kids, directing his question to Macy.

"Are you kidding? Of course, I wouldn't miss this for the world."

After many runs down the hill, Luke brought the kids back to their original meeting place.

"We figured it was time to come thaw out and warm up near the fire for a bit. And then maybe build a snowman. Right guys?"

"Yes! That was so fun, Mommy! You would've loved it." Travis said as Noah ran up to Macy and hugged her legs. She reached down to pick him up.

"Oh my goodness, your cheeks are freezing, Noah. Was it fun?"

"Mmhmm," Noah nodded his head.

"You want to build a snowman now?"

His eyes got big and Macy put him down so he could join Travis and Avery.

Luke was warming his hands at the barrel. "Holy cow, that's a workout."

"I bet! It was fun to watch," Macy smiled.

Luke looked back at her with a grin. "So how are things with you?" Luke asked.

"Pretty good. Work's good, Grandma's good. Did I tell you that Grandma found a villa? It's in a new subdivision so she is having a new one built. She's put a deposit down, but they won't start building until September. So, I'm getting started on the process for my home loan."

"Yeah? That's great."

"Thanks!"

"So, how is Jared?"

Macy got quiet for a second and thought about her response. Sometimes conversations like these felt like a competition between the two, as if one was better than the other if they were dating or whatever.

"Um, we broke up."

Luke quickly turned around, "You did?" he asked, somewhat surprised and more so relieved.

"Yeah, it just didn't feel right. It just felt like it was for all the wrong reasons." Macy was thinking to herself, *I'm supposed to be with you, not someone else.* "What about you and Susan? How is she?"

Luke stepped away from the barrel. "Well, we broke up too. She met someone else...in Walgreens of all places. But it was sort of in the coming, there had been a lot of distance between us the past couple of months."

"Wow, Luke. I'm sorry."

"Oh my gosh, don't be. I wasn't feeling right with it either, especially now that I've been at UPS and away from the restaurant and karaoke business. But probably mostly since I've been going back to church."

"Wait...you what? You're going to church? I've been going to church too!"

"Yeah, I know. That's awesome, Macy."

Macy felt a bit stupid; Luke knew the kids were at St. Patrick's. "Yeah, it's been great. Feels like home, ya know? Something normal and right for a change."

"Exactly! I completely agree. I'm playing drums again and singing on the worship team." Luke's mind was going a mile a minute. He didn't want this time to end. It was the first time in such a long time that he and Macy enjoyed each other's company and wanted to hear about each other's new beginnings and share in the encouragement. It felt so good to see the joy in her eyes.

This made Macy so happy but so sad at the same time. She was so full of emotion that she just wanted to cry.

"Luke, I'm so happy for you. That's really, really good to hear!"

It was cold being outside in the snow all that time, but Macy didn't notice. The emotions and thoughts made her heart race as the blood pumped quickly through her arms and legs and fingers and toes.

The two just stared at each other for a brief moment. Both feeling something very familiar: it hadn't died...it had just been locked away for so very long. The emotions created a curiosity within each of them. *What is happening? Who is this standing next to me? I feel like I've known them my entire life, and I recognize them; but then again, I don't.* His eyes were much clearer and brighter than Macy remembered.

"Maybe we should be calling it a day? The kids look exhausted." Macy broke the silence looking over at the kids plopped down in the snow.

"Yeah, I guess you're right. Come on, kids. We need to get you back home to warm up."

"Aw, but we don't want to go home yet," Travis whined.

"I know, but it's going to get dark soon, and besides, I have some hot cocoa waiting for us when we get home!"

"Oh alright." Avery said. "Come on, Noah."

Luke helped get the kids and all of their things in the car. He walked over to Macy's door and shut her door for her. She rolled down the window a bit.

"It was a good day," Luke smiled.

"It was. It really was," Macy smiled back.

"Love you, kids."

"I love you, Daddy," They all yelled back.

"Thanks for going sledding with me."

"Thank you, Daddy!"

"Talk to you later."

"Bye, Macy."

It was difficult falling asleep that evening. Macy and Luke would both find themselves lost in their thoughts, trying to make sense of some of the emotions that were resurfacing within each of them. While feeling joy and pride for the positive changes they both admitted to, there was also a wave of complete amazement at the timing of the day's conversation and the event in general that washed over them both. This would be a moment reminiscent of that night they first met almost thirteen years ago.

It had been a couple weeks since their sledding outing when Luke called Macy to ask if she'd be up to meeting so they could talk. Macy agreed to meet somewhere in the middle and preferably just the two of them. They decided to meet on a Sunday afternoon at the empty parking lot near the train tracks and sat in Macy's car and talked.

"Hey!" Luke said as he jumped in the passenger seat and quickly closed the door.

"Hurry. It's freezing out there." Macy replied.

"Very." Luke said. "How are you doing?" He asked, excitedly and a bit nervously.

"Pretty good. How 'bout you?"

"I'm great! I'm really glad you agreed to meet with me."

"Well, sure. What's up?"

"I don't know, Macy. The other day at the park was...well, it was...I can't really explain it. I've been thinking about it a lot, though."

Macy turned her stare back out the windshield now, "Yeah, me too."

"You have? I was so hoping you would say that."

"Yeah. To hear that you were back at church and playing and singing, it was awesome. I'm so happy for you and proud of you, Luke."

Luke stared and smiled with that sweet grin of his.

"The weird part is that we weren't trying to seek the other out; and well, that's not like us. You called because you wanted to take the kids out. I decided to tag along, and then, next thing we know it, we're learning about how each of us is trying to better our lives; that we were doing the same things...especially seeking God."

"That's what I was thinking about too. What do you think it means, Macy? All I know is that I can't stop thinking about that afternoon, and well, you. I can't stop thinking about *you*. I miss you so much."

Macy had tears in her eyes. She knew just how genuine he was being. This wasn't a game anymore. This was something their hearts had fought with for years—how do you love someone so very much but not hurt them.

"Luke, I'm not sure what any of this means? My mind is fearful of what my heart is most likely feeling. I don't know that I can survive going down that path again, that path that we've been on more than I care to admit."

Luke just stared at her. Looking in her eyes full of sadness and longing.

"I miss you too, Luke," Macy said as she took his hand.

It was like lightning all over again; the undeniable connection that came from their touch; like electricity sending paralyzing jolts through their veins going straight to their hearts.

With their hands still clenched together, Luke kissed Macy's hand. "You smell so good," he said. "What do we do now?"

"I'm not sure, Luke. I need to think all of this through." Macy still felt scared, like she still wanted—needed—to protect her heart. "I don't want to be heartbroken by you. I just can't go through that ever again." *But I truly have never stopped loving you.* She thought to herself.

"Yes, I agree. I don't ever want to hurt you again. I never did. I mean...I know that I did, but my intentions were never to hurt you."

The day they talked just so happened to be their original anniversary, one more odd phenomenon. Was it a sign? Macy couldn't shake the overwhelming feeling of divine intervention taking place right before her eyes.

Macy spent the next weeks praying.

"Dear God. What is happening? The only man I've ever loved is becoming the man I've always hoped he'd be, the man you intended for him to be. Thank you for getting him the job at UPS. Thank you for bringing him back to church. I'm just so grateful. I still love him. I've never stopped. Is it your will for us to reconcile? What if I get hurt all over again? What if he relapses and falls back into gambling? What am I supposed to do? In Jesus' name. Amen"

Luke prayed too. *"Father God, You are the provider of all things. You are the truth, the way and the light. Thank you for all you have done for me and for Macy and our babies. Thank you for keeping them healthy and sweet. Thank you for taking care of Macy while I couldn't be there to do it. I pray your Holy Spirit guide me, to help me understand these feelings that are surfacing, guide me to your will,*

Father. I only want to glorify you. Help me with my struggles...I want to learn to follow your way. Praise your son, Jesus' holy name. Amen"

He decided to write Macy a letter...

> Macy,
>
> Well, here it is! The letter that will probably change everything. This is the second letter that I've attempted to write to you, but all of my thoughts and feelings are knotted up. Like a double knot on the kids' shoes or something. I don't know what the hell is wrong with me, but I cannot sleep...at all!! It's now 4:15AM, and I've just left you a message on your office line—like an idiot. But I just don't know how to sort all of these feelings out.
>
> First off, I will never forget the conversation I had with my cousin Billy almost two years ago. He said, "Luke, do what feels 'right' in your life, not what feels 'good.'" Macy, so many times (up until now), we did what felt good. Or perhaps, for the moment! Do you agree? We've always (mostly) pacified each other, made each other feel safe inside our little world. While all along knowing that outside there was just complete chaos! Ya know? But lately, so much of my heart and <u>soul</u> has believed that you and I are just, <u>right</u>! I just cannot deny this feeling, and will not!
>
> Second, our kids. My God, Macy, what can I say? It is just so right for you and I to <u>raise</u> <u>our</u> <u>kids</u>... TOGETHER!!! We both have the same common interest in our children. We share 99% of the same goals for them. Also, we both want to nurture them in an environment that perhaps neither one of us has come to know. I feel completely confident about you and I being such a great <u>team</u> for them, don't you?
>
> My God, this letter might be a bad idea. Or I might be crossing some sort of boundary with you. But I just can't deny this <u>hole</u> in my heart, Macy. I sincerely believe that you are my first and <u>true</u> love!! My best friend through so much. I'm not necessarily asking you for a chance, if you will. But simply to consider all that's been said. By me, you, God, and maybe any other outside source. I'm so <u>in</u> <u>love</u>

with you, Macy! I hope that you can somehow find a way to love me the way that I love you. That totally sounds like an ultimatum or something. Please don't take it that way, okay? I just need you to know how I feel and what my heart says.

You know, I'm obviously overwhelmed too, as you can see. This is my way of dealing with it, I guess. I want so badly to say that I'll always be there for you, I really do. I guess we'll just have to see.

Your best friend and true love,

Luke

It was Macy's birthday and the one thing she wanted and needed the most was some time to herself. She bought a round trip train ticket to Illinois. Macy brought a book to read but found herself staring out the window replaying thoughts and past events from her and Luke's divorce to the very recent events spent with Luke. In addition to Luke's letter, they had been talking on the phone fairly regularly and had seen each other a couple times since their 'talk' in Macy's car.

The feelings of sadness and pain from lying and gambling were still very fresh in her mind. *He lied to me. He left me and his kids too many times. He kept us from being able to pay our bills or have a home together. He has a problem with addiction.*

Despite all those hurtful memories, it didn't erase the immense love and connection she felt with Luke. *But I just love him so much. He's the only man that knows me, really knows me. And, I'm the only one that really knows him. I want to be a part of him and a part of his life. We are one, and I don't think anything can ever separate that...not anything.*

Lastly, Macy thought about their babies—Travis, Avery and Noah. She felt sad for their hearts, their innocence and all that they had seen from their mom and dad. All of the fighting and screaming, too much anger and instability and not enough love and protection. They deserved so much better. She then remembered the night during the Christmas holiday that Travis had been more honest with her than she anticipated.

"Did you get everything you wished for this year, Travis?" she had asked.

"Well, yeah. All but one thing." Travis replied.

"Oh yeah? What's that?"

"I wished that you and Daddy would get back together and we could all live together again." It broke her heart to pieces. *Why can't I give this to my son?*

She remembered her reply. "I wish we could too, Travis. I wish things would've worked out the way I had hoped. I guess sometimes things just don't go the way we plan."

What an unsettling feeling. How could that have ever been resolved with him, she wondered? How could she ever help him through his sadness when she was feeling the very same thing?

Then Macy's mind took her thoughts to her grandma and their parents. *Oh my gosh! What are my parents going to think? They're going to think I've absolutely lost my mind. I've had to convince them to basically hate Luke.* She told herself. *If I tell them that he and I are back together, will they disown me? Oh dear God, what do you want me to do? Why is this even happening? I just want off this roller coaster. And what about church? I'm at St. Pat's and he's at Calvary—two radically different churches.*

After Macy received Luke's letter, she invited Luke to go to Mass with her and the kids. He had never been to a Catholic mass and truly had no idea what to do. He watched Macy for cues on what was coming up. If she pulled the kneeler down, he was ready to kneel. But then she'd stand and then she'd kneel. Luke would catch himself as he was thinking it was time to sit but instead kneel. He and Macy laughed about it after church. He would tell her how confused he was and ask, "What were those petition things again? I wasn't following."

In turn, Macy went to service with Luke a number of times (and secretly loved it). The music was current and alive and so was the message. They did things called dramas where they would act out a little scene that applied to the sermon. She loved how the service wasn't infused with memorized hymns or prayers, but the arts. People stood and raised their hands to God when they felt led, when the spirit was in their hearts. They clapped to the music, and most importantly, Travis, Avery and Noah loved the children's worship area. They had their own age-appropriate service while the adults were in the main church. But Macy's favorite part by far was getting to hear Luke play drums and sing. He was truly amazing.

When Macy got home from her trip to Illinois, she showered and then slipped into bed with her ear buds and music. *I just need to stop thinking about it all for a while. Stop analyzing and just allow these emotions and thoughts to work themselves out and, most importantly, get a decent night's sleep. I just want to get to sleep for once!*

Without Macy's knowing, Luke had gone to see Peter & Leanne. He had an agenda and greatly feared what the potential reaction and response would be from them; but he tried very hard to just say what he had to say and not have any expectation.

"So, what's going on Luke?" Peter initiated the conversation as they all took their seats; Peter on his recliner, Leanne on her spot on the couch, and Luke on the love seat across from Leanne.

"Well, actually a lot. So, I'm just going to say it. I'm here to tell you how sorry I am for all of the mistakes and hurt that I've caused. I never intentionally wanted to hurt anyone...especially Macy."

"Mmmhmm," Leanne was shaking her head in agreement.

"But, truth is...I still love her with everything I am and I don't want to live without her. I want to be her husband and I want nothing more than to take care of her and our babies."

"And, what's different this time, Luke. You know we've heard this before."

"Right, why should we believe you now?" Leanne chimed in.

"You shouldn't, I guess. You have nothing to go by other than my word and I know that's not worth much of anything to you, understandably. I can only say to please try to forgive me and trust me when I say that I love your daughter with all of my heart and that I have changed."

"It's going to take some time, Luke. That's all I can give you at this very moment," Peter said with that deep authoritative voice he had in times like these.

"I appreciate that... very much." He shook Peter's hand and gave Leanne a quick hug as she continued sitting on the couch.

Luke cried on his drive home, mainly from the nervousness and stress he had been holding back. *I've hurt their daughter—and all of them—and they're afraid to trust me again. I've got so much making up to do. I hope I can do this.* Luke took a shower and climbed into bed after tuning his radio to their favorite station. He laid there trying to forget Peter's rigid body language and tough scowl and Leanne's sad eyes and downcast face. Instead, he pictured Macy's face next to his and dreamt about her eyes and smile and her heart. As hard as it was going to be seeking forgiveness from Macy's parents, it was the right thing to do. Luke was proud of himself for standing up for his love for Macy and wanted to tell her about the visit but kept it a secret from her as he didn't want his intentions to be misinterpreted. This was between Luke and Macy's parents and nothing more.

"Hey, lil' mama!"

"Hey, sweetie!"

"How's your day going?"

"It's okay. How's your day going?"

"Good." Luke replied with intriguing enthusiasm.

"What are you so cheery for?"

"No reason. So, hey...I want to cook you dinner. Why don't you come over Friday night after work and I'll make you dinner and we can watch a movie or something."

"You want to make me dinner? Geez what the heck for? And, what about the kids?"

"My mom wants to take them to the Easter play they're doing at the church. I was going to ask if you wanted to go to it with me on Sunday, but anyways...about dinner. See you Friday?"

"Haha. Yes, sounds wonderful!"

Luke prepared his 'famous' chicken parmesan, fettuccini alfredo, and salad. He had candles lit and wine chilled. And the very familiar song, the same he played for her that afternoon in her dad's apartment, was playing in the background, 'Here and Now.'

"Wow, Luke! What have you got going here?"

"Hey, Beautiful!" Luke kissed her lips. "Perfect timing. I'm just getting the chicken out of the oven and the wine is poured. You want to have a seat and I'll get your plate."

"This all looks amazing and smells absolutely wonderful!"

"I hope you like it!"

Luke served her a plate and handed her a glass of wine as he sat down. "Let me bless the meal for us."

They both bowed their heads and closed their eyes while Luke thanked God for this time with Macy. "Thank You for this meal and help it to bless our bodies. Bless this time we have together, Father, and keep our hearts focused on You and Your will. Thank You so much for my best friend and mother of my children. May You continue to bless our lives with forgiveness and graciousness. In Your holy son, Jesus Christ's name. Amen."

"Amen."

"Dig in. Oh wait." Luke picked up his glass. Macy followed. "Cheers to you and me and new beginnings." They clinked glasses.

"Oh my gosh, Luke, this is amazing." Trying not to talk with her mouth full (one of Luke's biggest pet peeves), Macy was oozing over the Chicken Parmesan. "It's delicious. I have never had anything like this. You did an awesome job!"

"Thanks! Do you really like it?"

"Yes. Yes!! I love it!"

The two finished their meal and then moved into the living room. They took the wine and had an indoor picnic on the carpet. They talked—and kissed—and talked some more.

"Luke, listen. We need to talk."

"Yeah, I agree. We really do."

"If we're going to do 'this' again, we have to do it right. I can't have the past repeat itself again. I just can't go through that. And, more importantly, I can't put the kids through it. It's so not fair to them."

"Macy, I couldn't agree more and have been thinking about this a lot, probably too much. I thought *maybe* we could go see Pastor Eric to get his advice and help? He already knows some of our past and could help us not go down that road again. What do you think?"

"I think it's worth a try. I do. I'd like to seek counsel and he would be a good one to go to."

"Okay. I'll set up a time to meet with him."

"Thank you! For all of this. It's wonderful!"

"Thank you. I'm so in love with you, Macy. I want to take care of you. I hope you know that I have always loved you and always will."

"I'm so in love with you too, Luke. I always have been. I want you to take care of me. More than you know."

"Luke and Macy! It's so good to see you. How are you guys doing?" Pastor Eric asked as he took his seat behind his desk and Luke and Macy took their seats in the chairs across from him.

"Pretty good," Macy spoke up first, looking over at Luke with 'was that ok?'

Luke smiled back at Macy and nodded. "So, Eric, you know our history."

"Mmmhmm." Pastor Eric nodded.

"You know the problems I've had with gambling and what that ultimately did to our marriage. Well, we need your help. We want to work on reconciling our marriage. But this time, we want to do it right. And under wise counsel."

Pastor Eric smiled, "I am so very proud of you two. This is just absolutely wonderful news! I do know what you've been through, and I will tell you that it's not going to be easy."

"Yeah, we know that. It's already hard," Macy replied.

"So what do we do? How do we make it right this time?"

"I'd like to place you in a marriage group and a care group; but most importantly, I want you to start seeing a counselor. I'd like you to go to Stephen Brighton. He's a Christian counselor and I'm sure you'll both like him." He pulled his business card out of his Rolodex and handed it to them. "I'll give him a call to let him know that you will be calling him."

"Sounds good." Luke reached across the desk to take the business card. "Thanks, Eric!"

The following Wednesday evening was their first night at marriage group.

Luke and Macy anxiously walked up to the front door. They barely knocked before Mrs. Gabel opened the door. The Texan woman with big blonde hair and a giant smile extended her arms, "Welcome! You must be Luke and Macy. Aren't you two the cutest thing! Please come in and make yourself at home. This is my husband Jim. I call him Mufasa." Macy's shyness caused her to welcome the hug with grave hesitation.

Jim, the large Texan man with a gentle voice, extended his hand to greet them both. "So very nice to have you here. Come on in and I'll introduce you to the others."

There were snacks on the table, candles lit, and two chairs set right in front of the fireplace in the living room along with boxes of Kleenex in every corner. "You two sit here," Linda (Mrs. Gabel) pointed to the two chairs. "You'll be in the hot seat for a bit 'cause we wanna get to know y'all!" Luke and Macy just looked at each other, smiled, and telepathically passed a message to each other, 'what'd we get ourselves into?'

Everyone sat down and Jim began to tell the new couple how this group just started a marriage study and this was their second week into it. "So when Pastor Eric called us to let us know that you would like to participate with us, we figured we'd just take this time tonight to get to know you and for you to get to know the group."

"We'll let you two start," Linda chimed in joyfully. And, while looking to the others in the group, "then we'll all share a little bit about ourselves with you. Sound okay?"

"Um sure." Luke looked to Macy.

"Sure okay. I'll start," said Macy.

Luke and Macy both took some time sharing details from their extremely chaotic and destructive time together—having babies very early, the gambling, never having any money or a place to live, separation and then finally divorce. And, of course, the even more emotionally devastating times and experiences during their divorce. But, then they shared the more recent divine developments that led them to the Gabel's home that evening.

The group listened intently and was truly amazed that the couple was literally sitting in front of them that evening. Tears were shed and as scary as it was to tell these complete strangers their story, Luke and Macy felt a sense of comfort and finally felt as though they were supported and heard.

The rest of the group shared a little bit about themselves and then Jim prayed for Luke and Macy and the rest of their group. They opened up the prayer time for anyone to jump in with a prayer request or if they had anything they wanted to give to God. This was exactly what Macy had been yearning for.

Not too much was said the morning Luke and Macy made their first trip out to Stephen Brighton's office. Macy's Aunt Joan had passed away that Wednesday, on Luke's birthday and the hurt and pain was still very fresh in Macy's heart and mind. She was Macy's favorite aunt, so full of life and always laughing. Macy had so many fond memories with her Aunt Joan and her passing was just too soon for anyone in the family to deal with.

"I just can't believe she's gone," Macy said.

"I know, baby. I'm so very sorry. I know how much you loved her, how much our kids loved her."

"Yeah," she said as she looked down at her hands in her lap—she turned them over to look at her palms and then the tops of her hands. Macy kept playing over her uncle's sweet words towards his Joan, his best friend in the world. He loved her so much and just couldn't believe she was gone and how he'd live life without her in it. Macy kept thinking about those words while Luke drove to Mr. Brighton's. She'd stare at Luke and knew in her heart that she wanted him in her life. She didn't want to live life without him in it—as her best friend and father of her children.

This was now the second person in her life that she was with on their deathbed. It was such a scary thing but somehow she felt like she fulfilled something for each of them; both times were just completely life-changing experiences. But nonetheless, their family had lost an amazing woman who struggled to keep her pain and hurt left along the sidelines while she was always there for everyone else. She was funny and smart and had a light and enthusiasm about her that no one could match. No one.

They walked into the small house that was converted into an office and sat down in the waiting area. A tan, dark-haired man in glasses came into the room, "Luke and Macy? Hi, I'm Stephen Brighton. Why don't you come on back." He turned and directed them to his office.

"Here, you can have a seat there," he pointed to the pillow-filled loveseat, while he had a seat in his leather high-back desk chair.

Luke and Macy settled into their seats and fidgeted a bit with the pillows to get comfortable. Macy put one on her lap and Luke put the one that was behind him on the floor.

"So what brings you in today?" Stephen started the conversation, sensing the tension and anxiety amidst the two.

Luke looked at Macy and then at Stephen. "Well, we want to know how to make our marriage work. We've been divorced for almost four years now, and we are considering going down that path again...but, we want to do it right this time."

"Okay, do you feel the same way, Macy?"

"I do." She replied. "But I can't fathom getting remarried only to be hurt like we've been in the past."

They continued their session explaining a little of what's been going on with them the past couple months. Stephen ended the session by making their next appointment, "I'd like to see you next week. Does that work for you?" They both agreed and then Stephen said, "Okay, let me pray for you."

Luke and Macy would continue to see Mr. Brighton weekly.

"Honey, I can't tell you how excited I am about what's happening. For all that we have—all the support and encouragement." Luke squeezed Macy's hand.

"I agree. I keep asking myself if it's all a dream. We're finally getting all we hoped for and I pray we can make the best of it and not take it for granted." She stretched over the car seat to kiss his cheek and lay her head on his shoulder.

"I guess we need to tell some folks what's going on, huh?" Luke kissed her forehead.

"Yeah, I've been thinking about that too. I'm most worried about my grandma. I am afraid I got her all excited about having the kids baptized and First Communion planning, etc. I hope she's accepting of my, of our decision. She's the last person I want to disappoint or upset; especially with all that's she's done for me and the kids."

"I hear you, honey," Luke replied. "It's all going to be okay. God's on our side!"

Macy decided to have a conversation with her grandma that evening. "Grandma, I need to talk to you about some stuff."

"Okay. What is it?"

"Well, Luke and I have been talking again, as I'm sure you have noticed. And, well, we really want to work on fixing our relationship."

"Yes, it's not hard to notice you're both spending a lot of time together recently."

"It's scary. But, we're doing everything we can to get the necessary support and help to do it right. We're going to a marriage group now and a care group and we started seeing a marriage counselor today."

"That's really good, Macy. I'm proud of you for getting some help and support. You still want to buy the house, though, right?"

"Oh my gosh, absolutely. Nothing's changed with that!"

"Okay, good."

"Grandma, there's one thing that I'm really worried about now that all of this is happening with Luke and I. It's about church. We're not going to go to St. Patrick's anymore. We'll still be going to church and all. We're just going to go to Calvary—the church Luke sort of grew up in." Macy took a deep breath as she finished her sentence, bracing herself for Grandma's response.

"Macy, I understand. You can't very well do both now can you? I'm just glad that you're going to church—it doesn't matter which church you go to."

"Really, Grandma? You're okay with it."

"Macy, I can't tell you what to do. You have to make your own decisions in life. I appreciate your concern for me, but again, I'm just proud of you for going to church."

"Thanks, Grandma! You once again have been such a great support to the kids and me and I am so very grateful for all you've done and continue to do. Thank you so much!"

"For The First Time"
RECONCILED

The next couple months were filled with care group meetings, marriage group meetings and counseling sessions. Counseling was not fun at times, however. Luke and Macy would have scream-fits in the car on the ride home. It was just so very hard hearing the 'honest-to-God' truth and reliving some of the pain that forced them apart.

Along with all of the heavy rebuilding they had before them, there were also many fun events, too. One was planning Luke's 30th birthday party. Macy threw him a surprise party with all of their family and new friends. Macy's gift to him was a scheduled vasectomy at the local urologist. They had both talked about it and agreed it was the best way to go. "I'm pretty confident that God has given us all the babies we can handle and this surgery was part of His plan," Macy confirmed. They were doing all of these things—care groups, church, counseling—with the intent to get married again; their love and attraction for one another was inevitable, so this decision was one more area to make their future right.

While all of these things were going on between Luke and Macy, they did do what they could to keep it all discreet for their kids' sake. They were concerned for their tiny hearts and didn't want them to be overly excited or worried for their mom and dad. They saw their dad at church and he still took them places, just the four of them. And, of course, there were times he would come over to watch a movie or share a meal with them. But the times they were all together, there was definitely a peace in the atmosphere—a sense of togetherness and being connected again.

Luke's cousin was a photographer and she had offered to take photos of Luke and Macy and the kids after a recent conversation the two had had at Luke's surprise party.

"I guess we have never had a family photo taken." Macy said to Luke.

"You're right! Other than those candid shots taken at your sister's wedding or over the holidays," Luke replied.

"True. And those were taken so long ago. I wish we could get some photos taken, especially before we all lose our summer tans."

"Well, I just might know someone," Luke smiled.

Macy found them all coordinating outfits. The boys wore bright orange tops and Macy and Avery wore bright yellow tops and Luke wore a bright orange polo with thin bright yellow stripes. They boys wore khaki pants and the girls wore khaki capris.

They met at Kim and Liam's house during the later afternoon when the sun would be setting to the backside of their lush backyard—creating the perfect backdrop for their photo session.

Kim and Liam both took shots of just Luke and Macy, Luke and the kids, Luke and the boys, Macy and the boys, Macy and Avery, just the kids and, of course, the entire family—every possible combination. The kids were so good despite all of the 'move here, look there, fix your shirt, pull your pant leg down (we don't want to see your socks), and all the other annoying, but necessary, instructions the photographer gave them and not to mention the very warm weather.

It was just a couple weeks later that Kim and Liam had Luke and Macy over for a family dinner. They finished dinner and went outside to sit on the patio to relax. Kim handed Macy a photo album filled with all of the shots from their photo session. Macy couldn't hold back the tears. She slowly opened the cover to the 5x7 photo of all five of them, a bit nervous to look at them. They were beautiful! Absolutely beautiful. It's as if she were looking at her family in a new light for the first time, the way she had been dreaming of for so long.

She continued to turn the pages, hoping she wouldn't start bawling. You could practically feel the warm sun coming off the prints and their smiles were so big and bright, they gleamed; everyone was glowing. *Now that's one happy family,* she thought to herself. "Kim, thank you so very much! I can't even begin to tell you what this means to me. You have captured the kid's smiles and innocence perfectly. I can see our happy family more now than ever. I'm so excited for our future together. Thank you, thank you!!" Macy spewed graciousness all over Kim and Liam.

Luke had tears in his eyes too. He loved seeing Macy happy and tonight was a level of happiness he may have never seen from her. She was beaming with joy. It reaffirmed all over again his longing desire to make her and keep her happy for the rest of their lives...and not letting *anything* come between them.

By August, they had planned a family animal-themed stay-cation. Luke and Macy both took the week off of work to first take the kids to a drive-through animal park in a town that was about two hours away. Macy suggested renting a car, "I'm not driving my car through a park that has buffalo and zebras just roaming about." It was a good thing too, because when you entered the park, you could buy bags of feed to give to the animals, which they of course did.

Not two minutes into their drive through the park, there was pack of goats that made their way for the car, so they stopped to feed them. The goats just knew to go to the car to get food. They'd fearlessly stick their heads up to the car windows, sniffing out food.

The best part of driving through the animal park was when a buffalo came up to the car and literally stuck it's head, horns and all, in the driver side window where Luke was waving food.

Macy yelled, "Drive, Luke! Get out of here now. The dang thing is going to climb into the car with us!"

Luke laughed his head off out of nervousness. The kids didn't know whether to be scared or laugh along with him. "Oh my gosh. Look at the size of his tongue!" Luke exclaimed as he gave the buffalo some feed pellets and then drove off.

They laughed the entire day thinking about that giant buffalo head being inside the car. "His head was as big as Noah's entire body," Travis said and made everyone laugh.

They spent another day at the zoo; another day at an aquarium; and one more day at Grant's Farm with more goats. Luke and Macy finished out the week taking a weekend trip to the Lake of the Ozarks, just the two of them.

They drove with the windows down and music playing. Macy had made reservations at a little hotel that was on the lake and had a pool. They checked in and got their key. As they both walked into the quaint little room, they dropped their bags and Luke grabbed Macy around the waist and turned her so she was facing him and the two kissed.

"Wow!" Macy said smiling.

Luke smiled back, "How 'bout we go check this place out."

They walked through the back lot and down the hill to see the dock. There was a sign advertising daily boat rentals, so they decided they'd take a day and get out on the lake. "Let's do this tomorrow," Luke said.

"Okay, sounds fun to me. Wait...do you know how to drive a boat?" Macy asked.

Luke was wondering if she was joking and felt a bit insulted, so he quickly responded, "What? Yes, I know how to drive a boat."

"Okay, just checking." Macy smiled.

"Let's go get a bite to eat over at the little seafood place I saw next door."

They made the walk to the restaurant. The place was empty. Luke and Macy both ordered a beer and a shrimp dinner and enjoyed their meal along with light-hearted laughter and sweet hopes for their future. When they got back to their room, they decided to go for a swim. The water was warm but so were their lips as they kissed and hugged and wrapped their arms and legs around each other. It would be the first night they spent together in which they both felt was much longer than they care to admit.

The next morning, Luke went to the office to secure a boat rental. He returned with a key and some snacks. Macy was all ready to go. They spent the whole day on the lake—much longer than they had anticipated.

"Luke, look at all those little fish jumping behind the boat," Macy yelled over the engine.

Luke looked back, "What the heck?"

"Are you slowing down?" She asked as she saw a couple fishermen waving at them and shaking their head. She couldn't hear what they were saying, but she read their mouths, "No, you can't go there."

"What is the deal?" Luke asked, confused.

At that point, some guy at a nearby campsite was yelling too, "You can't go that way, dude. Get out of there."

"What are they talking about, Luke?"

"Oh my gosh, Macy. We're in the mud!"

"What? In the mud?"

Luke turned off the engine and went over to the side of the boat. "I'm going to have to dig us out." He said, as he took his shoes off and hopped over the side of the boat. But when he jumped in, there was no splash, nothing. He was standing – on the water. It was like he jumped out onto flat land or something. They were in the mud alright and the water was only about four inches deep.

246 • amy jo hawkins
Macy laughed hysterically, "Oh my gosh, seriously? How the
heck did we get this far on four inches of water?!" Macy couldn't
stop laughing at the sight of Luke jumping over the side only to be
standing on the water.

"Well that's obviously why those little fish were jumping all
over the place." Luke laughed, too, as he started digging out mud
from the prop.

One of the guys from the campsite decided to help Luke. Once
they were freed from the mud and could push the boat into deeper
water, the fishermen yelled across the lake to direct Luke where to
drive. They got back into deeper water but not without a little bit
of hurt pride. "How embarrassing! How are people supposed to
know not to go that way?" Luke asked sarcastically.

Macy just laughed.

Luke and Macy would finish their trip with an intimate dinner
at a nice Italian place down the street from their hotel. They sat at
one of the back tables and held hands across the table.

"Luke, is everything okay? You seem a little out of it." Macy
said to Luke.

"Yeah, baby, I'm fine." Luke responded. He had something up
his sleeve, a surprise, but didn't want her to notice quite yet.

They were eating their wonderful meal and sharing toasts,
gazes and loving conversation.

"I've had a really good time with you this weekend, Macy."
Luke shared.

"Oh, me too, Luke. I'm really glad we were able to get away
just the two of us."

"I've really enjoyed the past months with you too. It's been
wonderful rekindling our relationship and spending time working
on making it better, making it right. And I just love our kids so
much, Macy. I love you more than anything; you and the kids are
everything to me."

"I know you do and that we are, Luke." Macy was wondering what was up with him...he seemed so nervous about something. She was hoping it was about—

"I want to ask you something," he said as he reached down into his lap and put a little black box on the table. "Macy, will you marry me? I can't imagine my life without you, and I want to share it with you and only you."

The joy overwhelmed her and, without any thought, she leaned over the table and got in Luke's face and said, "Absolutely, I will marry you!" and she kissed him. "Yes, Yes, Yes!"

Luke took out the ring and put it on Macy's finger. "It's gorgeous," she replied.

By this time, most of the restaurant was clapping and cheering for the newly engaged couple. They all raised their glasses as Luke and Macy joined them in a toast. "To her saying, Yes!" a man at the table next to them yelled. "Cheers!" they all said as they clinked glasses.

Macy couldn't wait to get home and tell one person in particular of this news. "Travis is going to be overwhelmed, Luke. I mean...they all will be ecstatic, but Travis was the one who shared his dream of us getting back together. We get to make his dream come true, Luke!"

"He's going to be so happy."

"I can't wait to tell him."

After saying their hellos to all of the kids, Macy and Luke went into Macy's bedroom and called for Travis.

"Travis, would you come in here for a minute, please."

"Okay, coming." Travis yelled from the living room.

"Hey buddy, your mom and I want to talk to you about something."

They all sat on the bed. Macy started the conversation.

"Travis, remember what you said to me over Christmas when I asked if you got everything you wanted?"

"Um, I think so." Travis thought about it looking at his dad and then back at Macy. "Oh, I said that I wanted you and dad to get back together." Travis was confused, wondering why his mom was asking.

"Well, your daddy proposed to me today and do you know what that means?"

Travis thought for a second and then said, "That he asked you to marry him?" he asked, eyes wide and big smile. "Are you getting married?"

Luke and Macy looked at each other and then Luke confirmed Travis' answer.

"Yes. Your mom and I are going to get married and we're all going to be together again. Is that okay with you?"

Travis had tears in his eyes. "Oh my gosh, Yes! I'm so excited. Can I tell Avery and Noah?"

"Well, why don't you let us do that. We wanted to tell you first because we know how hard all of this has been on you; how hard it's been on all of us. But we're working on it and want to make it right again." Luke said while Macy sat staring at these two beautiful men before her. It wasn't just Travis' dream coming true, it was hers too and it was all starting to set in.

"Okay!" Travis said.

"I love you so much, Travis," Macy hugged him.

"I love you too, Mommy!"

Luke leaned over to hug them both and kissed them on their heads.

The following few months were jam packed with wedding plans. Luke and Macy decided the perfect time for their wedding would be November 25th, the weekend following Thanksgiving. What more could they be thankful for than the reconciliation of their marriage and so much more. Macy was still just a bit worried that three months would be too short of time to get everything done, but Luke was adamant about sooner than later—exclaiming that he had no desire to live in sin and was ready to move forward with their future.

Macy asked her sister Kyle to be her matron of honor and youngest sister, Merriam, and her good friend from work to be bridesmaids. Avery would be her junior bridesmaid. Luke asked his cousin, Shane, to be his best man as well as sing a couple songs, and his younger brother, Jason, and good friend, Bill, to be groomsmen. Travis would be his junior groomsman and Noah would be their ring bearer.

A mother of one of the couples in their marriage group was a seamstress, so she made the bridesmaids dresses for her. Macy found the exact wedding gown she had been envisioning at a local bridal shop and it was on sale! Her mom made her veil and Avery's dress.

Luke and Macy's family were becoming more and more accepting of their plans to remarry—it was pretty hard not to while witnessing the joy in their kids' faces and all that Luke and Macy were doing to make this journey as healthy and God-centered as possible.

Pastor Eric had already agreed to officiate their wedding, but Macy wanted to have the ceremony in a church. Calvary met in the same auditorium the guys played basketball in; therefore, lacking in some of that traditional church feel. They signed a contract at a nice Baptist church to use for their ceremony.

Macy designed and printed the invitations herself. The cover read: *"Love knows no limit to its endurance, no end to its trust. Love still stands when all else has fallen."* 1 Corinthians 13:7-8. The inside read:

Macy Jo Hawthorn
and
Lucas Dean Hawthorn
Together with their children
Lucas Travis
Avery Leigh
Noah Blake
Invite you to share with them
a celebration of love

The marriage will take place
On Saturday, the twenty-fifth of November
At two o'clock in the afternoon
First Baptist Church

Please be our guests
For Dinner and Reception
At seven o'clock in the evening
Biltmore Manor

Macy also wrote and printed little booklets and titled them "Our Story" for keepsakes to be placed at each table setting. She and her mother-in-law and Luke's aunt shopped for fresh flowers and made the bouquets and centerpieces.

They talked with a couple DJs and finally locked down their favorite being sure to note that there would be no Duck Dance, Hokey Pokey or Electric Slide played at the reception. Luke and Macy couldn't stand those corny traditions. But, of course, they *were* open to karaoke.

Luke and the boys took care of the tuxes and the music. Kim and Liam would be their photographers. And one of the guys from their marriage group offered to videotape the ceremony and reception. Mr. Gabel agreed to give the blessing over the meal for the reception.

Kyle reserved them a hotel room for the night of their wedding and prepared her matron of honor speech for the reception.

The girls in their marriage group ordered the balloons that would be released after the ceremony. Judy would do the reading and Macy's cousins would be greeters and have guests sign the Congratulations book.

Every detail was taking shape perfectly and in such a short amount of time. God's hand was completely on every aspect and certainly on Luke and Macy's hearts.

Along with all the wedding planning, Luke and Macy were also very busy paying off the debt that was inhibiting the approval needed for their home loan. The day she received the call at work from her loan officer, she hung up the phone and yelled across the floor, "I'm going to be a homeowner!" She and Luke were getting married, they were having the ceremony they had always wanted and to top it all off, they would have their own house too. Grandma and Grandpa's house would be theirs. Macy was completely overwhelmed with joy!

Macy's grandma sorted and packed her things for storage while her new villa was being built. She also gathered blue prints, appliance warranties, utility bills and instructions on how to work this or where to find that for Macy.

The kids started at their new school—which Luke and Macy promised would be the last move they'd make for a long time. Since they were all now attending Calvary, Luke and Macy decided to send the kids to public school. If the kids were to have any of Luke's musical and athletic gifts—which they knew they did—they both agreed that there would be more opportunities for them to explore those talents in the public school system instead of private schools.

Travis and Avery were loving every bit of it. They rode the bus together and really liked their teachers. Macy and Luke loved them too.

It then came time for Macy to close on the house. She and Grandma met at the title company as they exchanged checks. Macy handed over her down payment for the loan and Grandma received her check for the sale of her home. They were now the official owners of the house her Grandpa built. God was answering prayers so swiftly that Macy's heart could barely keep up.

Then, one Sunday afternoon, while over for a family dinner, Peter and Leanne pulled Luke and Macy aside to tell them that they would like to take care of paying for the reception.

"You guys don't have to do that," Macy said.

Peter replied, "We know we don't have to, but we want to, Macy. It's the least we can do with all that you have going on. It will be our gift to you."

"Wow, Peter. That's awesome. Thank you so much!" Luke replied with much gratitude.

"And, we'll keep the kids for you on your wedding night if they need a place to stay." Leanne offered.

"Oh, Mom. That would be great. They'd like that for sure."

"And, oh, I almost forgot. We got you something." She went to the other room to grab a little package and handed it to Macy.

Macy opened the little box with the ceramic figurine of a bride and groom.

"You can use it as a cake topper."

"Oh, mom. It's so cute. I love it! Thank you so much."

"We wish you all the best and will be praying for you." Leanne shared as she hugged her oldest daughter.

"Thanks, Dad." Macy hugged Peter.

"You're very welcome." Peter said, not wanting to sound too excited but with a smile.

Peter reached to shake Luke's hand, "Let's go see what your little ones are up to," leading them all out the sliding glass door to the back patio.

It was Friday, November 24th, the night before their wedding. Luke and Macy met with the church wedding coordinator first. She showed them the bride room and groomsmen room and then introduced them to the audiovisual man who would be handling the mics and sound for the ceremony.

The couple then joined Pastor Eric, Travis, Avery, Noah, and the rest of the bridal party and their parents to rehearse. Shane started things off by singing a couple songs while the bridesmaids walked down the aisle to be greeted by their escort in front of the altar. The groomsmen assisted them up the couple of steps and then took their places on either side of the altar. Then came Avery's turn to walk down the aisle. Her brother Travis waited there patiently to escort her up the stairs. *What a perfect gentleman,* Macy thought to herself watching him lead and care for his sister. Sweet Noah made his way down the aisle carrying the pillow with him. His head was held high as he had one of those giant grins of his gleaming from ear to ear.

Now it was Macy's turn. She and her dad made their way down the aisle to greet her groom at the altar. Luke looked scared and taken with excitement all at the same time. Pastor Eric said a few things and then Judy read a little from her piece that she wrote.

Pastor Eric continued with instructions, "We will then share the vows and exchange rings and then Luke will sing his song to Macy. I'll pronounce the happy couple as husband and wife, and they will then kiss and exit. Each of you will follow the opposite way you entered. I believe then Luke and Macy will have balloons for everyone to release outside after the ceremony."

Luke and Macy were staring and smiling at each other holding hands. Macy looked over at Pastor Eric and realized he was looking for confirmation that his last statement was, in fact, correct.

"Oh, yes. Sorry. Balloon release after the ceremony. That's correct." Macy blushed.

Macy went to sit with the kids. "You all did so wonderful. I'm so very proud of you. Did you think it went well?"

"Yes. It was fun," Avery said.

It was time to go their separate ways for the night. They all said their goodbyes with hugs and excitement for tomorrow's big day.

"Get a good night's sleep, Macy. And you get some rest, too, Luke." Judy said to them.

"I'll try," Macy said.

"Yeah, me too," Luke said.

"I'll see you tomorrow, my love," Luke said as he kissed Macy's hand.

"Yes, you will. And I can't wait to see the look on your face when they open the door and you see your bride for the first time." Macy replied kissing his cheek.

"Sleep well," Luke kissed her lips.

"You too."

Luke and the boys went to his mom's house. Macy and Avery went back to the house. Both houses were busy laying out everything they'd need for the ceremony and their overnight bags for staying at Mama and Papa's. Everything was set and organized so well—one of Macy's gifts.

"Hallelujahs"
REMARRIED

It had finally arrived. The first day of the rest of their lives.

Macy was up and feeling refreshed. She actually *had* gotten some good sleep the night before. She put on an old button-down top and drove to the hairdressers with veil in hand. Her friend's aunt kept her hair long and only pulled up the front and the sides—securing her veil with many, many bobby pins.

"Nothing's getting that veil out," she said. "Not even a tornado's getting this baby loose," she said as she yanked and pulled on it.

Macy gave her head a shake and said, "Yep, I think your right, that's not going anywhere. It looks really beautiful. Thank you so much, Mary Ann. I love it."

"Aw, you're welcome, honey. Best wishes for a happy life with your young groom! And, take care of those babies."

"Oh you know it. Thanks again!"

She headed back home to help get Avery ready. Avery showered and then Macy blew her hair dry and curled the ends of her little bob cut.

"When we get to the church and finish getting dressed, I'll put a little make up on you, okay?"

"Okay," Avery replied. "When are we leaving, Mommy? Are the boys going to be there when we get there?"

"We'll leave in just a little while, sweetie. We girls will be there a little earlier than the boys because we take longer to get ready." Macy smiled.

"Come on, boys. It's time to get up. Time to get ready for the wedding." Luke said.

Travis was already up, but Noah was still sound asleep. "Travis why don't you go ahead and get in the shower. I'll get Noah up and make some breakfast."

"Okay, Dad!" Travis headed to the bathroom.

Luke made them some scrambled eggs, thinking the smell would help Noah awake from his slumber. It worked. "Watcha making, Daddy?" said the little voice making its way into the kitchen.

"Well hello, sleepy-head. I'm making you some eggs. Sound good?"

"Mmmhmm. Can I have toast too?" Noah asked.

"Sure, lil' man. Travis is in the shower now. When he's finished, you and I can take ours. Have a seat and I'll get you a plate."

The boys all showered and Luke did a great job styling their hair and packing their bags.

"You ready, Avery?"

"Yeah, Mommy."

"You have your bag for Mama and Papa's?"

"Yes, I put it by the door."

"Well, let's get going to the church then."

Avery and Macy climbed into her packed car and got to the church, right on time. The other girls were making their way in as well.

The coordinator greeted Macy and Avery and helped them get their things back to the bride room. They sat their things down and then the coordinator did one last walk through with Macy to make sure everything was placed just as she had wanted it.

Kim and Liam arrived and they both split up to take pictures of the guys and the girls as they got ready.

The church looked beautiful. It was decorated for the Christmas holiday with green wreaths and red ribbons and white lights everywhere, it was absolutely gorgeous.

"Now let's get you back to your dressing room before the groom gets here and sees you before the ceremony!" She said to Macy.

"Boys, let's go. I have everything in the car. I just need you two in it."

"Coming Daddy. I'm trying to find Noah's other shoe, though."

"Other shoe? What are you talking about? Didn't you pack them in your bag?"

"I thought so. I have this one but can't find the other," Travis said holding up the left shoe.

"Oh my gosh." Luke went out to the car and started digging through their bag. "Found it," he yelled from the car.

"Okay, Noah. Let's go!" Travis grabbed his hand and they all climbed into the car.

The boys all made it to the church on time; the groomsmen and ushers too.

Luke had been practicing his song in the car on the way to the church. He, Shane and Kelly (the pianist) had a few more run-throughs to work out any nerves.

"It's going to sound beautiful," Shane reassured Luke.

"Thanks, man! I'm so glad you're singing too. I wouldn't have wanted it any other way."

"My pleasure, cuz!"

The man running sound queued up a song that Macy chose in honor of their deceased loved ones, "Angels Among Us." This was the cue for the coordinator to allow guests to take their seats and before long; friends and family began to fill up the pews.

Macy and the girls took their final bathroom breaks and made final touches to their makeup and started handing out Kleenex.

The boys made their way out to the altar.

The coordinator lined up the girls outside of the door as the music began.

This is it, Luke thought to himself. Standing on the altar step, he said a little prayer, *"We're going to be husband and wife again. Macy is going to be my bride. Thank you, God. Help me keep it together. Help me remember the words to my song. Help me to forever honor this woman selflessly and unconditionally. I don't know how we got here today, but I thank you with all that I am. Thank you God!"*

"Father God, Luke's in there waiting for me, waiting for me to be his bride again," Macy prayed quietly while waiting at the end of the line. *"He's going to take my hand in front of our family and friends and You and be my husband once again. You have given us so much and now our dreams of having a real wedding in a church with bridesmaids and groomsmen and a Pastor and a dress and flowers are coming true. I am so grateful! Thank you for our wonderful babies. I pray that I can be the mom they deserve and I pray I can be the wife to their father that you've intended for me to be and give them an example of family and commitment the way they deserve. Father, help me love and honor this man unconditionally forever and ever."*

Shane had just finished singing "For the First Time" and the piano now gave Macy her cue to proceed through the doors in her Father's arm down that aisle. The coordinator gave both Macy and Peter a nod, "you ready?" and opened the double doors for her entrance. Her eyes were in Luke's direction the entire time, as his face was the very first thing she wanted to see.

Macy watched Luke take a breath and close his eyes in an effort to hold back the tears. Macy was so excited she just grinned from ear to ear.

Macy and her dad made their way down the aisle, smiling at all of her friends and family along the way.

Pastor Eric opened the ceremony by talking about the couple standing before him and how they were all standing before God, "The God of second chances." Macy nodded in agreement. "God has brought this couple back together to remarry today and for that I am truly grateful."

He then asked who gives this woman to this man, and Peter replied, "Her mother and I do." Peter kissed Macy on the cheek and shook Luke's hand. Then Luke smiled at Macy, taking her hand to lead her to their spot on the altar. He looked at her again and whispered to her, "You look so beautiful."

Luke's mom, Judy, then approached the microphone. She shared the poem she wrote for the two of them and a couple passages from the Bible.

Remember what brought you here all the forgone years,
Remember what brought you here the joy and the pain and the tears.
It is just for a time such as this by His grace you stand,
He alone allowed the past to orchestrate His plan.
Forget not child who brought you here His plan is without flaw,
He waits in patient silence as close to Him we draw.
He never missed a moment of your pathway to this day,
So never think that your maker would look the other way.
It is we who go away from Him in his protective care,
And, all the while He's never more than a moment away in prayer.
Remember those who have gone before your loved ones here in spirit,
The quiet rush of angel's wings; be still and you can hear it.
Remember the time it took to make friends tried and true,
And, know that your best friend of all today is marrying you.
Forget what's kept you looking at your past in terms of failure,
Remember that's' behind you now the things in store are greater.
He's the God of second chances remember He is He,

Don't expect one another to be what He must be.
Cherish the joy in your children's eye as they watch their parents
   teach,
The sacrificial love you'll show is out to others you will reach.
There's no love that's greater than the one that see past fault
And, given without condition the kind our Savior taught.

Judy finished by reading From God's word, Ecclesiastes 4:9-12, "Two are better than one because they get a better return for their work. If one falls down, his friend can help him up. But pity the one who falls down and has no one to help him up. Also, if two lie down together they will keep warm. How will one keep warm alone? And, though one may be overpowered, two can defend themselves. A cord of three strands is not quickly broken."

"Luke and Macy, remember the third strand."

"This family's life scripture is chosen by Travis, Avery and Noah, Matthew 6:33, "Seek first His kingdom and His righteousness and all these things will be added to you also." Macy wiped her eyes.

Pastor Eric agreed with Judy's choice of scripture and complimented her on the "beautiful poem that she so eloquently shared with us today." He then talked about the symbolism that was to take place next with the lighting of the unity candle.

"Just as you leave your parents and cleave with your spouse, the unity candle shows us just that. You were given life by your parents and now your lives will light the candle and you will live as one."

Shane began singing "Hallelujahs" and Luke and Macy carefully walked over to their unity candle. Macy was very careful to not let her veil get in the way of the flame. Together Luke and Macy lit the candle—they were to be one.

After Shane finished singing the beautiful song, they exchanged their vows. Luke got a little choked up when repeating 'in, eh hem, in poverty, and in prosperity." But, they both got through it. Luke then took the mic and sang his tearful song to Macy. Again, all of the excitement kept her from crying. She was also worried that if she cried even just a little, the floodgates might open and never close. He changed the words to fit in her name towards the end..."All the love I have, all the love that I have for you, Macy." It was perfect. Luke did amazing and filled up the church with his incredible voice making it seem as though time stood still.

And, now came the words that Luke and Macy had been waiting to hear...when Pastor Eric said, "By the power vested in me, I am so very proud to pronounce you husband and wife." He was barely able to get out, "You may kiss the bride," before Luke was grabbing Macy's face and kissing her with every intention of making the moment a permanent memory from here on out. Their first kiss as husband and wife...again, but now in front of God, their family and their friends.

The weather had turned a little colder and there was a light mist and sprinkle falling.

Guests hugged and congratulated the couple. Everything was amazing. What a beautiful ceremony. "I'm so proud of you both and wish nothing but extreme happiness for the rest of your lives," Judy said hugging each of them with tears in her eyes.

"Sorry the weather couldn't have been a little nicer for you," one person had said to Macy.

"Oh, don't apologize for that. I think the rain is a good thing. It's washing us clean of our past so we can start our new lives with much growth and newness!" Macy replied.

While they signed the marriage certificate, their friends from marriage group handed out balloons to everyone. Macy and Luke grabbed their heart-shaped balloons and followed their kids out to the front entrance to meet all of their guests.

"Okay, folks, on the count of three, Macy and I are going to release our balloons and then you release yours immediately after." "Ready, Macy?" Luke asked.

"Yes, I'm ready," Macy shook her head, smiling.

He quietly counted, "one...two...three."

He and Macy released their balloons. And then the kids let theirs go and then all of their guests. They all watched as the pearl colored bubbles floated up...only to see their outlines as they got closer and closer to the gray sky.

"Thank you all so much for being here. We're off to take some pictures now, so we'll see you at the reception in a couple of hours."

After making a few stops for chips and salsa and margaritas at a local Mexican restaurant, the bridal party arrived at the reception. The DJ announced their arrival and called off each of their names as they danced their way up to the head table.

The hall looked beautiful; candles lit and balloons strewn all about. The centerpieces that Macy and Judy and Luke's aunts and cousins had made with fresh ivory and pink roses looked just as she hoped they would. The cake was tall and displayed the bride and groom Precious Moments figurine Leanne gave to Luke and Macy a few days prior. And everyone there looked happy—they were having a good time and ready for the newly remarried Luke and Macy's entrance.

Mr. Gabel wrote a prayer to bless the new couple and the meal. It was so sincere and heartfelt. He read from Genesis and then Proverbs 31:10, the wife of noble character: "that she is worth far more than rubies. Her husband has full confidence in her and lacks nothing of value. She brings him good, not harm, all the days of her life." Luke and Macy were so very grateful for he and his wife and all that they had done to help make this day possible.

Next, Macy's Matron of Honor, Kyle, gave a toast. She talked about how she and Macy and Miriam put their parents through some pretty tough stuff growing up. Then she reminded Macy of what their mom always said, "If he really loves you like he says he does, he will come back for you." Macy shook her head in agreement and looked at Luke smiling.

She went on to say, "If you love something, let it go. If it comes back, it is meant to be. This Thanksgiving we all have so much to be thankful for. Macy and Luke had a tremendously rough time before and we know that. God is giving you another chance. Cherish your love, your family and each other. You have taught us all that love doesn't fail. We are so proud that God has shown himself to us, in the two of you. Let's raise our glasses to the blessed couple. I love you guys."

Luke and Macy finished dinner as best they could with all of the congratulations and hugs. They made their way around to the tables to express their gratitude and thanks to everyone for supporting them and being a part of this very important day.

Instead of throwing the bouquet, Macy dedicated it to her late Aunt Joan who had passed away earlier that year. Not only was she an amazing woman whom they all adored and loved, she and Macy's Uncle Gerry were also married on November 25th. It was a sweet gesture that everyone appreciated, especially Leanne— Joan was her younger sister and best friend.

Tim, their friend from marriage group, walked around the hall with the video camera getting guests to record their well wishes and congrats or anything else they'd like to say to the new couple. They danced and danced and sang karaoke. The kids danced and had just an absolutely wonderful time. The photographers, Kim and Liam, took a plethora of pictures.

The favorite part of the evening for Luke and Macy was when the DJ turned off the music for a minute to say a few things. "Folks, if you don't mind, I have to say something." Everyone stopped what they were doing to turn their attention to Ray their DJ. "You know, I don't know Luke and Macy that well at all. I've only talked to them a couple times, but after reading this—he held up the little booklet that Macy had made—I am absolutely touched. You two are amazing and I plan on keeping this with me forever, as a reminder to hope and know that things can work out. I wish you two nothing but the absolute best. And, thank you for allowing me to be a part of your incredible day!"

Luke and Macy nodded their heads in appreciation as Ray held up his glass in their honor. "How amazing was that?" Macy whispered in Luke's ear.

"Very!" They felt even more blessed in that very moment. *Never take this for granted. Never,* they both thought to themselves.

They were on the dance floor dancing with their friends and laughing and singing when Luke grabbed Macy and squeezed her tight. They stood still and he stared into her eyes for a second and said, "I love you so much, Macy Hawthorn! I cannot wait to spend the rest of my life with you!"

"I love you, Luke Hawthorn! More today than I ever knew possible." She brushed her hand along the side of his face and held his neck. "And, I cannot wait to spend the rest of my life with you."

It was time for the reception to end; time to get things packed up and go home for the night. Macy's parents took all of the gifts back to their house, along with a very tired Travis, Avery and Noah. Judy and her siblings took care of getting centerpieces handed out to guests for them to take home and gave balloons to the kids.

Luke packed up his bride and off they headed to the Marriott to check into their room. "What an amazing day it's been! I am so very proud of our babies, aren't you?" Macy asked Luke.

"Oh my gosh, Yes! Everything was perfect, Macy. And, I think everyone had an amazing time! And what about DJ Ray's little speech? Can you believe that?"

"I know. It totally caught me off guard and made me want to cry! This day just couldn't have been any more perfect!"

They got their key and made it to the room.

"I am starving, Macy. Aren't you?

"Yeah actually, I am. I barely ate any of my delicious dinner. What do you think we can order this late?"

"I know! I'm ordering us Pizza Hut," he said as he picked up the phone.

Macy laughed. "Okay, I lied, the day just got more perfect." How could they not have Pizza Hut on such a significant day? "Well, while you order, I'm getting out of this dress and veil and getting into a hot bath."

"Okay, baby. Let me know if you need any help," Luke grinned.

Macy got in her robe and shared pizza with her husband. They laughed and kissed as they filled their bellies and eventually drifted off to sleep for the night.

Luke lay there watching Macy sleep. He brushed some of her hair back over her ear. He was the first thing Macy saw as she was awakened by his touch. He leaned down to kiss her on her forehead. "Good morning, Mrs. Hawthorn." Macy stretched and blinked a couple times, "Good morning to you, Mr. Hawthorn," she said as she snuggled closer, laying her head on his chest.

"How'd you sleep, my love?"

"Oh goodness, really, really well," she said kissing his neck and smiling.

She looked up at him. "What about you, how'd you sleep?"

"Oh me too... really well!"

"Well, then why that face?"

"Hmmm? Oh what...I don't know." Luke was in a daze, staring at nothing.

"Well, are you okay?" She touched his face.

Luke grabbed her hand from his face and pressed her wedding ring to his mouth as he kissed it. He held her hand to his face and then looked at Macy and said, "I'm better now!" Looking back down at that symbol of commitment, she was his again and he was hers. "Better now, my Lady."

... To be continued.

ACKNOWLEDGEMENTS

My Heavenly Father, who created me uniquely perfect and for this very purpose.

My family, who has supported me, my husband and our children in ways that no one should ever have to.

My editor, Maggie Singleton, for taking on my very first work with personal and professional joy.

My mentor, Dr. Bryan, for not going anywhere. I would not be where I am today, nor would I be taking the path I currently am, without his insight and wise counsel.

Jillian Schoettle, talented friend and artist who brought my idea to an exclusive, colorful life.

Gertrude Gusewelle, my very dear 'lover-of-life' friend and photographer who captured our family so perfectly in just the right light.

ABOUT THE AUTHOR

Amy Jo is from a small town in the west suburbs of
St. Louis, MO. She was raised in a modest home attending
private school from kindergarten through high school. Life
experiences and the people around her are a direct correlation to
what shaped her as a woman and ultimately her life's passion; thus
her first book *It Doesn't Have to be That Way* was born. She still
lives in that same small town with her husband and their three
adult children where she is also a full-time student working
towards a degree to impact and mend couples, building
stronger marriages and families alike.
Follow her at amyjohawkins.com.

39232892R00174

Made in the USA
Charleston, SC
03 March 2015